On Being a Therapist

ON BEING A THERAPIST

FIFTH EDITION

JEFFREY A. KOTTLER

OXFORD
UNIVERSITY PRESS

OXFORD
UNIVERSITY PRESS

Oxford University Press is a department of the University of Oxford. It furthers the University's objective of excellence in research, scholarship, and education by publishing worldwide. Oxford is a registered trade mark of Oxford University Press in the UK and certain other countries.

Published in the United States of America by Oxford University Press
198 Madison Avenue, New York, NY 10016, United States of America.

First Edition published in 1986 by Jossey-Bass, a Wiley Imprint
Second Edition copyright 1993 by Jossey-Bass, a Wiley Imprint
Third Edition copyright 2003 by Jossey-Bass, a Wiley Imprint
Fourth Edition copyright 2010 by Jossey-Bass, a Wiley Imprint

Library of Congress Cataloging-in-Publication Data
Names: Kottler, Jeffrey A.
Title: On being a therapist / Jeffrey A. Kottler.
Description: Fifth edition. | New York, NY : Oxford University Press, [2017]
| Includes bibliographical references and index.
Identifiers: LCCN 2016029437 | ISBN 9780190641542 (alk. paper)
Subjects: LCSH: Psychotherapists—Psychology. |
Psychotherapy—Practice—Psychological aspects.
Classification: LCC RC480.5 .K68 2017 | DDC 616.89/14092—dc23
LC record available at https://lccn.loc.gov/2016029437

1 3 5 7 9 8 6 4 2

Printed by LSC Communications, United States of America

Contents

Preface

THE CLIMATE FOR being a therapist has changed so dramatically that the field is all but unrecognizable to those who began their careers when the first edition of this book was published 30 years ago. This was a time when clients were mostly white, female, and upper middle class, when therapy was believed to take a long time (at least months, if not years) to be considered viable, and when insurance companies would pay 90% of whatever we charged, with no lifetime limit or restrictions on frequency of sessions.

Now we practice in an era when more indigent, immigrant, and working-class clients are being served, often presenting much more severe problems. In addition, many caseloads are filled with court-ordered and involuntarily referred clients. Whereas once upon a time therapists followed Freud's lead of specializing in the so-called worried well or the neurotic middle class, we now reach a far more diverse population, representing every conceivable cultural, age, ethnic, racial, religious, socioeconomic, and sexual orientation background. Whereas it had once been the case that therapists must master the intricacies of a handful of different theoretical orientations, with increased blending and integration of models into more pragmatic, evidence-based practice, it is now just as important to learn the unique and most significant aspects of the various cultural backgrounds of our clients.

We are also asked to treat an increasing variety of complaints, many of them not particularly amenable or responsive to therapy in the past: domestic violence, physical and sexual abuse, trauma, sexual identity issues, substance abuse, eating disorders, personality disorders, self-harm, and dissociative disorders. Moreover, we are being required to make a difference in increasingly brief periods of time. Whereas long-term therapy once was measured in the span of 5 to 10 years, now it is often restricted to the same number of months, or even weeks.

Managed care has completely restructured the ways we operate as therapists, not only limiting the time we spend with clients but also dictating what sorts of things we are permitted to do. In most managed care situations, the course of treatment is strictly limited, and any extension of the allowable number of visits must be approved by some external authority. Everything is about accountability, empirically supported evidence-based treatments, and measured outcomes, all within specific time parameters.

Technology has also revolutionized the field in the past few decades and will only alter the landscape further in years to follow. More and more often, we are using software or websites to communicate with managed care payers, send our reports and invoices, and aid our diagnostic decisions and treatment planning. Both therapists and clients are using the online sources as a means of instant consultation, as well as for delivering and receiving therapy. Texting, emailing, social media, and instant-messaging are becoming increasingly common as favored means of communication, even as a way of conducting sessions. We are spending more and more time in front of a computer screen and less and less time engaged in face-to-face, intimate engagement with others. This might make us more efficient, but it certainly changes the nature of our work and our lives—and not all for the better. In many ways, the life of a therapist is far more stressful with so much continual accessibility and so little downtime.

The Mysteries of Being a Therapist

Since the first publication of this book, the boundaries between theoretical orientations have begun to crumble further. Most of us could once easily identify ourselves as a strong follower of one particular persuasion—as psychodynamic, existential, cognitive-behavioral, or one of a few dozen others. Nowadays almost everyone is eclectic and pragmatic, or at least integrative, no matter what the espoused ideology. We might call ourselves constructivists, behaviorists, feminists, or humanists, and we might describe ourselves as psychodynamic, cognitive, Gestalt, narrative, or relational therapists, but the reality is that we now borrow concepts and ideas from a variety of approaches, depending on the context, culture, and presenting complaints of our clients, not to mention our own mood.

One thing that has not changed much is that the process of psychotherapy still flows in two directions. This is obviously the case in the direction of influencing the client, but it is also true with respect to affecting the personal life of the clinician. This impact can be for better or for worse, making the helping professions among the most spiritually fulfilling as well as the most emotionally draining human endeavors. Some of us flourish as a result of this work. We learn from those we try to help and apply what we know and understand to ourselves. And some of us become depleted and despondent. Over time, we may become cynical or indifferent or stale.

We have long recognized the impact of various therapeutic ingredients in the changes that a client will likely undergo. We know that such factors as the therapeutic alliance, synchronized agreement of goals, reliable and accurate feedback, empathic responding, sensitive questioning, and constructive, sensitive confrontation will often lead to greater self-acceptance and even to personality transformations in a client. But what impact do these processes have on the person facilitating them? Can the clinician be an active instigator of the therapeutic process without, in turn, being affected by its ripple effects? Can therapists be immune to the influence of prolonged exposure to human despair, conflict, and suffering? Can we resist the inevitable growth and self-awareness that come from studying other lives? Can we remain the same after being in the presence of so many who are changing? Whether we like it or not, the decision to be a therapist is also a commitment to our own growth.

I remember that when this book was first published, lo these many years ago, the reviews were somewhat mixed, sometimes reflecting the passionate opinions of the reviewer that there are just certain subjects that we shouldn't be talking about in a public forum. I drew some consolation from another reviewer at the time who called me the "conscience of the profession," and I've always liked the idea that I was willing to discuss taboo topics, even if sometimes awkwardly. One of my earliest heroes was the little boy in Hans Christian Andersen's tale of *The Emperor's New Clothes*, the truth speaker who says aloud what everyone else can plainly see but will not acknowledge. Likewise, early in my career I felt so lost because the things that I struggled with most never seemed to come up very often in supervision, workshops, or resources—and they were certainly never discussed in my training. I wondered constantly why it was so rare that therapists talked about their failures, or why we argued among ourselves so much about whose approach was superior to all others, or why it didn't feel safe to talk about all the ways that doing therapy was making me a better person, or why others seemed to be so limited by the literature and research from our field when I noticed my most influential teachers came from novels, travel experiences, adventures in my own life, and especially lessons learned from clients.

Coming Attractions and Latest Innovations

During the years since I last revised and updated this volume, there have once again been many changes in the ways we operate. Who could have ever imagined that many practitioners would be conducting sessions via online video, texts, chats, and—perhaps coming soon—via virtual reality and avatars. One can imagine a time in the not too distant future when everyone will have a device in their home, or implanted in their head, that will respond to any query, whether offering directions to the drugstore or advice for dealing with mental health issues.

PERSON: "Siri, I'm depressed. What should I do?"
DEVICE: "You sound tired. *I'm* tired. It's 3 a.m. and you should be sleeping, not talking to me."
PERSON: "Sorry. I just keep thinking over and over about ..."
DEVICE: "Have you tried a warm bath and some hot milk to help you sleep?"
PERSON: "What I'd really like now is a real drink."
DEVICE: "Now, now, don't go there."
PERSON: "Where?"
DEVICE: "Genetic tests have already demonstrated your susceptibility to alcohol addiction. And then with your family history you are further at risk."
PERSON: "Okay, then, what's on HBO?"

This book now incorporates the latest research and developments, plus quite a bit of new material that reflects my own understanding of cutting-edge innovations. The first of these is a new chapter on storytelling, since I now believe that what therapists really do most of the time is (1) listen to people's stories, (2) help them to collaborate on a different narrative version that is more self-empowering, and (3) introduce stories in the form of metaphors, disclosures, modeling, and teaching tales. Given that the vast majority of our waking moments are captured by stories in the form of shows, films, novels, conversations, gossip, song lyrics, fantasies, and dreams, the brain has actually evolved as a "storied organ" that makes the vicarious experience feel real.

Over the years I've become increasingly aware that therapists are not the only ones who read this book. Quite a number of clients—past and present—have also discovered it as a way to better understand and get the most from their experiences. I'm aware that many therapists have actually recommended the book to their clients; others have received them as gifts. And quite a few have written to me over the years asking what they can do to get the most from their sessions. Many others had questions about the process and wondered if certain things going on were "normal" or appropriate, or even what they might say or do to better improve their outcomes. I have thus added a new chapter (Chapter 14) that is specifically focused on how to become a better client. I would hope that therapists find it helpful as well to better prepare our clients to get the most from our work.

Like its predecessors, this expanded volume is written for all practitioners of therapy—social workers, counselors, psychiatrists, psychologists, psychiatric nurses, family therapists, human service professionals, pastoral counselors, and other mental health specialists. It will be of utmost value to students of these professions, who may be preparing for a career by learning helping skills without fully appreciating the personal consequences. Those who have experienced therapy as clients, or who are contemplating such a formidable adventure, will also find the premises contained herein of special interest.

Chapter 1 begins with a discussion of what it means to *be* a therapist, the inner journey with all its joys, benefits, and challenges. It explores the personal motives for becoming a therapist, as well as the cultural, political, and social context for the relationships we create and maintain. This chapter also describes the inherent risks of working as a therapist and presents a unified framework of the change process as a backdrop for exploring further ideas about modeling and influencing power in Chapter 2. Essentially, all systems of therapy work because they share several elements: the powerful presence of a therapist, an effective therapeutic alliance, and structures for constructive risk taking both within sessions and in the client's life.

Chapter 3 further explores the implications of the role of the therapist as a model by examining the relationship between personal and professional effectiveness. Just as professional skills help therapists improve their personal relationships, their real-life experiences are invaluable tools during sessions. This is the best fringe benefit of the field: constant exposure to change continually stimulates us and promotes greater personal growth, which in turn makes us more powerful models.

The new material I mentioned earlier relating to storytelling and its power to persuade and influence people, both in therapy and everyday life is discussed in Chapter 4 (new to this edition). Traditions within various cultures around the world become the context for understanding the virtually universal employment of stories as the primary means by which to instruct and heal others. Readers are encouraged to develop their storytelling skills as a means to make therapy (and their lives) more dynamic, interesting, and powerful.

Chapter 5 was a new addition to the book in the previous edition, one that further expands discussion of how therapists are profoundly changed by their clients, both personally and professionally. Clients are our best teachers and supervisors in that they help us become more responsive to their needs (if we are flexible, adaptable, and paying close attention).

The next set of chapters all explore special challenges that are part of being a therapist. Chapter 6 reviews many of the hardships that are part of this work, including the strains of fatigue, one-way intimacy, and personal restraint. Chapter 7 was another new chapter to the previous edition that focuses specifically on therapists' struggles with imperfection, negative outcomes, disappointments, and failures. There is an overriding theme that such experiences provide valuable feedback that makes us both more personally resilient and professionally effective. Chapter 8 concentrates on so-called difficult clients, those we experience as unusually challenging and frustrating. Chapter 9 examines issues of burnout and boredom—not only how we can address them but also, more importantly, how we can prevent or minimize them in the first place.

Chapter 10 was also recently added, speaking in greater depth about the secrets of the profession, *that which is not said*, the topics that are often considered most taboo and forbidden: that much of the time we are flying by the seat of our pants; that we don't often understand how and why therapy really works; that sometimes we feel like frauds and hypocrites; that inside our heads we are far more critical of others than we pretend; that we don't often do what we say we do in sessions. Chapter 11 follows this discussion with lies we tell ourselves and others and games that therapists sometimes play.

To balance all this exploration of deep, sometimes disturbing and uncomfortable topics, Chapters 12 and 13 discuss ways in which therapists can revitalize and take better care of themselves. They describe practical suggestions for initiating more personal and professional development, encouraging creative growth, and finding deeper meaning in our lives and work. In this latest edition, there is also increased focus on the therapist's role and responsibility to promote issues of social justice, human rights, and systemic changes within the community and world at large. Chapter 14 ends the book by speaking directly to clients about how to get the most from their experiences.

Given that this volume is often used in a variety of classes and seminars, as well as available to the general public and popular among book clubs, the appendix contains more than a dozen discussion questions that can spark interesting conversations as well as deep reflection on how some of the ideas mentioned may intersect or challenge some of your own cherished beliefs.

Acknowledgments

I GRATEFULLY ACKNOWLEDGE the assistance of the many professionals, representing various mental health specialties and theoretical orientations, who agreed to share their thoughts and experiences regarding what it means to be a therapist. Although many of these clinicians and therapist educators wish to remain anonymous, their words speak loudly throughout the chapters that follow.

I'm also appreciative of the input and suggestions from the reviewers who helped improve the book in so many ways. Many of them have been using this book as primary and secondary texts in their classes for over a decade and so were able to provide deep and meaningful input into ways to make it even better.

I'm especially indebted to my longtime editor, Dana Bliss, with whom we've shared so many previous projects, all of which represent a true creative partnership that has resulted in some of my favorite work. I also wish to thank many of the Oxford University Press staff who were instrumental in the production process: Andrew Dominello, Stefano Imbert, Dan Petraglia, and Sarah Russo. Finally, I'm indebted to the hundreds of readers who have written me over the years, providing valuable feedback as well as sharing their own stories.

Jeffrey A. Kottler
Huntington Beach, California

1

The Therapist's Journey

THERE ARE MANY healers among the indigenous people of the world who would find it utterly ridiculous that anyone would ever *choose* to become a therapist. They believe that becoming a helper or healer is a calling, but one that is fraught with danger and burdens. After all, clients come to us in pain and despair, hoping we will cure their suffering and leech away their toxic energy. They have unrealistic expectations about what is within our power to do. They are often in *very* bad moods. And they come to talk to us, in part, because they don't feel that anyone else has the patience or interest to listen to them.

And yet—and *yet*—there is no other profession that can be as fulfilling and satisfying, no other job that provides as many opportunities for continual learning and growth. Being a therapist is truly a lifelong journey, one in which we accompany others on a road toward enlightenment or peace or salvation. It is a journey into the unknown with many obstacles along the way. Like any journey, there are hardships for each pilgrim, but also many joys. We are afforded the opportunity to live myriad different lives through the relationships we have with our clients.

We are offered glimpses, even deep searches, into the questions that haunt people the most. We experience a level of intimacy with our clients that few will ever know. We are exposed to levels of drama and emotional arousal that are at once terrifying and captivating. We get to play detective and help solve mysteries that have plagued people throughout their lives. We hear stories so amazing that they make television shows, novels, and movies seem boring by comparison. We become companions to people who are on the verge of making significant changes—and we are transformed as well. We go to sleep at night knowing that, in some way, we have made a difference in people's lives. There is almost a spiritual transcendence associated with much of the work we do.

Personal Motives for Being a Therapist

Our journey to become therapists began for most of us, not with the urge to save the world or help people, but rather to save ourselves. Many of the motives for becoming a therapist are unconscious and even beyond the reach of supervision or personal therapy that skirted over such unresolved or disguised issues (Adams, 2014b; Sussman, 2007). Frequently they involve lingering struggles with early loss or unfulfilled narcissistic needs for recognition and approval (Barnett, 2007; Kuchuck, 2014). Half of therapists polled in a large-scale survey confessed that their choice to become a therapist, as well as their subsequent professional development, was motivated largely by the resolution to work through their own problems (Orlinsky & Ronnestad, 2005). One common area frequently mentioned is the desire to understand oneself more fully and feel understood by others.

Ghent (1999) contends that therapists are masochists and gluttons for punishment. What else could possibly explain our willingness to spend so much time exploring the darkest recesses of human experiences? Ghent asks, "What other occupation has built into it the frustration of feeling helpless, stupid, and lost as a necessary part of the work?" (1999, p. 236). Commenting on this observation, Hamman (2001) remarked that therapists are willing to subject themselves to the trials and tribulations of their work in the search to become more authentic and real.

Another motive for becoming a therapist relates to feeling a greater sense of power and control, not only over others but also over yourself. One experienced clinician admitted with some reluctance that this was what clearly drew her to the profession. "After all," she said, "if you're always focusing on other people's problems, it's easy to wriggle out of focusing on your own. People think I have it all together—Ha! After a while, maybe I started to believe the same thing, even if part of me knows that it isn't true. I guess what I'm saying is that being a therapist means enjoying intimacy without the loss of control that intimacy usually requires."

Besides the feeling of being in control, there are other reasons that therapists cite for ending up in this profession. We might have been inducted into caretaker roles in childhood and so are only doing what came to be (or was trained to be) natural. As was mentioned by the therapist just quoted, we can enjoy deep levels of intimacy without being hurt. We get to be voyeurs and enjoy living other lives vicariously; each week clients come in and tell us the most amazing stories. As if that isn't enough, we also enjoy the benefits of post-traumatic growth as a vicarious experience, observing the ways that our clients develop so much resilience dealing with their life challenges (Bartoskova, 2015; Joseph, 2011).

Developing a Second Sight

Central to all that I will say on the interaction between therapist and client is a relatively unified view of change. This framework particularly emphasizes the power and influence of the therapist's personality as a facilitator of growth. The force and spirit of who the therapist is as a human being most dramatically stimulate change, especially the personal attitudes that we display in the relationship. Lock a person, any person, in a room alone with Sigmund Freud, Carl Rogers, Fritz Perls, Virginia Satir, Albert Ellis, or any other formidable personality, and several hours later the client will come out different. It is not what the therapist does that is necessarily important—whether she interprets, reflects, confronts, disputes, or role-plays—but rather who she is as a person. A therapist who is vibrant, inspirational, and charismatic; who is sincere, loving, and nurturing; and who is wise, confident, and self-disciplined will often have an impact through the sheer force and power of her essence, regardless of her theoretical allegiances.

The first and foremost element of change, then, is the therapist's *presence*—her excitement and enthusiasm and the power of her personality. Rollo May (1983) spoke of presence in a different sense: the complete experiencing of the client's being—not of his symptoms or problems but of his essence. The therapist enters the relationship with clarity, openness, and serenity and comes fully prepared to encounter a soul in torment. The client comes prepared with his own expectations for a mentor, a guru, a doctor, a friend, or a wizard.

It is sometimes surprising to realize the ways that doing therapy produces an altered state of consciousness not only in our clients but also in us. When things are really moving along well, when concentration and connection are at their peak, we may experience a kind of synesthesia, or second sight, in which a state of hyperarousal leads to greater intensity of our awareness. We are able not only to hear and see, with exquisite sensitivity, what is going on in the session and within the other person but also to transcend the ordinary senses to achieve greater clarity. Many indigenous healers of the world speak of being able to develop "second eyes" in which they can actually see sickness in others, as well as smell and taste it. During those times when empathy is at its peak, when we have entered the trance-like state of total immersion in the relationship and concentration in the conversation, when we can almost read the client's mind and anticipate what he will think, feel, say, and do next, there is a similar synthesis of perception.

The Power of Belief

The therapeutic elements of indigenous healing are part of every helping system. Regardless of the locale and cultural context, whether in the Amazon River Basin, Himalayan Mountains, Kalahari Desert, or a large city, helping usually takes the form of instilling hope among those who feel only despair. The shaman, physician, priest, teacher, and therapist all believe strongly that what they offer to those who are suffering will bring comfort and even promote a cure. They have faith in their powers to make a difference and promote change. Just as important, they are able to persuade their clients that this is the case.

In the context of therapy, some classic theorists (Fish, 1973, 1996; Frank, 1993) concluded most therapeutic systems are designed to maximize the client's expectations for a successful outcome. This optimism and hope, coupled with the client's own positive beliefs, are considered to be among the common factors of all forms of therapy (Greenberg, Constantino, & Bruce, 2006; Kirsch, Wampold, & Kelley, 2015; Miller, Hubble, & Duncan, 2007; Steingard, 2015). We set this active placebo in place not only through our confidence and persuasive skills but also by the way we manage the helping environment. Diplomas, books, dress, arrangement of the office—all feed the client's expectations that this is a place of serenity and wisdom.

The specifics of what we do next—whether encouraging catharsis, self-control, or self-confrontation; whether using interpretation, reflection, or goal setting; whether focusing on thoughts, feelings, or behavior—probably elicit less client insight and action than does our belief that they will. The client has faith in us, as professionals of integrity and knowledge, as experts with the power to heal.

If we were merely magicians or faith healers, then what use would there be to study the scientific and clinical aspects of our profession, much less to train so rigorously in its methods? But of course, what we do only *appears* to be magical because of its many dimensions. I hear colleagues and read authors all the time who speak with such authority and confidence about what they do that makes a difference. They say things so casually, such as, "This was the client's problem, and this was the clear diagnosis, so this is what I did that made the difference." That has not been my experience of being a therapist at all. Certainly I have my theories and favored explanations to account for what happens and why, but if I have learned anything about this craft over so many years of practice, it is to appreciate and honor the complexity of what we do. I think we could spend a lifetime studying a single case and still not ever get close to understanding everything that happened and why. By this time, you've already learned to love this sort of ambiguity and complexity or you've found other work.

In the absence of certainty about what is best, in the presence of someone who is needy and vulnerable, there is a compelling urge for us to *do* something. It has become the zeitgeist of our times to embrace evidence-based practice, empirically supported treatments, technical eclecticism, strategic interventions, structured therapeutic tasks technological innovations, behavioral management, and other forms of helping that emphasize technique, especially those that are purported to work quickly and efficiently. In many ways, we have permission to adapt our style and methods according to the client's needs and clinical situation. Lost in the rush toward technical innovation are the human dimensions of the relationships between people.

Despite our best efforts to research the phenomenon of the therapeutic relationship, to isolate operative ingredients, the fact remains that something magical and wonderful does take place when we create a certain kind of alliance with clients. This healing force is not unique to our profession; doctors, teachers, lawyers, and even hairdressers, taxi drivers, and bartenders offer some degree of comfort and aid in their relationships with clients—apart from the contracted services they provide. This healing relationship between people goes beyond mere catharsis: human beings have an intense craving, often unfulfilled, to be understood by someone else.

Cultural, Social, and Political Contexts

In many cases, therapeutic responses are also greatly influenced by the cultural, social, and political context of the client and therapist. Most therapeutic approaches are no longer applied in universal ways but are adapted according to the values and needs of those from varied socioeconomic, ethnic, racial, and religious backgrounds and of a range of gender and sexual identities. The goal of such clinical flexibility is not only to customize therapy to fit the particular needs of an increasingly diverse client population but also for practitioners to confront their own prejudices and stereotypes.

I realize that the preceding statements are so commonly and obligatorily included in every book that they have lost all meaning. It has become so politically correct to espouse the standard party line regarding diversity issues that we may fail to appreciate the real depth, complexity, and influence of the challenges we face on almost countless different levels. We are not supposed to make sweeping generalizations about groups of people, but the reality is that every practitioner understands that there are certain similarities in the ways that particular people of certain backgrounds react in therapy.

A new client walks in your door, perhaps a 54-year-old Vietnamese female with a strong accent, shy smile, and averted eye contact, or maybe an African American teenager wearing sunglasses (it is nighttime) and earphones attached to a mobile device, or envision a guy in a tailored suit with a Rolex watch and perfectly coifed silver-gray hair. It is difficult, if not impossible, to avoid forming immediate impressions. Some of these prejudgments are based on prior experiences with clients who appear to be similar; some are based on far more personal influences, such as the values of our own families of origin or perhaps our own ethnicity.

There is a myth operating that therapeutic approaches or ingredients are essentially the same—you just fine-tune or adjust them a little for so-called diverse groups. A Vietnamese immigrant walks in? Expect deference and try to work within a family context. A young black man from the inner city comes in? Expect a little resistance and hostility, especially to a white therapist. The CEO-looking dude with the polished wingtips? Expect power and control struggles because of his narcissism and sense of entitlement. But these minor concessions to diversity (and that's what they are—minor, token efforts) only scratch the surface. The greater truth is that we would sometimes do better by throwing our theories out the window and meeting each person not just as a representative of his or her cultural group but as a completely unique individual with an assortment of cultural identities that include far more than ethnicity, race, and religion.

I was working with an older Vietnamese woman who was very self-conscious about her English fluency. In fact, she was difficult for me to understand, and I suspect a good part of our communication consisted of smiles and shrugs. This left me little choice but to abandon the usual ways I might work and to experiment with alternative methods that were less reliant on verbalization.

We struggled through the first few sessions as the woman's story emerged. She was a recent immigrant and a survivor of the war while a child. She was now the eldest woman in her household, which meant that she was responsible for everyone else, even though she was to remain obedient to the eldest male, who happened to be her son. There were clear lines of authority based on gender and age, and this was creating some problems both within the family and for her own dreams for a career.

The whole concept of traditional therapy was an anathema to her. Here I was, an older male authority figure, trying to negotiate a relationship in which she was the most important partner in the process. Given her own cultural traditions, we were doomed to frustration unless I could find a way to meet her on terms that were mutually acceptable. Once we found this common ground, whatever I learned had little applicability to my next client—an angry African American woman who felt that the system I represented was giving her a hard time.

We win a few, we lose a few. Quite literally. But whatever we do, it is hardly business as usual in the sense that we can never expect to learn a way of being a therapist and think that we can operate in similar ways with an increasingly diverse client population. This is both humbling and endlessly fascinating, making it virtually impossible for us to reach a place where we can ever be certain about the therapeutic path we are taking.

In addition, the increasing reality for many minority and economically disadvantaged people is that they are locked out of the system and have little access to any mental health services no matter how desperate they might be. One psychiatry professor laments that so many of his students end up in private practice serving the wealthy and "worried well," charging exhorbitant fees for those who treat the sessions as a status symbol or hobby (Dembosky, 2016).

Minority and working-class clients are often even more out of luck. In one study that investigated therapists' willingness to take on new clients, Kugelmass (2016) had people call for appointments using either a name associated with a black woman (LaToya Johnson) or a name that might imply a white woman (Amy Roberts). The callers also used scripts that signaled they were working class or else more affluent. Perhaps it isn't all that surprising that that the upper-middle-class whites were accepted as clients twice as often as the black or working-class individuals. It was especially surprising considering that they all had the identical health insurance, so there was no financial advantage to serve one person over than another. It was plain and simple that this was another example of racial and class discrimination by those of us who are supposed to advocate for the most needy and oppressed.

Client Risk Taking in the Change Process

No matter which approach we adopt, and no matter what background our clients come from, we still operate in such a way as to motivate people to take constructive risks. When a person gives attention to unresolved issues of the past, she often must work through resistance and apprehensions. To dismantle rigid defenses, interpret unconscious motives, or reflect on unexplored feelings may involve pushing the client to the brink of her endurance. She must confront parts of herself that have been deeply buried, and she must risk the consequences of relinquishing coping strategies that have worked fairly well until this point. There is a risk (or perhaps even a certainty) that some destabilization will occur. In order to attain real growth, the client must often be willing to experience intense confusion, disorientation, and discomfort. She leaves behind an obsolete image of herself, one that was once comfortable and familiar, and she risks not liking the person she will become. She will lose a part of herself that can never be recovered. She risks all this for the possibility of a better existence, and all she has to go on is the therapist's word.

When the client seeks to modify specific goals and behaviors, the risks are even more evident. To change any single aspect of one's behavior is to set in motion a chain reaction of subsequent aftershocks. One woman had been procrastinating for years in therapy, reluctant to take any action. As is usually the case, all her difficulties were interconnected—the dead-end job, desire to move away from her parents, relationships with men, and the desire to lose weight. To make a change in any one of these areas would mean she would risk having everything else possibly fall apart. The idea of losing even 15 pounds was frightening to her because it would mean that she would be more attractive, feel more confident, have demonstrated the capacity for self-control, and have proven the power to change. She just could not face the consequences of changing any part of her life because that would mean that every other part might have to change as well. It was much easier to come to therapy each week and please her therapist with good intentions, a cooperative attitude, and a wonderful capacity for generating insights that would not necessarily lead to change.

The therapist's job is to do everything in her power not just to promote self-understanding but to encourage experimentation. The client must not only reflect but act. This task is accomplished through both the quality of the therapist's interventions, designed to reduce the perceived threat and increase the willingness to experiment, and the genuine commitment to risk taking that the therapist makes in her own life. A professional who believes in the value of risk taking is one who has had varied experiences in taking calculated chances when the need arises. This courage, as it is modeled in the sessions, hopefully begets courage in the client.

Risks of the Therapist

Doing therapy is risky work indeed. We sit in a room all day long with people who spill out the most disturbing, horrifying, tragic stories imaginable. They tell us of their abuse and suffering, their sense of hopelessness. They may deliberately deceive or manipulate us, or at least provide very sketchy and misleading details. Over time, many practitioners become desensitized to human emotion and experience an acute overdose of feeling; they learn to keep boundaries firmly in place and turn off their emotions. Even when we maintain such a guarded and cautious stance, there are times when contact with our clients penetrates us deeply—sometimes in ways we neither acknowledge nor understand.

I was cross-country skiing in the woods with my wife. The sun was blazing, reflecting off the snow. We were breathing hard, enjoying the scenery and the synchronized movement of our bodies. It was an absolutely peaceful and spectacular day, requiring continual concentration to stay upright, balanced, moving along the trail. Quite suddenly, without any warning, I abruptly stopped in my tracks and started crying. Needless to say, my wife was a little surprised.

She asked me what was wrong, especially considering that a few moments earlier I had been feeling such joy. I finally blurted out the question, "Are you going to leave me?" She looked at me as if I were a raving lunatic and replied, "Of course not!" She reassured me with a hug and tried to find out what was going on. I explained that lately in my practice a number of female clients had been working on issues of freedom and independence. They felt trapped in their marriages and resented their husbands' needs for approval and dominance. After years of struggle with and resistance from their husbands, they had chosen divorce as the only solution for liberation. Again and again, I heard their words ringing in my ears: "Why is he so oblivious to what I want and what I feel? He thinks things are so great between us just because he finds me home at night. When he finally realizes how serious I am about making changes, it will be too late. He has no idea how bad things are, and he doesn't want to know."

For weeks, the effect of hearing these words in several different keys had been accumulating, and it had begun eating away at my own illusions of security. Was I, like the husbands of my clients, on the verge of divorce while blissfully denying my problems—while enjoying an afternoon in the woods? Fortunately, my concern was unnecessary, but I felt shell-shocked from the close proximity to other people's battlefields. One benefit of such fears is that they helped me to become even more determined to work on honest communication in my marriage and friendships.

Physicians take careful steps to protect themselves from the infection, disease, and suffering of their patients. Rubber gloves, surgical masks, and probing stainless steel instruments keep germs at arm's length. But sometimes there is a seepage of pain. For some practicing physicians, all barriers between themselves and their patients become eroded because they let themselves feel too much when their hands explore inside the visceral organs of their patients. Yet because they are admonished against showing any signs of "weakness" associated with emotional expression, they retreat into the stairwells or bathroom stalls to cry in private. More and more often they now hide behind computer screens or mobile devices while they enter data.

Throughout the process of therapy, the relationship is our main instrument of cure. Although we try to insulate ourselves, and we are successful in doing so most of the time, leaks inevitably occur. As our warmth, caring, and power radiate toward the client, facilitating the kind of trust that will lead to more open exploration and constructive risk taking, so, too, do we experience intimacy, discomfort, and countertransference reactions that permanently alter our perceptions and internal structure. The more clients talk about subjects that touch on our own unresolved issues, the more insecure and uneasy we may feel about ourselves.

To take on a client, *any* client, is to make a tremendous commitment to that person, which in some cases could last weeks, months, or even years. For better or worse, no matter how the client behaves, we feel an obligation to be available, understanding, and compassionate. From the moment a client settles himself in the chair for the first time, we take a deep breath, knowing that what is about to occur is the beginning of a new adventure. We will share moments of special closeness and others of great hardship. The client may, at times, worship us, scorn us, abuse us, ignore us, play with us, and want to devour us. And through it all, regardless of what is going on in our own life—sickness, births, deaths, joys, disappointments—we must be there for the client, always present.

If we ever really considered the possible risks in getting involved with a client, we would not do so for any price. Never mind that we will catch their colds and flu—what about their pessimism, negativity, and annoying symptoms? One just cannot see clients week after week, listen to their stories, and dry their tears without being profoundly affected by the experience. There are risks for us that we will not recognize until years later. Images stay with us until the grave. Words creep back to haunt us. Those silent screams remain deafening.

Even now, this moment, as I write these words, I see the blur of faces crossing the page. I hear the sobs of a father whose teenage son died in his arms. I see the cascade of hair that hides the face of a young woman who spent a significant part of every one of our sessions crying copiously. I feel the shudder of revulsion when a man confessed that he enjoyed exposing himself to little girls. I relive the story of a woman whose family was murdered in front of her. I feel the imprint on my lap of a 3-year-old girl I held just before telling her that she was an orphan after her home collapsed during an earthquake. I feel the helplessness, horror, and frustration flooding me all over again. Some of these were people I saw more than a decade or two ago, yet they still inhabit my heart and mind. They will be with me until my last breath.

What do we do with the stories we hear? How do we hold them? How do we live with them? The answer, in part, is with difficulty.

Therapist Vulnerability

Watching a therapist enter his office with nothing but a briefcase, one would never imagine that he is preparing to enter into mortal combat. Things appear quite civilized and controlled on the surface, what with the polite greetings and all. But once the action starts, the sparks that fly may leave third-degree burns. In a small room, there is nowhere to seek shelter. The therapist uses only his naked self (figuratively, of course) as the instrument of treatment, a condition that requires tremendous self-control and induces considerable vulnerability. To meet the client in a therapeutic encounter, we must leave behind some of our armor and defenses. We must go out from our centeredness as far as we dare. In our effort to be open and receptive, to participate with the client in the relationship, to venture forth as far as we are able, we risk losing our own sense of self along the way.

Great wracking sobs could be heard through the door, not an unusual occurrence in a mental health clinic, except that the client had left 5 minutes earlier. Only the therapist remained—alone, behind the closed door. Tears streamed down his face. He was huddled in a ball on the floor. The therapist had been conducting a particularly intense session with a man who was mourning the loss of his unborn son. As he was helping the client accept the miscarriage and find hope in the future, the therapist realized at some point that he was no longer speaking to the client but to himself. His own girlfriend had unceremoniously decided, upon ending their relationship, to abort their baby. The therapist had long ago worked through his loss, pain, and disappointment. Yet it all came tumbling forth again as his client struggled with a similar issue. Against all restraint, all objectivity, all desire to help the client, he lost the separateness between himself and the other.

It would be senseless to complain about the side effects that stem from personal involvement. After all, many of us entered this profession in the first place because of an interest in resolving our own issues along the path of helping others. I am reluctant to admit that although I did and do feel a commitment toward altruism, a significant part of my motivation to become a therapist came from my need to make sense of the world, to stave off my fear of mediocrity, to find acceptance, to satisfy my desire for control, to win approval and gratitude. I ask myself why I care so much about writing these words, why I continue to write books, and I laugh at the pat yet incomplete response: because I have something to say that others might find useful. But that is hardly the whole truth. I also desperately want to be liked, and I thrive on external validation. Finally, I want to feel good enough.

When a client comes in and struggles with these very themes (because I am looking for them, I see them everywhere), I rejoice in the opportunity to do some more work on myself. There are times, however, when I lose perspective and become so intertwined in the relationship that I must take a few steps out of range in order to untangle my own vulnerabilities from those of my client. Sometimes, when I am counseling or teaching, I stop for a moment to consider whom I am really speaking to—more than a few times I must admit that it is to myself.

The therapist is vulnerable not only to the loss of self but also threats to her self-esteem. We may profess to be neutral and to have no vested interest in outcomes, but we care quite a bit about how things turn out. It is impossible to care deeply for people without caring about what they do. When clients are demanding and critical, dissatisfied with their lack of progress, or blaming us for not being a miracle worker, we feel disappointed, if not inadequate. When clients do not improve, or get worse, we not only feel their pain but also take it personally that they are not cooperating with our therapeutic efforts. This is in spite of our attempts to remember the golden words, "We do our part; the client must do his" or "It is ultimately up to the client to change." All of this might very well be true, but we have a lot at stake as well. We can act unconcerned when a client does not improve, shrug our shoulders and go about our business, tell ourselves we are doing all we can, then head for the beach. But others will make decisions about our competence and attack our credibility even if we do not.

The client's family members, for example, having been in the unenviable position of having to live with the client while we only see her an hour per week, cannot afford much patience. It is easy for us to tell them, "Give it time. This has taken a long time to develop into a problem, and it will take awhile to resolve." They will thank us politely as they mutter under their breaths, "This guy doesn't know what he's doing." Then they will express their opinions to all who will listen, exasperated and exhausted. Considering that everyone knows a therapist whom he or she likes, the family's confidence will be further undermined by friends who suggest that they consult someone else who *really* knows what she is doing.

And let's not pretend that it doesn't hurt when a client abruptly quits treatment with the following farewell: "Gee, I know you've tried so hard to help me. And I agree it's probably all my fault. But since I've been seeing you, I've only gotten worse. You asked me to be patient, and I think I have been, but it doesn't seem to help. My cousin is seeing another therapist who was recommended to me. I'm going to be switching to her. Thanks for all you've done." Now not only will the other therapist find out how ineffective you have been (because she may not assume that the lack of progress was the client's fault), but soon the referral source will call wanting to know how things are going. You can make up some excuse about primitive defenses or resistance that you may even believe, and maybe the referral source will buy it, but deep, deep inside is a quiet little voice that will whisper, "You blew it." If such an episode occurs in the same week in which you have a few too many cancellations, you are well on our way to a major bout of self-doubt.

Of course that is only half the picture (I hope much less than half). Just as we are vulnerable to disappointment because we care so much, we are also open to the incredible joy we experience being witnesses, if not partners, to the amazing things our clients accomplish in such a short time. Every single day of our working lives we hear incredible tales of courage and accomplishment, breakthroughs that could only have occurred because of our support and intervention.

The Experience of Being *a Therapist*

The therapist's journey is filled with mystery and challenges. It follows a developmental pattern that usually progresses through several stages, each of which provides its own challenges and opportunities. For the beginner one of the initial tasks involves learning how to metabolize everything we take in without undue stress and hardship. Lyman (2014), for example, describes the ways her life changed since she'd been training to be a clinician. Although she admits feeling a certain pride and satisfaction in all that she has learned and accomplished, she also acknowledges there's been considerable suffering and confusion. She's noticed feeling increasingly impatient and intolerant of others who are not as psychologically minded. On the other hand, at the latter stage of his career, Messer (2015), feels "on top of his game," more able to relax and let go in all areas of his life in ways he'd never been able to do before. This is actually a common report among aging practitioners who have developed confidence and expertise in their work that spills over into other areas of their lives (Kottler & Carlson, 2016).

We act as models of courage and as adventurers, blazing trails that might inspire others to follow us into the unknown. One therapist I spoke to, Fran, shares her fascination with the inner experience of being a therapist: "I love what it feels like, how it changes us, how it penetrates us. I see the job, or the profession, or the calling, as just being this amazing gift for those of us who are privileged enough to do this work because of these gems and things that we learn."

Fran laughs, remembering what it was like trying to describe to her children what it is she does for work. It really is quite amazing when you think about it. I have had a number of conversations with healers in other cultures, trying to explain what it is that I do in my own work. I recall one shaman from the Bushman people who literally fell off the rock he was sitting on, laughing hysterically, when I told him how I work by listening to clients, helping them sort things out and talk about what is most bothersome. The shaman called over others from his village, yelling out, "Come on over here! You gotta hear what this white dude shaman character says" (that's a rough translation). Once assembled with his friends, he urged me to repeat what I do in therapy. He was absolutely dumbfounded that I didn't bring together the whole community as witnesses to the healing. There was no dancing, shaking, chanting, or drumming in my description of psychotherapy. There was no calling to the spirits. There was no fire built for the healing ceremony (although I thought about telling him about a kid who once lit a fire in the wastebasket of my waiting room). Again the shaman grabbed his belly and everyone laughed at my expense. Finally, when he caught his breath, he asked me if I had ever helped anyone with just this talk. It gets you thinking, doesn't it?

I have never really trusted anyone who claims to understand how therapy works. I think it is far too complex. What the client brings to us in a session is so overwhelming and so full of content and feeling that we can't hold it all. So we have to find ways to live with that—to live with all this uncertainty, all this mystery, all this ambiguity. At the same time, our clients are demanding answers and solutions.

"So," a new client speaks up loudly to make sure you are paying attention, "now that you've had a chance to hear what's bothering me, can you fix it?"

"You mean right now?" you ask, a little confused.

"Well," he shrugs, "if you can't take care of this for me today I guess I could come back one other time."

Part of the job of inducting someone into the role of being a good client is teaching the individual a little bit of patience as well as how to work the process. But all the while we're saying this to our clients, we're talking to ourselves, too, about how to live with the ambiguity of our own lives, trying to make sense of what it is that we do.

2

Struggles for Power and Influence

AS WE ARE all well aware, growth occurs spontaneously without professional help. Many theories offer explanations of this phenomenon. Most people who are struggling eventually recover on their own; it just usually takes longer than if they sought assistance. Psychological growth may be part of our genetically programmed survival instinct or may be reinforced by the environment and society. People are transformed by recovery from trauma or adversity or even by travel experiences. There are developmental, phenomenological, sociobiological, behavioral, and countless other explanations for spontaneous, unstructured change processes. To complicate matters further, the interpersonal influence that operates in therapy moves in *both* directions. Just as the therapist attempts to do everything in his power to change clients, so, too, do clients seek to control the therapist for their own purposes. They do this for a number of reasons:

- To persuade us to take sides in their struggles with others and agree that they are right and others are wrong
- To convince us that we should be more like them, thereby confirming that they don't have to change
- To win our love and approval, providing the sort of validation that they have been hungry for their whole lives—especially from an authority figure
- To affirm that they are more important than all other clients and that we like them best as the "favorite child"
- To manipulate us into meeting their needs or hidden agendas, often in the form of affirming their own sense of power
- To work through unresolved transference relationships by knocking us off our pedestals

There is a two-way interchange of social influence that exists between client and therapist in which we are each trying to persuade the other to take a particular position or adopt a favored viewpoint. At the same time that we are working to influence our clients to think, react, or act in some way, they are unconsciously or deliberately fighting for control of the sessions. In classical psychodynamic terms, the client attempts to act out the transference and mold the therapist into someone else. Each participant in this process may even begin to imitate the speech and behavioral patterns of the other.

Of course, the nature of interpersonal influence and reciprocal power has changed in the last few decades. We therapists are no longer regarded with the same unwavering respect and deference as we used to be when we were treated as gurus and godlings. Sure, we still have the power to inspire awe in some clients who come to us, but not all—especially those who are court ordered or involuntarily referred.

Those clients who do come of their own free will are more informed by education, media, online research, self-help books, and talk shows; they are empowered to act as their own self-healers and want therapists to serve in the role of consultants or coaches, available as needed via text or messaging. Although this attitude fits well within the scope of some practitioners, such overexposure can ruin the mystery behind what we do. Therapists are no longer universally regarded as authoritative experts, but rather as partners in the democratization of therapy. This is not altogether a bad thing, but it does present some additional challenges in a profession where our maximum influence comes, in part, from our stature in others' eyes.

Therapists as Professional Models

As the Socratic era of teaching by personal example, Freud's proposal of identification processes, and Bandura's reworking of social learning theory have shown, people are strongly influenced by exposure to other, more powerful people. Thus one main force of childhood is the overpowering urge to grow up and be just like mommy or daddy, sister, Wonder Woman, Spiderman, a favorite teacher, or the kid down the block. Even in adulthood, models in the media continue to exert a powerful influence on people's behavior.

Even after we learn to stop idolizing our heroes and parents and to prize new values of independence and self-sufficiency, models continue to exert a powerful influence on the way we dress, speak, feel, and think. In fact, the mentor system is the core of most therapist education: teachers, advisers, supervisors, authors, and colleagues shape who we are and the way we practice our craft. For many therapists, the first decade of our professional lives is spent imitating the master clinicians. We generally do this long before we ever consider what we really believe in our own minds and hearts. Yet it is interesting how even as we mature in our development as therapists, we still seem to have a strong tendency toward idealizing our heroes and heroines, as evidenced by the long lines at conferences to obtain autographs from luminaries in the field.

In the early stages of the identification process, we idealize the model and make that person even larger than life. Who among us cannot remember the ways we idealized, if not worshipped, a teacher, mentor, author, or supervisor who inspired us like no other? Under such circumstances, this model had extraordinary influence in our lives, not just in terms of our professional development but also personally. There is also a dark side to the modeling phenomenon. (Isn't there always?) Models give lots of reinforcement to those who express an interest in becoming just like them, perpetuating miniature selves who go out into the world and preach the True Word and convert others to the cause. If you have ever attended a therapist conference, then you can easily recognize the various schools of thought, just like schools of fish, swimming in synchrony. There is no doubt that there is comfort in such company, being one of many who have found the one true path to enlightenment.

Charisma invites vulnerability and trust; it is thus both a potential instrument of constructive influence and a dangerous form of manipulation. Narcissism pervades our domain. Therapists, teachers, and other professional models, such as actors and athletes, thrive on gratitude and accolades from fans and disciples. You would only have to attend any workshop or conference to see the ways that otherwise powerful professionals in their own right pay homage to the "rock stars," who are treated with reverence. The only difference is that public figures receive financial compensation equal to their aura. Therapists are limited to the ceiling established by their hourly rates or their salaries. The balance of payment is usually received in the intangible benefits that accrue from hero worship.

When Therapists Can't or Don't Practice What They Preach

It is galling to hear "crazy shrink" stories in which a therapist is portrayed in the media or in social conversations as being more disturbed than any of his or her clients. This isn't helped by the not uncommon experience of encountering colleagues who, let us say, are rather eccentric, if not not downright strange, in the way they conduct their lives. They may be rude or lazy, or sometimes just clueless about how they are perceived by others.

In an article about how emotionally unstable, narcissistic, and wounded many therapists are, one woman is quoted by Maeder (1989) as saying that every time she goes to a party, invariably the most foolish, embarrassing, and crazy person in attendance is a therapist. As further evidence for his arguments, Maeder quotes a president of the American Academy of Psychotherapists addressing the members of his own organization: "When I first visited a national psychiatric convention, in 1943, I was dismayed to find the greatest collection of oddballs, Christ beards, and psychotics that I had ever seen outside a hospital" (p. 37).

Popular movies and television shows often portray therapists as harmless, neurotic characters who can barely hold their own lives together. Journalists seem to delight in uncovering scandals that show the chinks in our armor, or sometimes far worse. In one article in the popular press about a charismatic, prominent psychoanalyst (Boynton, 2003), the author writes a scathing indictment of the profession based on the abusive behavior of one disturbed professional who regularly had sex with his clients, breached confidentiality by talking about celebrities he was seeing in therapy, and verbally berated and abused people who were coming to see him. Of course, this whacked-out therapist deserves to have his license revoked and to serve prison time, but the impression sometimes given is that people like this are somehow representative of our profession.

We also perpetuate the myth of therapist ineptitude by criticizing members of competing helping professions or therapeutic approaches who are not members of our own tribe. Psychologists, psychiatrists, social workers, counselors, family therapists, psychiatric nurses, and addiction specialists often attack one another for perceived (or actual) differences in training. Likewise, there has been an ongoing war for decades among psychodynamic therapists, cognitive-behavioral therapists, behavior therapists, humanistic therapists, constructivists, feminists, and so on, as to who has cornered the market on truth. Perhaps these debates are useful in clarifying universal features embedded in all therapeutic work, but there is one area of hypocrisy that I can't abide: it just burns me when I encounter a professional (or parts of myself) who asks clients to do things that he himself cannot do. What kind of image do we project to the public when we cannot demonstrate in our own lives the most rudimentary degree of empathy, sincerity, and emotional stability? What sort of hypocrites have we become when we ask people to do things that we are unwilling or unable to do ourselves?

So many of the joys, as well as hazards, of our work result from the consequences of being professional models who allow ourselves to be affected by our clients. We want to show them, by the way we live our lives, that it is possible to be proactive taking charge of our own behavior. Clients know little about the details of our existence, our dreams, our disappointments, or what we are like in social situations, yet they know our spirit intimately. They can sense our moods and feel our tranquility, confidence, and energy. They may not know what we are really like, but they know us at our absolute best. We do not yell impatiently at our clients as we might at our own children. We try not to meet our own needs at all during sessions. And clients come to love us, to worship our idealized selves. Even though we understand the illusions and myths we may be creating, we still have a wonderful opportunity to be more like the people clients think we actually are—completely loving, giving, peaceful, and in control.

Balancing Omnipotence and Humanness

Traditionally, the therapist has been seen as the contemporary equivalent of the oracle perched on a mountaintop; clients are the pilgrims who journey in search of enlightenment. Mistrusting their own inner voices and lacking self-direction, clients have looked to their gurus for guidance and see them as embodiments of power. There are ancient traditions in almost every human culture of not only worshipping gods but also showing reverence to those who are considered conduits to the spirit world and to those who are considered sages, shamans, or healers.

We will explore later how one of the principal hazards of our profession is the narcissistic belief that we really are special. After all, it's tough not to take ourselves so seriously when so many people treat us with such awe and deference. The therapist's office is an unreal world in which distractions are minimized and rituals are carefully observed. The therapist controls most of the show. Although the client chooses the content, the therapist directs the script and the interpretation of the lines. We are used to being in control and are accustomed to having people defer to us. We feel special because we are often treated that way.

Most therapists do good work. Clients get better. They feel grateful and ascribe their improvement to something or someone outside themselves. We are more than willing to take partial credit; it is good for promotions, new referrals, and our sense of potency. The problem is not in feeling that we have made some difference in a client's life but in forgetting that we are not the paragons we pretend to be. When we direct the interacting, questioning, controlling, confronting, nurturing, and even summarizing at appropriate intervals for 8 hours a day, it is an abrupt shock to our systems to find ourselves, once we are at home or with friends, struggling to be heard like everyone else.

We are used to being listened to. Some people even take notes on what we say, and we can test them later to make sure they were paying attention. After a while, we start believing that we really *are* important. Clients reinforce the idea by telling us how much they were helped. Then we remember how fragile the illusion of omnipotence really is. Even if it is initially useful for clients to idealize their therapists, we must help them and ourselves see a separate reality.

Modeling takes the form of presenting not only an ideal to strive for but also a real, live person who is flawed, genuine, and sincere. Occasionally, the therapist can use self-disclosure to close the psychological distance between herself and the client. Such sharing can often lead to increased feelings of mutual identification, as well as build great intimacy and authenticity. Many clients are greatly relieved to learn that their therapists have been the victims of the same self-defeating behaviors that they are now trying to overcome. You may have noticed a similar phenomenon as a reader in the ways that I disclose my own doubts, uncertainties, and struggles in this book. If I have done this effectively, then you feel greater permission to be more open, vulnerable, and honest about your own unresolved issues. If I am perceived as self-indulgent or inappropriate, then I risk losing your trust and confidence.

By serving as a model of humanness, with accompanying imperfections, we can help clients (or readers) feel less overwhelmed and more optimistic that relative personal mastery is indeed within reach. We thus walk a fine line between exuding a certain assurance and personal competence and coping with unique eccentricities. We must battle with the consequences of acting like an impromptu guru much of the day and then successfully make the transition to flawed normality during the rest of our time. Otherwise, friends and family find us very annoying.

The Therapist's Strength of Character

Most of the great teachers we have ever read, known, or heard of were charismatic individuals. Plato, Socrates, Confucius, Freud, Gandhi, and Marx were geniuses in mastering their fields' knowledge, but their true talent was in imparting their wisdom and recruiting disciples through the force of their personalities. (Historically, at least, inspiring adulation has often been primarily a male-dominated enterprise.) Contemporary teachers in every field demonstrate the power of attractive personalities in promoting learning. Their followers are as much seduced by their voices, smiles, humor, and charisma as they are fascinated by what they say.

The leaders in the fields of counseling and psychotherapy have made many significant contributions through their research and ideas. However, nobody would have listened to them if they had not been captivating people. Their unique ways of expressing themselves, their passion and excitement, their energy and spirit, their commitment and confidence, gave life to their ideas. It was their eccentric quirks, their personal struggles, their humanity that were also appealing. They not only managed to develop theories that perfectly suited their own values and interpersonal styles but also were absolutely brilliant at "recruiting" others through the force of their personalities.

During the past decades, a colleague and I have completed over a hundred interviews with many of the field's most notable figures, representing two dozen different theoretical orientations. We have asked these master therapists to tell us about their worst sessions (Kottler & Blau, 1989; Kottler & Carlson, 2002), most unusual case (Kottler & Carlson, 2003), best therapy session (Kottler & Carlson, 2008), spiritual transformation (Kottler & Carlson, 2007), most creative breakthrough (Kottler & Carlson, 2009), the client who changed them the most (Kottler & Carlson, 2006), their advocacy and social justice efforts (Kottler, Englar-Carlson, & Carlson, 2013), and what constitutes a true master in the profession (Kottler & Carlson, 2015), as well as one who ages and matures successfully (Kottler & Carlson, 2016). The participants in these studies included theoreticians who represent a broad range of viewpoints and styles. After spending countless hours with these individuals, listening to their experiences, identifying common themes in their stories, observing their sessions, and analyzing the results, one of the surprising—even shocking—discoveries was that many of these theorists don't even practice their identified models any longer! They have moved on to other things. They have been influenced by their colleagues during panel discussions at conferences. Most of all, they have transcended technique to emphasize far more the human and relational features of their interactions with clients. In other words, they may no longer use their developed theory in pure form, but more than ever they use their caring, compassion, and other personal characteristics.

I am not saying that a therapist must be eccentric or outrageous in order to be maximally effective. It is one of the most perplexing (and wonderful) aspects of our work that one can adopt so many different therapeutic styles with equal effectiveness. There are great therapists who were provocative and pushy (think Fritz Perls or Carl Whitaker), and there were others who were softer and sincere (think Virginia Satir). There were therapists who were talking rational computers (Albert Ellis), charming rogues (Jacques Lacan), kindly grandfathers (Carl Rogers), or Wizards of Oz (Milton Erickson). It doesn't matter so much which path the professional took to develop a therapeutic style as long as it was one that brought out the best in him or her.

All good therapists have a way of communicating similar greatness—in their own unique way. They have developed their own style of helping people feel that what they have to say is worth listening to no matter how much effort is required to hear it. They accomplish this through the intrinsic appeal of their inner voices. All effective therapists intuitively find a way to capitalize on the strengths of their character. Freud's self-analytic skills, Rogers's genuineness, Ellis's capacity for rational thinking, Whitaker's playfulness formed the nucleus for their respective theories. So, too, do all clinicians translate their inner selves into a personal style of helping.

The Ideal Therapist Model

Even with all our differences in values, interests, histories, professional affiliation, and training, most therapists share similar attributes as powerful helping models. Many researchers, theoreticians, and practitioners have attempted to describe the dimensions of an ideal therapeutic personality (Beutler, 1983; Corey & Corey, 2016; Heide, 2013; Kottler, 1991; Kottler & Carlson, 2015; Norcross, Bike, & Evans, 2009; Orlinsky & Ronnestad, 2005). Carl Rogers mentioned such qualities as genuineness, authenticity, openness, and acceptance. Robert Carkhuff specified empathic understanding and the ability to respond. Jerome Frank felt that confidence was the key to a therapist's persuasive power. Abraham Maslow believed that the more general striving for self-actualization was a crucial trait.

Whether through a deliberate and systematic indoctrination in certain beliefs or as a by-product of interpersonal intimacy, clients come to know our basic values about life, no matter how much we try to disguise them. Some practitioners deny that this is so, claiming that perfect neutrality and complete objectivity are possible. Perhaps those who practice within a strict psychoanalytic framework are indeed able to withhold most of their values from their clients. However, as a veteran participant in psychoanalytic therapy many years ago, I can attest that although my therapist tried to keep herself out of the sessions, I knew exactly what she wanted me to say and do and the choices she preferred that I make. Being an expert approval seeker from way back when, I worked very hard to be as much like her as I possibly could—including entering her profession so that I might embrace even more of her values.

If this assumption is true—that clients take on our values as a consequence (deliberate or incidental) of participation in treatment—we had better be sure that what we espouse is well grounded in reality and generally healthy. It's also interesting to consider that there is often a match between a therapist's theoretical orientation and his or her personal values, beliefs, qualities, and relational style (Heinonen & Orlinsky, 2013). It wouldn't be surprising to learn, for instance, that cognitive-behavioral therapists describe themselves as logical and pragmatic, whereas humanistic practitioners identify most strongly as being warm and accessible.

Regardless of chosen approach, ideal therapists are comfortable with themselves and appear tolerant, sincere, serene, tranquil, and self-assured. This quiet confidence is counterbalanced by a contagious zest for life. Passion. Excitement. Electricity. Enthusiasm. They radiate from body and soul.

We have the client's attention. He is attracted to our compassionate and a loving nature. Offering much more than the wooden skills and platitudes of advanced accurate level empathy, unconditional positive regard, and other primary facilitative factors, we genuinely care about the client's welfare. These feelings go beyond restrained professional respect for someone who trusts us. The client can feel our caring, our intense desire to give of ourselves.

But love is not enough. If it were, parents could heal their children with intention alone. Therapists are wise and knowledgeable. They are experts in human nature. They are perceptive and sensitive. They are students of science and the arts, of the abstract and the ambiguous, and especially of language. They hear things that are inaudible and see things that invisible to others, and they do so with great accuracy.

Therapists are also known for their stability and grounding. They are patient, so, so patient. They exhibit great self-discipline, yet, enigmatically, they are also spontaneous and playful. Creativity, humor, flexibility, honesty, and sincerity are other qualities that therapists strive toward. And as a function of these attributes, therapists are in an optimal position to demonstrate those skills and behaviors that are most persuasive and influential in promoting change.

Our main job is to make ourselves as attractive and powerful as possible in order to lend greater potency to our interventions. We communicate on two levels simultaneously. First, there is the content of what we say: the accuracy of our interpretations, the truth of our confrontations, and the appropriateness of our metaphors make a difference in client awareness, insight, and behavior. On a more subtle, preconscious level, the client also attends to our style. Much of our interpersonal influence, our power as models, operates in the nonverbal realm. It is the way we speak as much as what we say that communicates confidence and favorable expectations. It is the way we carry ourselves that implies genuineness and sincerity in our movements.

We try to teach goodness, honesty, and trustworthiness in our sessions. Such qualities cannot be faked very easily. That is not to say that deceitful therapists are never effective, because some are. But to the degree that we can make our spirit and energy purer, we enable our words to carry even more power. As professional helpers, then, our primary task is to be more personally effective and loving human beings. We should show compassion not only in our work but in our lives. If we are to be consistent and genuine, then our family, colleagues, friends, and even strangers on the street deserve the best of us as well.

One of the ironies of our profession is that we become highly skilled at giving our clients undivided, concentrated attention without interruption, yet we may rarely do the same with our family and friends. The people we care about the most get us in diluted form, distracted and self-involved. As I was writing these words, my 3-year-old granddaughter found me hiding in the study and asked if I would pay hide-and-seek with her.

"Let me finish what I'm doing ...," I started to say, and then abruptly caught myself, realizing how out of whack my priorities were in that moment. I would never put a client off, so why would I think this little girl was any less important to me? This is exactly the kind of revelation that I try to teach so often to my clients.

How Modeling Works in Therapy

Several researchers, such as Bandura (1977), have described the uses of modeling in specific, behaviorally defined situations. These social learning theorists are fond of investigating those factors that enhance the acquisition of learning, the quality of performance, and the transfer and generalization of behavior. For our purposes, however, we are less concerned with the details of vicarious reinforcement processes than with the broader understanding of the different ways in which modeling operates in therapy.

For example, on the most ambiguous and elusive level, the therapist's energy has a significant impact on the client's mood and conduct. Therapists who sit peacefully and sagely, speaking in silky and serene tones, seem to tranquilize even the most agitated clients. Anxious, high-strung people, those with fears, phobias, and panic disorders, respond well to calm models. They learn from our manner of interaction, the way we sit and stand, the pace of our speaking and listening, just how a relaxed person functions. In contrast, when a therapist's energy is animated, electric, vibrating throughout the room, even the most passive people will wake up a bit. Clients respond to the personal energy we generate. They admire our intense vibrancy and the self-control to modulate it. As models, we remain living examples of constructive human energy.

Clients deliberately and sometimes unconsciously adopt their therapists' speech patterns, favorite expressions, even mannerisms and dress habits. Groups of graduate students can be identified with their advisers with only brief verbalizations as cues. After decades, we can still trace remnants in our vocabularies to the influences of significant mentors. I still occasionally catch myself mimicking one of my previous mentors or supervisors as if he or she still lives within me (which of course is actually true). Considering that this kind of imitative learning occurs without deliberate encouragement, imagine the incredible potential power of more strategic therapeutic modeling.

The simplest form of modeling occurs in those instances when the therapist spontaneously demonstrates desirable behaviors. During a typical session, regardless of the content, a client may receive instruction in effective confrontation, appropriate questioning, or comfortably handling silence. The therapist subtly (or directly) draws attention to his or her own assertive posture, internally based language, concise statements, or creative thinking.

The use of simulated experiences in therapy provides even more specific imitative learning. Psychodramatic and other rehearsal or role-playing structures usually contain a segment that is demonstrated by the therapist. A restrained and timid client who is practicing a confrontation with a family member will be asked during periods of frustration to observe the expert model in action. The therapist will then show a variety of ways to defuse conflict and maintain control.

Therapists have been known to employ a number of interventions that have modeling principles at their core, including (1) rehearsing role playing that emphasizes recurrent themes, (2) showing videos or simulations that demonstrate desired target behaviors, (3) teaching discrimination skills through observing models, (4) reviewing recorded segments of the client engaged in new behaviors, (5) using puppets or other enactments in play therapy, (6) using anecdotes or stories to illustrate principles, (7) embedding metaphors in communication to model effective behavior vicariously without the client's feeling threatened, (8) employing language carefully to demonstrate self-responsibility. Finally, we model acceptance and a caring attitude toward clients, hoping that they will internalize these qualities to neutralize their own self-critical natures.

Metaphorical anecdotes can range from fairy tales to more personal self-disclosures that minimize the psychological distance between therapist and client. By modeling openness, strength, even vulnerability and the sharing of intense feelings, the therapist invites the client to follow her lead. Trust, perceived similarity, and empathic understanding can be vastly improved through restrained, well-timed, and appropriate therapist sharing that is devoid of self-indulgence. As long as we don't inappropriately take attention away from the client, we can increase our trustworthiness, attractiveness, and credibility through such self-disclosures (Berg, Antonsen, & Binder, 2016; Bloomgarden & Mennuti, 2015; Farber, 2006; Gelso & Hayes, 2007; Henretty, Currier, Berman, & Levitt, 2014; Somers, Pomerantz, Meeks, & Pawlow, 2014). Naturally, how clients receive and interpret self-disclosure depends a lot on the quality of the alliance that has been established (Myers & Hayes, 2006).

The Uses of Power

Modeling strategies also share a belief in the benevolent and judicious use of power. A clinician's power is first sanctioned by legitimate bodies, such as licensing boards. The diplomas on our walls are sometimes perceived as endowing us with certain mystical powers to read minds. We are viewed not only as legitimate professionals with special privileges but as figures of authority. Depending on the client's previous experiences with other models of authority (school principal, safety patrol, drill sergeant, boss, parents, and teachers), the therapist's power also can instill feelings of resentment and rebellion. This is especially more likely in cases when the therapist and client represent different cultural, ethnic, or socioeconomic backgrounds.

It's also important to keep in mind that we may sometimes inflate the amount of power and control we think we wield considering that somewhere between an estimated 60 to 70% of therapy outcomes are attributed to *clients' characteristics* and what they bring to the table. Depending on the severity of their problems and their preexisting conditions, their level of motivation, resilience, and commitment, their beliefs and optimism, their perceived self-efficacy and internal control, clients largely determine their own prognosis. Of course they can only do so much on their own, and that's where we enter the picture.

Power is what infuses us with the persuasion and influence to motivate and inspire clients to change. When used in the spiritual rather than a manipulative sense—that is, for the client's self-articulated good rather than for meeting our own needs—power is the driving force behind much of what we do. It gives weight to what we say and commands sufficient attention that clients will allow themselves to be influenced by our messages in ways that hardly ever happen in the outside world. Eventually, there is a gradual transfer of power in which clients take on the roles and responsibilities that we have modeled. They have internalized the best parts of us.

If we accept our responsibility as therapist-models and agree to use our influence for the good of our clients, we are then committed to increasing our personal and professional effectiveness. We are involved in the process of integrating our various roles and making ourselves as appealing and as influential as we are capable of becoming.

3

Personal and Professional Lives

THE PRACTICE OF psychotherapy permits a unique lifestyle in which one's personal and professional roles complement each other. There are few other careers in which the boundaries between work and play, between professional and personal life, are so permeable. All the powers of observation, perception, and sensitivity are equally useful with clients, family, or friends. The skills we use in our work, such as empathic listening or flexible problem solving, prove invaluable when helping the people we love. In a similar vein, all our personal experiences, travels, learning, conversations, readings, and intimate dealings with life's joys and sorrows provide the foundation for everything we do in our therapy sessions.

Many have described the practice of therapy as a calling rather than a job or a profession. It is often observed that we are driven to understand the human condition, within those we help, but also within ourselves. We have an insatiable curiosity about, and a need to make sense of, life experiences and to help others do so. This process moves in the opposite direction as well: by helping people put their lives in perspective, unlock the hidden secrets of their psyches, and understand themselves more thoroughly, we are helping ourselves do the same. We are often searching for answers to life's ultimate questions since one of our jobs is to find or create meaning for a living. Finding others who will help subsidize this quest only makes this journey less lonely and more comfortable. Searching for truth in the tradition of Lao-tzu, Buddha, or Confucius is admirable, but it is a lot more fun when we do not have to do so as paupers.

Confusion of Roles

Personal and professional roles become fused when the therapist is always on duty and thus unable or unwilling to have a life outside work and beyond the role of helper. In their classic study of practicing therapists, Henry, Sims, and Spray (1973) discovered that many adopt a one-dimensional attitude toward all their relationships, whether they involve clients, friends, or family. There is a distancing aura in which the clinician detaches himself not only from the therapeutic encounter but also from home life. There is also remarkable consistency in the way clients change in sessions and in the way therapists made their decisions to enter the field. Most practitioners were more strongly influenced by personal considerations, such as cultural heritage or rejection of parental values, than by any professional models. In most therapists there seems to be a burning desire to work through personal conflicts, a conviction that helping solve others' problems can help one solve his or her own problems. There is a tendency to merge the personal and professional dimensions of life into a unified perception of self and world.

This reality can become annoying, if not problematic, when strangers or acquaintances discover that you are a therapist (or training to become one). Your seatmate on a flight casually asks what it is you do for a living, and you reveal your job. "Oh yeah?" he says, with that look in his eye you've come to recognize. "You know, I have this teenaged kid and he just doesn't listen to me. I bet you see that sort of thing all the time. I was wondering. . . ."

You try to bury your face in a book or video, but before you know it, your new best friend is asking for help, if not sage advice. During the early part of our careers, this is almost flattering, but eventually we come to realize that if we are going to survive for very long in this profession, we must learn to set boundaries.

Our early life experiences and events shaped not only what kind of persons we've become but also the unique ways that we have chosen to help others. Likewise, each of our current life passages and experiences continue to influence our work, whether as a result of becoming a parent, going through a loss or divorce, navigating a life stage transition, dealing with illness or aging issues, or any other challenge (Gerson, 2009; Kuchuck, 2014). It's also interesting the way seemingly inconsequential, serendipitous things hit us just as hard and change how we think about ourselves and what we do.

Within sessions we experience all kinds of strong emotional reactions to what is transpiring in the room, including joy, pride, satisfaction, elation, as well as crushing disappointment, anxiety, and discouragement. The various times when therapists are most likely to have powerfully strong positive emotional reactions have been dissected and catalogued, occurring in circumstances that are both predictable and sometimes surprising (Vandenberghe

& Silvestre, 2013). The most obvious examples are when clients improve significantly, especially when we can trace a direct connection to something we said or when we did something extraordinarily well crafted: we feel the pride of professionalism. Other times include when we:

- Experience deep, resonant intimacy and a strong connection to a client
- Genuinely enjoy a client's company and admire his or her resilience, courage, and honesty
- Identify with a client's issues, feeling a shared common bond
- Advance our conceptual understanding of the process as a result of something that occurred
- Resolve an ongoing conflict as a result of determined persistence
- Hear deep appreciation from a client acknowledging progress that has been made
- Facilitate a creative breakthrough through playfulness, humor, teasing, or joking that is well received
- Experience an altered state of consciousness or transcendence in which we are able to totally lose ourselves in the process

We are sometimes moved to tears in session because of the powerful emotional energy in the room. In fact, three-quarters of therapists report that at some time they have actually cried with a client, although it is likely the real figure is even higher because of a reluctance to disclose such a perceived loss of control (Blume-Marcovici, Stolberg, & Khademi, 2013). One study investigated the circumstances under which therapists had been so moved by the proceedings that they cried and discovered that the vast majority of times it was in response to the client's story or when the client expressed strong emotion. Eighty percent of the the psychologists surveyed also had no regrets about letting their tears flow since they believed that this incident sparked quite favorable reactions from their clients (Blume-Marcovici, Stolberg, Khademi, & Giromini, 2015).

Most of us remember times when we were so powerfully impacted by something that occurred in a session that we couldn't help but feel choked up. Sometimes this happened as a result of something going on in our personal lives that resonated with the conversation in some way. but just as often it is our intense empathic attunement that leads us to feel what clients are experiencing. This is, of course, both a gift and a burden, depending on how we process the feelings and use them in session—or refrain from doing so if such disclosures might be inappropriate or distracting.

There is some fairly compelling evidence that when therapists are having difficulties in their personal lives, it can reduce their ability to function optimally in sessions, to remain grounded and clear. Our capacity for relational attunement is compromised, just as it becomes far more difficult to remain present and focused. Likewise, when we feel isolated and disengaged in our personal lives, clients are more likely to report weaker alliances than if we were involved in a number of rich, meaningful relationships (Nissen-Lie, Havid, Hoglend, Monsen, & Ronnestad, 2013). Perhaps not surprisingly, the quality of our lives in the outside world truly has a huge impact on our emotional reserves and professional effectiveness.

The fusion of personal and professional dimensions in a therapist's life affects not only her lifestyle, emotional stability, and values but also the course that her sessions take. It is naïve to pretend that the client assumes complete responsibility for introducing the content and direction of treatment. We may begin with what the client believes is his problem, but in no time we take over to lead discussions toward the topic that we think is most important—whether it be the client's feelings toward his parents, underlying thought patterns, or specific behaviors at work. Furthermore, except for the most conservative practitioners who follow the tenets of their theory to the letter, there is a certain amount of inconsistency and unreliability in our helping efforts, depending on what our mood is at the time, what is currently going on in our lives, what we have recently finished doing or thinking about, and what we are planning to do next.

It is no extraordinary revelation to admit that events in our lives affect the outcome of our work. Why, then, do we pretend as though therapy is simply the application of scientifically tested principles and reliable therapeutic interventions to the specific circumstances of a client's life? We act as though the process is always the same; as though there is always a progression through identical stages, resolution of conflicts, challenging of the same dysfunctional beliefs; and as though the therapist is always a constant. Many leading therapists believe that reliability in helping methodologies is the most important issue in the field.

Regardless of what we may wish to believe, the practice of therapy is a distinctly human enterprise that is significantly affected by myriad random and personal variables. Although it is laudable to work toward greater consistency in the way we treat clients, a therapist is a fallible human being subject to quirks, biases, errors, misjudgments, and distortions of reality. Even with the best education, training, supervision, study, and self-analysis, a therapist is hardly the anonymous, perfectly stable, neutral, all-knowing, and accepting creator that clients prefer to see.

Consider, for example, the potential impact of various personal events on professional behavior. Several intercurrent events, such as marriage, divorce, childbirth, illness, and family death, affect a therapist's life in profound ways, which in turn affects the client's behavior. Any physical change, such as a leg cast, missing wedding band, weight loss, even a haircut or new outfit, will hardly be ignored by clients. Certainly, such life transitions and crises cannot be fully shelved by the person experiencing them, even for 50 minutes while someone else is talking.

Perhaps the best evidence of how a therapist's increased vulnerability can change the nature of treatment is the observation that the majority of therapist–client sexual improprieties occur with therapists who have been recently divorced. It is also inconceivable that a therapist who has a baby growing within her or has pain radiating up his spine or has severe financial difficulties or has experienced the death of a loved one is going to conduct therapy in exactly the same way as he or she would if these conditions did not exist.

How do we know when there is personal and professional role confusion that may be interfering with our work? How do we recognize when our unresolved issues are playing themselves out or our lived experiences are distorting our judgment? Here are some questions to consider:

- Are you expecting things from your clients that they are unable or unwilling to do, yet interpreting their behavior as resistant, defiant, reluctant, or obstructive?
- In what ways during sessions do you feel strong personal reactions that parallel those expressed by your clients?
- How is your empathy with certain clients compromised, or even impaired, making it difficult for you to feel respectful and caring toward them?
- In what ways are your inaccurate interpretations or reflections the result of your own projections and overidentification?
- How do you experience feeling blocked, stymied, helpless, and frustrated with certain clients, and what does that say about *you*?
- When do you feel bored, restless, and unable to remain present in sessions, with certain clients, at particular periods, and what does that say about you?
- What does it mean when you can't seem to remember the details of a particular case, but others are easily retrievable?
- How often do you speak derogatorily about a client?
- In what ways have you lost (or misplaced) your compassion?

All of these questions address one theme that is the focus of this chapter, namely that our personal and professional lives intersect in ways that represent one of our greatest resources and also one of the most challenging hardships.

Oh, You're a Therapist?

As therapists, we do two kinds of helping: formal therapy within our professional domain, complete with all the trappings, and *kinda therapy*, in which friends, relatives, acquaintances, and even complete strangers ask us for advice. Of course, we attempt to sidestep this advice ambush with a feeble protest: "I'm not on duty right now," or "I think it would be best if I referred you to a colleague," or "Giving advice is not really what I do." But the reality is that we are never really off-duty. We cannot just stop using what we know and can do. Almost against our will, we find ourselves sorting out arguments or listening to people's complaints.

One new therapist, for example, struggled with the confusion surrounding her personal and professional roles. She had volunteered her time to work with terminal patients. Once it was discovered what she did for a living, she was assigned to a family to help them work through issues related to death and dying. What was her role in this helping effort? She was not actually their therapist, more like a friend. Could she ask them personal questions, or would that be prying? Maybe she should extricate herself from the situation altogether, so confusing was her ambiguous role.

This fusion of personal and professional roles underlies some of the risks inherent in intimacy with clients. Sorting out dual relationships has become one of the most prevalent ethical issues of our time (Gabriel, 2005; Herlihy & Corey, 2014; Zur, 2014). Our family members and friends constantly ask us for advice. Although we may do our best to beg off, the truth of the matter is that we may well enjoy being needed. I love it when people ask me what to do; because I don't allow myself to give advice to my clients, and because hardly anyone ever listens to me anyway, I feel happily self-important that someone else thinks I know something that he does not. I pretend I am a little annoyed by those who ask me how to handle their children, confront their bosses, or straighten out their lives, but I appreciate that they think enough of me to ask.

Risking and Intimacy

Intimacy means being open, unguarded, and close to another. To facilitate trust, the therapist must feel comfortable facing intimacy without fear. This closeness helps clients feel understood and appreciated; it teaches them that true intimacy is indeed possible, that a relationship based on regard and respect is desirable. Through the mutual risking that takes place between the two partners in the relationship, both learn to appreciate better what closeness can bring.

Because therapeutic relationships are intensely personal and often quite intimate encounters in which participants feel a mutual attachment, there is intrinsic tension and confusion associated with the way they are structured. We know more about our clients than we know about many of our friends. We spend more time each week engaged in meaningful conversation with a given client than we do with most of the other people in our lives, including family and cherished friends. Before you deny this proposition, consider how often you arrange to be someone on a regular basis with whom you (1) talk only about personal matters of great significance, (2) do not allow yourself to be distracted by any intrusions, including any phone or mobile device, and (3) confront each other when you sense that someone is being evasive or less than truthful. Even with the asymmetrical, inequitable, one-sided professional dimensions of our relationships with clients, they are nevertheless moving, personal interchanges. They carry many of the risks that are operative in any such intimate encounter, regardless of the safeguards and boundaries we install.

The levels of intimacy in a therapist's personal and professional lives may not coincide. Whereas most of us may be quite willing to let ourselves feel close to our clients, we may not be so successful at committing ourselves to the intimacy of social and family relationships. Still, if we stay in the field long enough, we eventually confront our reluctance and defenses. One therapist admits with candor, "Being a therapist saved my life. I was about to go into the theater, which is most unhealthy, and rewarded all the phony, manipulative, narcissistic parts of me. When I chose therapy, it demanded that I deal with issues that I never would have changed in another environment. I made a choice for health."

This is another area where the discomfort of confronting your hypocrisy comes into play. There are most certainly aspects of your personal life that are less than satisfactory—you don't have enough friends, or you aren't involved in a committed romantic relationship, or you experience conflict with a friend or coworker, or your relationships don't feel deep or intimate enough. These are exactly the same issues that clients bring into sessions every day. And when they do, you most likely tell them that in order to experience deeper, more satisfying intimacy, they are going to have to take risks revealing themselves in more honest, authentic ways. Now: what about you?

Boundaries Between the Personal and the Professional

The boundaries that we define and enforce are as much to protect ourselves as our clients. There is often a fear of losing control, of impulsively slipping over to the dark side in spite of our best of intentions. A client hugs you—and it feels *good*. You don't want to stop. Your brain tells you, "Danger! Danger! Abort hug!" yet your body is responding without your consent.

We sometimes confuse boundaries with walls—that is, rules about the relationship designed for safety and efficiency as opposed to those artificial (and perhaps unnecessary) limits that function as armor. In alternative paradigms such as feminist or relational-cultural theory, practitioners often advocate greater mutuality in the relationship.

There is a bias, if not a mandate, in the profession that dual (much less multiple) relationships are a bad thing that can compromise therapy, confuse clients, and lead to abuse. Yet many of the breakthroughs that occur in therapy take place because of changes in context, setting, or structure of the sessions. In a collection of cases about the most creative interventions of the most innovative practitioners, many of the breakthroughs took place outside the normal boundaries of traditional psychotherapy (Kottler & Carlson, 2009). Bill O'Hanlon describes how Milton Erickson used him as his personal gardener for a year in order to teach an obscure metaphorical lesson. Brad Keeney used home visits to a reluctant family in order to engage them productively in therapeutic work. Sam Gladding went outside with a resistant adolescent to take photos. Steve Madigan convened a whole community to provide needed support for a depressed client. All these approaches are consistent with the healing practices of most cultures around the world in which therapists (aka shamans) do all their work in a natural setting rather than on the artificial, contrived stage on which therapy takes place (Kottler, Carlson, & Keeney, 2004).

We also have to keep in mind that violating boundaries in the therapeutic relationship is the most common complaint to ethics committees (Wang, 2008). It may be clear that it is *never* appropriate to have a sexual or romantic relationship with a client, or to blur the boundaries between the personal and professional. Yet there are all kinds of tricky questions that therapists must face on a weekly basis. Most clinicians would agree, for instance, that you wouldn't go out for a meal with a client—*unless* the client is struggling with an eating disorder that requires in vivo coaching. You wouldn't accept a gift from a client—*unless* it is of "negligible" monetary value and a rejection would be viewed as anti-therapeutic. You wouldn't drive a client home after a session—*unless* you saw him standing at a bus stop in the middle of a blizzard. It is the exception in these examples that makes things complicated. Clearly the boundaries between the realms of the personal and the professional are not as discrete as they would seem.

Learning to Hide

It is our greatest gift, yet also our most difficult burden, that we must face ourselves every day. There is a part of ourselves contained in every client story and a continuous recognition of our own unresolved issues in almost every session. Ideally, such awareness would lead us to work through our personal issues in supervision, if not personal therapy. At the very least, we spend a portion of every day working to process what we've experienced with clients, constructing meaning not just for the client's good but also for our own growth.

Yet nobody is better equipped than we are to bury ourselves in other people's problems as a way to avoid our own. Likewise, we have at our disposal a whole collection of tools by which to keep people at a distance, deflect attention, deny responsibility, or escape being nailed down.

A friend of mine who works as a musician has frequently found himself surrounded by therapists conversing about their work. I once asked him what this was like, listening to us talking about what we do. He started to laugh and shake his head. "Compared to playing Rachmaninoff's *Third Piano Concerto*, what you guys do is easy."

"Easy?" I said. "Are you kidding?"

"Yeah, sure. All you do when someone pushes you into a corner is you say, 'This isn't about me, it's really about you.'"

I was speechless. Then I started to laugh. There was some truth to what he said about how we are experts at putting the focus back on others. I was thinking about all the times I had offered this interpretation to avoid answering questions or revealing more than I wanted. I was always amazed at how well it worked.

"And then the other thing you guys do," my friend continued, "is the exact opposite. You make everything seem like it is about you, as if you were so damn important that anyone really cares what you're feeling or thinking."

"Feeling resentment, are you?" I replied automatically.

"See, there you go with option one, putting it back on me." "Sorry."

"It's okay. You can't help it."

"So," I reminded him, a little uncertain that I wanted to take this further. "You were saying the other thing that therapists do."

"Yeah. You say, 'Hey, this isn't about you, it's about me.' "

I must say that this was an elegantly simple summary of two basic strategies that are an internalized part of the ways that therapists automatically respond. It reminded me of all the other ways that we actually avoid deeper intimacy and keep others at a distance.

One therapist, Myron, describes the parallel process he experienced for many years, trying to reconcile his failing 10-year marriage with his practice as a specialist in couples therapy. "We were so desperately unhappy," he admitted, "and so convinced that it was the other's fault, that we had no choice but to seek help. Unfortunately, the therapist proved to be much too skilled for my good, and at one point she asked a simple question that unlocked some dark shadow inside me that felt as though it would choke the very life from me."

This confrontation turned out to be a point of no return. "It propelled me into the murky grounds of self-exploration. I learned everything there was to learn about that shadow, but never went near it again."

Yet the deeper Myron explored his own issues and fractured marriage, the more frustrated and unsatisfied he felt. He was aware of the recurring destructive cycle he was living, just as he recognized such patterns in his clients, yet he felt powerless to change anything. "It almost seemed a daily occurrence that I would sit wisely in front of a couple and support them through the pain of their relationship and then return to the unresolved and deepening pain of my own marriage."

Myron felt like a fraud and hypocrite, unable to apply in his own life what he was teaching to his clients every day. He felt like a failure not only as a therapist but also as a client and human being. As much as he read and studied about dysfunctional relationships, as often as he helped other couples navigate through their suffering, he could not find a way through his own issues. It wasn't until he discovered that his wife was having an affair that he felt jolted sufficiently to take necessary, courageous steps he had been avoiding. "Our old marriage died in that moment and was then rebuilt from the ground up into the marriage we both wanted over the ensuing year."

Myron shared how everything he learned as a therapist had helped protect and insulate him from suffocating fear that had escalated since his own session years earlier. "I realized that what I was doing as a therapist was trying to do my own process vicariously through the pain of my clients. I was trying to resolve something without experiencing the fear and powerlessness of actually confronting it. It's not that I've learned anything new as much as now I understand infinitely more."

What Myron understands, and now acknowledges, is that his training and experience as a therapist allowed him to hide from his own unresolved issues. He knew all the tricks of the trade designed to elude and evade. He knew exactly how to deflect blame, dance around core issues, and avoid having to face himself and his own role in sustaining mediocrity in his marriage.

Doing Good

The risks that come with the territory of being a therapist emanate primarily from getting perilously close to the flame that burns deep within the sorrow of each client we see. Yet in spite of the many hardships and occupational hazards of this work, we also experience tremendous satisfaction, not the least of which is the urge to strive for greater fulfillment. Just as satisfying is the wonderful feeling of doing good for others.

Altruism is certainly a driving force behind our motives and actions as helpers. There is nothing like that feeling of elation that we sometimes experience when we know beyond any doubt that our efforts have helped redeem a human life. Whether the result of a prolonged commitment to a relationship that spans years or a single gesture that yields immediate results, the joy we feel from knowing that we have made a difference goes far beyond mere professional pride; sometimes this "helper's high" creates an incredible surge of tranquility, inner peace, and well-being. Such "prosocial behavior" can lead to all kinds of benefits, including greater longevity, boosted immunity system, and an improved sense of well-being and life satisfaction (Schroeder & Graziano, 2015). This is especially the case when we extend ourselves to someone in need without any financial remuneration or external reward.

I was walking down the street one day, lost in fantasies about what flavor of ice cream I would have, when I saw a flash of color and movement ahead, accompanied by screams of indignation. I rushed to the scene and discovered two children, a girl of about 7 and a boy of 6, fighting on the sidewalk. The larger and stronger girl quickly dispatched her foe and then in triumph scattered the contents of his book bag all over the street. Papers flew everywhere like mutant snowflakes, falling down and around this little boy, who was sobbing in frustrated helplessness.

I gathered up as many of his things as I could find, stooped down on my knees, and handed him his reloaded bag. He looked at me, startled at first by my intrusion into his misery. Then he broke out into the most glorious smile I had ever seen and probably will ever see again. I felt his gratitude wash over me. As I continued on my journey, tears now ran down my face. I was just so thankful that I happened to be there at that moment so I could help him. I was able to do some good. In that simple interchange, lasting not more than 2 minutes, I had a relationship with another person that was helpful. In an influential way, that effort of doing good helped make the world a better place. During subsequent periods of frustration, I have thought about that little boy's smile, and somehow the risks and aggravation I must put up with have seemed worthwhile.

In truth, I've become addicted to this feeling of doing good, the helper's high, constantly looking for other ways that I can make a difference. That's one reason why I have been spending so much time working in remote areas, supporting at-risk children, leading trauma teams, and bringing students with me to help families in distress. That we receive no compensation for our efforts—and pay our own expenses—would seem to make the trials and tribulations far less endurable. We put up with strikes, civil wars, political upheaval, and shortages of food and supplies, sleep in tents or teahouses in the freezing cold, spend hours every day walking up and down steep mountains, and subject ourselves to the most tragic stories imaginable, and yet it is precisely because this is a labor of love that the satisfaction is beyond anything else I have ever known or experienced.

Even when we are paid for our work (usually inadequately), there is still that feeling of pride and accomplishment that, in our own small way, we are helping to diminish suffering and make life for some people more tolerable, if not meaningful. Amid the bureaucracy, paperwork, politics, finances, client resistance, and any personal side effects that we feel from doing this kind of work, we still get the biggest kick from the realization that something we said or did, in isolation or as an accumulative effect, made a difference to someone else. This desire to be useful is, in fact, the primary reason that most of us entered this profession in the first place.

This is one reason why I so love to give directions to people who are lost, and why I have worked so hard to become good at this skill. Rather than feel annoyed when someone stops me on the street for directions or peeks into my office for guidance regarding how to find a particular room, I rub my hands together in glee (and I'm not just talking figuratively). Because the nature of doing therapy is such that I sometimes can't tell if I really have helped anyone (clients lie, or they don't know, or it sometimes takes a while to understand the effects), I really enjoy any opportunity to offer assistance and know that within a limited time I can make a definite difference.

After I spent more than 5 minutes giving one person explicit, detailed directions about how to find a conference room, including suggestions for what to observe along the way, the recipient of my instructions looked at me as if I were crazy with so much idle time on my hands. That wasn't it at all, but rather that I really enjoyed telling someone *exactly* how to get to where he wanted to go with total certainty that he would eventually get there.

Therapist Self-Healing

For the most part, therapists live relatively flexible lives. Except for those therapists who work in corporate, government, or other large organizational settings, most therapists in universities, schools, community agencies, and especially private practice can exercise considerable control over their schedules and work priorities. Supervision and structure are usually minimal. Like the artist and musician, the therapist needs freedom to flourish and create.

The marriage between the personal and the professional in the life of a therapist is never clearer than in the benefits that the career provides for its practitioners. Far beyond any monetary, prestige, or freedom needs that are satisfied are the opportunities for growth. "I practice psychotherapy not to rescue others from their craziness," says Sheldon Kopp, "but to preserve what is left of my own sanity: not to cure others, but to heal myself" (1985, p. 12). If what Kopp says is true, that doing therapy helps the therapist become more sane, then just how does this process take place?

We return to the mundane details of what a therapist actually experiences during the day, not only the dramatic moments of truth when a client finally understands and feels grateful but also the frustrations, repetitions, and stalemates. First of all, therapists have to sit still for long periods of time, and from this we learn physical self-discipline. Rivaling the most accomplished monk, a therapist develops phenomenal powers of focused concentration. We resist the intrusion of external distractions—cars honking, doors slamming, clocks ticking, uncrossed bare legs sitting across from us, phones ringing, email or texts chiming, unanswered messages winking—and as though in a meditative trance, we gently nudge our minds back into the present. With stoic self-control, we ignore internal distractions—grumbling stomachs, painful bladders, unfinished conversations, undone errands, the past, the future—and return once again to the task at hand. From such deliberate and studied engrossment, we develop a razor-sharp intellect that is only improved by the things we must learn to remain effective.

Therapists field questions like line drives during batting practice. We leap and duck, catch some and sidestep others. "When will I get better?" "Why do I hurt?" "How do you feel about me?" "What am I here for?" "How do I grow old?" "What should I do?" "What would *you* do?" Whether we respond to these questions aloud or not, we must nevertheless answer them—either then or later. We can flee, but there is nowhere to hide. Every working day holds for us a confrontation with the issues we fear most.

Every time we speak to our clients, we heal ourselves, for there is an audience of two. We talk about what we know or what we think we know, but we teach only what we understand. We feel a tremendous incentive to answer life's most difficult questions and understand things and people. If we analyze the content of our sessions, regardless of clients' presenting symptoms, we will find our most disturbing themes and the things we best understand.

I take inventory of my caseload.

Tina is learning to stop thinking obsessively, or at least to stop obsessing about her obsessions. She has made progress in that now she only talks about her obsessions during therapy sessions. Whenever I try to get her to talk about something else, her symptoms spill over into her work and marriage. We have learned not to tamper with what is already working, even if it is sometimes boring to listen to. Tina has learned to accept and live with her irritating symptoms. From her, I have learned to live with my irritating symptoms, too.

Michelle has taught me a lot about patience. After a year together, I finally gave up trying to control or structure our talks. Each week, she tells me that something is bothering her, but she will not say what it is because she does not trust me. I complain that I cannot help her if she will not trust me. She says, "Fine. I'll go find someone else who won't require me to trust him." She keeps feeling better, but I cannot figure out why.

Feeling trapped in her marriage, Rachel used to cry the entire session. But now we play a wonderful game together. Each week, she comes in having already decided to take on one of two parts. If she decides to be the dutiful but misunderstood wife, then I attempt to help her feel satisfied with the status quo. She then leaves the office resolved to initiate more open communication with her husband. But the harder she tries, the more frustrated she becomes. (The husband is only interested in his work, in his Model T Ford, and thrice weekly in the missionary position.) Inevitably, she returns the following week prepared for divorce. We then discuss why she should follow that course of action, but we both know she will change her mind before the week has ended. Twice I attempted to confront her about this circular pattern, but she punished me for my impatience by canceling the next appointment.

Elena is thinking of dropping out of school because she has so little money. It has taken her years of preparation and planning to negotiate the time and space within her family so that she might devote some time to herself instead of taking care of all her siblings and the household responsibilities. Now she is seriously considering abandoning all the hard work and negotiations it took to begin her studies. When I confront her, she looks at me and shakes her head. I know exactly what she is thinking: "How can this *gringo*, this old white guy with his books and comfortable life, possibly understand what I am going through?" She is right, of course: I can't possibly understand Elena's world no matter how hard I try. How can I relate to what it must be like to go back to a home where she shares a room with two siblings, where, if she's lucky, her father will not beat her too badly or take one of her sisters for fun and games when he's in a drunken stupor? How can I possibly appreciate the meaning of school to someone whose daily survival is a major challenge?

I tell Elena that I understand, when I can only begin to appreciate her plight. I wonder what I can do for her as a therapist. Bring her false hope? Encourage her to take a road that is far beyond what she can reasonably expect to walk? I realize that she is resigned to what she must do; I am the one who is not willing to accept her choices. Whose problem is this? I wonder.

These few cases are a profile in diversity familiar to most therapists. Yet there is also similarity in the issues clients confront—and repetition in the things we hear ourselves say again and again. If only we would take our own advice.

Taking Our Own Advice

Even the most creative, inventive, and spontaneous clinicians will teach similar lessons to most of their clients. Our moral imperatives, favorite platitudes, and well-worn words of wisdom find their way into many sessions. Regardless of the client or presenting complaint, there is repetition in the themes we present, which could include some of the following:

- If you do not take care of yourself, nobody else will.
- You are alive for a very short time and then dead for a very long time after that.
- Symptoms are useful in getting your attention.
- Symptoms will not go away until they are no longer needed.
- We are all afraid to be alone.
- If you don't expect anything, you will never be disappointed.

- One hundred years from now, nobody will care what you did with your life.
- The material world is seductive.
- Feeling powerless is a state of mind.
- We spend our lives trying to control our hormones.
- No matter what you do or say, half the world will like it and half the world won't.
- You will never have your parents' approval.
- You will never ever be content for very long.
- It is hard to love without being vulnerable.
- Change does not occur without risks.
- Failure or mistakes represent useful feedback for the next attempt.
- Everything worth doing is difficult.

We disregard our own advice not only by ignoring the messages we repeat but by failing to implement them in our lives. It hurts to be a hypocrite. Day after day, we admonish clients for doing less than they are capable of, while an echoing voice nags at our conscience: "What have *you* done lately?" We critically help clients define those behaviors that they would most like to change and end up doing likewise for ourselves. How can we expect clients to understand ideas that we have not fully mastered?

Besides taking our own advice and applying what we teach to our own lives, we naturally do many things that lead to self-healing. Out of necessity, we are good at valuing and organizing our time. Because of our training and exposure to the consequences of self-neglect, we have an elevated capacity to perceive our own stress. We thus remain sensitized to certain warning signs, such as sleep disruption or excuse making or agitation or something in the body and mind feeling out of balance. Once these potential problems are identified, we can immediately take steps to correct them. Therapists work with colleagues who happen to be experts at giving support and nurturance. From the perspective of human contact, we work in an enriched environment. In theory, anyway, our professional relationships should offer the potential for personal fulfillment. There should be opportunities for constructive feedback, benevolent guidance, and lots of hugs.

Unfortunately, there is often a discrepancy between what should be and what actually is. Therapists can be as cruel, manipulative, insensitive, self-involved, and political as the rest of the human race. Some of the best people you know are therapists, and also some of the worst, those who attempt to use their skills and power to exploit and hurt others. Fortunately, we are trained to deal with deception, game playing, and politics with minimal threat to the self. When we do find ourselves subjected to abuse by others, there is nobody better prepared to counter this behavior and metabolize it in such a way that damage is minimized.

Family Fallout

In addition to the usual countertransference reactions that a therapist experiences in response to client behavior and issues, when we work with families or groups of clients, we also must contend with an enmeshed, multi-person system that is potentially unpredictable and explosive. The group or family therapist must deal with more acting out in response to his being in an authority role and must simultaneously deal with myriad feelings and reactions to each person in the group as well as to the group members' interactive patterns. Moreover, his own family-of-origin issues, as well as current family experiences, influence his work.

In the therapy group I'm leading, Fiona catches my eye and smiles in a flirtatious way. I feel flattered, then uncomfortable and guarded. I notice that Fred sees the little interchange and smirks. Fiona smiles at him, too. I feel a little jealous about that, then chagrined that I am irritated with Fred. At that moment, Cassie pipes up with another distracting question. I am tired of her insensitivity, so I confront her. Fiona rushes in to defend her, so I turn to her. I realize, just before I am about to confront Fiona as well, that I am still haunted by her earlier flirtatious gesture.

I have now lost the threads of where we were headed. I feel overwhelmed by how much there is to attend to and all the complex and varied reactions that I have to each person in the group, how they relate to one another and to me. These effects do not end once the group ends, but continue to plague me throughout the week.

We try to keep a vigilant eye on personal fallout to protect our family and friends from the intensity of our professional life. Yet with all the restraint we must exercise in order to follow the rules regulating our conduct during working hours, it is difficult not to be insensitive, surly, or self-indulgent with our loved ones. All day long, we have stifled ourselves, censored our thoughts and statements, and disciplined ourselves to be controlled and intelligent. And then we make an abrupt transition to go home. Much of the pressure that has been building all day long as clients have come in and dumped their troubles finally releases as we walk through the door. If we are not careful, our families will suffer the emotional fallout.

Among all the strategies that therapists use to manage their own stress and difficulties from work, by far the single most common coping method is relying on friends and family for support (Norcross & Guy, 2007; Turner et al., 2005). Understanding this makes it even more critical that we invest the time and effort to make sure that we respond to loved ones with the same degree of caring, sensitivity, and respect that we would show our clients.

Personal Metaphors and Professional Work

After all the training we receive in diagnosis, recognizing defense mechanisms, perceiving things as they are, and defusing game playing, we are creatures exquisitely designed to smell self-deception and set things right—not just when the meter is running during therapy but instinctively when we are alone. Even if we do not deliberately keep track of how our work is currently affecting our emotional health or how our personal life is affecting our therapy, such an evaluation will take place effortlessly. We find ourselves feeling self-conscious in a social situation, feel our hearts beating quickly, and immediately start talking to ourselves the way we would to a client. Or we make an interpretation during a session that is obviously off the mark and then begin to question what inside us led our clinical judgment astray.

The content of our therapeutic metaphors comes from our personal experience. Much of what we say to clients is strongly influenced by what we have read and seen, whom we have encountered, and what we have done that very week. A client complains in anguish of feeling trapped, and I find myself describing the lyrics from a popular song or a scene from a current movie. I plant trees over the weekend and weave together for a disoriented young man an example of how each living thing requires nourishment, minimal shocks to the system during transplanting, and individual attention. I spend the morning surfing, surrounded by dolphins playing in the waves around me, and I tell a therapy group how peak performance increases with an absence of critical judgment; the less I think, the better I surf. I return working abroad where the people have nothing, own nothing, and yet seem so much more content than the people I know back home; this is a powerful example to drive home in my sessions with the disenfranchised and discouraged. The places I visit, the weather, dreams, memories—everything that filters through my senses affects what I do during sessions. My work in any given moment is the product of who I have become up to that very instant. As I change, so does the style of my therapy.

We, like our clients, change only at a pace with which we are comfortable. If we move too quickly, the personal fallout can reach dangerous levels. Yet it takes such incredible energy and commitment not to lose ground, much less to change one's position. We all move just as fast as we can, although we sometimes seem to stay in the same place, reworking the same issues again and again.

In one mental health clinic, a dozen colleagues were asked how their personal values, old baggage, and new dreams influence their style of helping. The question was based on the reality that the choice of one's therapeutic approach is hardly based solely on intellectual compatibility but is also strongly influenced by one's personality, beliefs, priorities, cognitive style, and favored mode of expression. Humanistic therapists, for instance, tend to see themselves as "genial" in all their relationships, whereas cognitive behavioral clinicians describe themselves as "practical" and solution-focused practitioners rather "forceful" (Heinonen & Orlinsky, 2013).

Given the influence of our own personal history on our professional behavior, it is perhaps not shocking to discover that one psychologist in the clinic lost her mother to cancer while still a child and somehow finds a way to diagnose most psychopathology as a form of mother–child deprivation. She views her primary role as providing the maternal nurturance that she herself so longs for.

A social worker has had great difficulty dealing with authority and anger. Not coincidentally, he specializes in work with adolescents who inappropriately act out their hostility. Another psychologist has struggled since childhood with obsessive thinking and her fear of going crazy. In her practice, she requests the most disturbed referrals and prefers working with psychotic disorders. A family counselor prizes humor and spontaneity above all other human experiences and so functions as a court jester to make people laugh. Most of us can identify with such correlations between the major themes of our personal lives and our professional style of practice. Despite our best efforts to separate the two roles, the barrier remains fluid, flexible, and even permeable.

The Human Dimensions of Being a Therapist

I recognize the compatibility between the personal and professional in my own life for a number of reasons. First and foremost, it makes my work more fun. I find greater meaning in everything I do when I can relate it to the rest of my life. I like the feeling that I am always working, always thinking, and always trying to make sense of what is happening. And yet I am never working because even time spent with clients helps me learn more about the world and myself.

Second, I monitor the interaction between my personal and professional lives to protect both my clients and my family. I know I have unresolved personal issues that get in the way of my being more effective with my clients. I must constantly guard against my self-indulgences, egocentricity, and narcissism. I sometimes catch myself saying and doing things in sessions for my own entertainment. I ask questions only to satisfy my curiosity. I let clients dig themselves into holes just to see how they will get out. I inflate my sense of importance so that clients will admire me more. I sometimes see clients longer than is absolutely necessary because I welcome the income. Oh, I justify all of these actions, convincing myself that they are all for the client's good. I don't worry as much about this personal fallout because I am aware of it. I do genuinely worry about those instances when I don't catch myself meeting my own needs.

In all these factors that connect the personal with the professional, the therapist juggles conflicting desires and multiple urges, motivated by altruism as well as by egocentricity and self-interest. It is difficult, if not impossible, to filter personal elements out of a therapist's professional work or to restrict clinical perceptions and skills to the office. If truth be told, our therapeutic perspective on life is our greatest asset and our greatest liability. Being a therapist affords us the opportunity for continual spiritual, intellectual, and emotional growth. We become more intuitive, better risk takers and communicators. We experience excitement, human intensity, confidence, and self-fulfillment, all at great expense. The consuming nature of therapeutic work reminds us of a common truth that we may repeat to clients: every joy sometimes has its price, whether we pay now or on the installment plan.

4

On Being a Therapeutic Storyteller—and Listener

CAROLINE SEEMED NICE enough even if she was unusually quiet and insulated. I couldn't actually recall her interacting with anyone on our team, pretty much keeping to herself, smiling shyly when anyone made a point to address her directly. She had been invited to join our mission at the last minute by a friend of hers who was part of our volunteer group.

I was leading some executives who had all been actively involved in raising money to provide scholarships for our more than 300 mostly lower-caste girls in Nepal who were at greatest risk to be trafficked into sex slavery or forced into early marriage. The reward for these corporate leaders who had worked hard to raise awareness of the girls' plight was to meet the children and their families and see what impact the donations and support were having on their lives.

Ordinarily Caroline would not have been permitted to join our team since she had not actually raised any donations, but it was hard to turn down the request after I heard about her story. She had been on a road trip with her husband and two young sons, aged 2 and 4, when the next thing she knew she found herself waking up in a hospital bed. She was told that she had been in a car accident and was the only survivor: her husband and two little boys had died.

It is perhaps not unexpected that Caroline became a recluse. She cut herself off from everyone and everything while she mourned alone in her empty house. She refused all offers for help and all attempts to reach out to her by friends and family, so it was particularly surprising when she agreed to come to Nepal, especially considering that the work involved spending intimate time with children. After it was explained to me how this would be the first time she had ventured from home in more than 6 months, and how wounded she was, I couldn't possibly refuse her.

During the previous week Caroline did spend time with the children, reading them stories, talking to them about their schoolwork, conducting home visits, and sometimes even holding young ones on her lap. I kept an eye on her, and she seemed to be doing okay even though she was so reserved with the rest of the group. Several times I had tried to strike up a conversation with her, but it didn't appear to go anywhere, so I backed off and let her have all the space she seemed to need.

After traveling to villages for almost a week, we had set up camp on a mountaintop with spectacular views of the Himalayas across the skyline. This was to be our base for the next few days while we spent time conducting home and school visits in the region. I had been to this spot many times before, and it was one of my favorite places in the world—an ethereal place where the clouds covered the valleys below and the snow-blanketed and glaciated peaks rose to impossible heights in all directions.

I awoke early in the morning when it was still dark and there was a light covering of snow on the ground. I had a favorite ritual of climbing to the top of a nearby mountain where there was a *stupa*, a Buddhist shrine, perched on the side of the cliff with 360-degree views of the Himalayas rising above 25,000 feet. It was the most amazing place to watch the sun rise.

As I was lacing up my boots I could see Caroline standing outside her tent watching me. I approached her tentatively in the dark, not wanting to spook her or wake any others who were still sleeping. "Put on your boots and jacket," I whispered to her. "I want to show you something."

We climbed for almost an hour up the steep, sheer mountainside in the dark, breathing heavily but not saying a single word to one another. I would occasionally look back over my shoulder to make sure she was still with me, but otherwise we just concentrated on the next foothold and handhold. When we finally reached the summit there was just the beginning of purple lighting the horizon, with the first glimmers of pink underneath. We were both bent over trying to catch our breath.

I signaled Caroline to follow me to the edge of the cliff where the small temple was situated. It was a tiny monument with a likeness of the Buddha inside and a large gong hanging by the side of the building. "It is said," I told her, "that if you ring the gong you can awaken Buddha to hear your prayers." Caroline cocked her head to see if I was kidding but I just shrugged and pointed to the wooden mallet attached to the gong by string.

To give her some privacy I walked to the edge of the cliff and sat down with my feet dangling over the side. As I looked down I could see holes in the glowing pink clouds that offered views of the valley thousands of feet below. Then I heard the low reverberations of the gong; I could almost feel the sound echo through my spine. I looked back and could barely make out Caroline standing thoughtfully by the stupa with the mallet in her hand. She struck the gong one more time and then carefully placed the mallet in its holder before she walked over and sat down next to me with her feet also dangling over the side. We sat that way for several minutes watching the sun rise and the sky lighten before I heard her start to cry. I looked over at her, not sure what to say, what to do, so I just put my arm around her and held her while her sobs grew deeper, wracking her whole body. To me it felt like the same kind of vibrations from the gong running up my spine.

I didn't say a single word. I didn't ask any questions. In fact, I realized that so far that early morning we had not spoken a word to one another other than my invitation to her to come with me and then to follow me over to the stupa. I just held her and let her cry. I watched the mountains and the clouds and the light. I tried to remember the sound of the gong. I concentrated on my breathing. And then I started to sob as well.

During the preceding days I had seen so many things that had broken my heart, so many children living in such horrific poverty. Often when I am doing this kind of work I feel so helpless and powerless. My boundaries collapse and I feel pain like none I have ever experienced. Then, all of a sudden, sometimes I just lose control. Something in me was triggered when Caroline started crying. I could feel all her pain leeching out of her body. I just couldn't imagine what she must have been going through, feeling so alone.

I started to feel self-conscious, if not uncomfortable, in my position. My arm was starting to go numb. I wanted to help her somehow, but I didn't know what I could possibly say that could make any kind of difference, or that wouldn't sound so feeble. It was then I could hear Caroline clear her throat. I held my breath and waited.

"They are here," she said. "I feel them. I feel them with me right now." Then she turned to look at me. "My little boys," she added. "My husband. They are here with me right now." All I could think to do was nod my head.

We walked down the long, serpentine trail back to camp, arriving just about the time the rest of the group was washing up before breakfast. Caroline went back to her tent and I went to talk to our guides about the day's itinerary. Caroline and I never spoke about what happened at the stupa, never talked about what she'd said. But something remarkable changed for her after that morning. She began to interact with the group. She became more animated. I heard her actually laughing at times. For the rest of the visit she was always the first one to dive into the gaggle of children, holding them, holding herself.

It was the most remarkable "cure" I've ever had the privilege to be a small part of. It was a relational cure I am certain, although I'm not entirely sure whether it was her connection to me, to the children, or the spirits of her lost family that healed her. But it's her story that sticks with me and continues to haunt me.

Each of us is privy to so many tragic, powerful stories that are shared with us by our clients. We "hold" these stories, take them in with our minds and hearts wide open, all the while doing our best to protect ourselves from the collateral impact and side effects. But far more than that, we also help to restructure, reframe, and coauthor the stories in more constructive, heroic forms that honor the lessons learned. This is the essence of narrative and constructivist therapies but is also part of any therapeutic approach, regardless of the particular names ascribed to the process. In one sense, our main job is listen to the stories presented as well as to offer our own that are designed to have maximum influence.

We Experience the World as a Series of Stories

I settled on the idea of rethinking what I do, and how I do it, one day when I was out for a run along the beach. Like almost all the things I choose to write about, the seeds for my reconceptualization were planted when trying to sort out my own personal reactions and curiosity to a confusing phenomenon. I had just finished reading a trilogy of novels about a zombie apocalypse in which a virus had turned most of the world into the walking dead. I spent weeks immersed in this alternative universe to the point that I was totally beguiled by the idea of how I might survive such a catastrophe. Although I would later learn that there are actually some highly adaptive and functional aspects to this literature, and to almost any form of vicarious entertainment including video games, television shows, films, and novels, at the time I still found myself recovering from the chills and thrills of the continuous tension. I mention this as both an explanation and an apology for my behavior.

As I was running along the beach, a runner approached me from the other direction. Once he drew closer I could see him smiling; as we passed one another he held out his hand to offer a "high five," as if to say, "Aren't we both awesome, out here running while everyone else is still sitting at home?"

I thought to myself that this was pretty cool since it almost never happens. Runners are notorious for our grim, suffering expressions, rarely acknowledging anything other than the placement of our feet and labored breathing. Against my will, a thought popped into my head: "What if he has a zombie virus that he just passed along to me?"

Utterly ridiculous, even slightly insane, I know! But the thought, once embedded in my brain, just wouldn't let go. I noticed that I was rubbing my hand against the front of my shirt, as if to wipe away the imagined virus. I could only shake my head in wonderment: "Kottler," I thought, "you've lost your mind! Here it is a gorgeous day, enjoying a run, encountering a friendly compatriot, and all you can think of is that he infected you by touching your hand?"

As crazy as the idea might sound, it then occurred to me that if this really was some kind of deadly virus, wiping it on my shirt would hardly keep me safe. So I stopped to rub my hand in the sand before immediately turning around and heading back home, all the way whispering to myself, "Don't touch my face, don't touch my face."

Okay, I admit: it *does* seem like I lost my mind. And you may be wondering how this can possibly be related to therapy and storytelling. My point is that stories can sometimes seem so vivid and immersive, so powerful and persuasive, so emotionally evocative and impactful, that they seem like they are real. And here's the kicker: it turns out in the research that followed, I learned that I am hardly alone in the way I was so completely involved in this fictional tale that I couldn't let go. As far as the brain is concerned, there is an impressive body of evidence to demonstrate how it has evolved over time as essentially a storied organ. Humans have developed the means to accrue vicarious experiences, whether climbing mountains, visiting faraway, exotic places, chasing a serial killer—or being pursued by one, even surviving a zombie apocalypse, all within the safety of a chair. Mirror neurons in the brain function as "as if" receptors, simulating experiences that might better prepare us to face danger or adversity (Gazzaniga, 2008; Hess, 2012; Hsu, 2008; Iacoboni, 2008; Nigam, 2012; Rizzolatti & Craighero, 2004). We may never have to deal with raging zombies, vampires, werewolves, or serial killers (all manifestations of predators) or face floods, cyclones, riots, wars, or other disasters, but it helps allay fears to consider the ways we might cope.

You'd only have to reflect on the stories that have irrevocably changed your life to jump on board this bandwagon. There are films, shows, and novels that leave us forever different, opening up new avenues of thought and feeling. We watch programs, plays, or movies or read novels that leave us dissolved in terror or tears. There are fictional characters on the screen or in books that really *do* feel like our closest friends. The appeal of reality shows or celebrity attachments similarly reveal the very strong emotional connections that people feel toward those they've never even met. And once again our brain treats these relationships as if they feel (almost?) real. Indeed, there is some evidence that fiction is actually even more powerful than nonfiction or self-help books precisely because of the high emotional arousal and complete immersion in the experience (Appel, 2008; Appel & Richter, 2007; Mar, Oatley, Djikic, & Mullin, 2011; Paul, 2012; Vanderbes, 2013).

That's just part of the story, so to speak. Stories are so much a part of our daily lives that we don't stop to think about all the ways we are influenced, persuaded, affected, and sometimes manipulated by various narratives. Gossip consumes something like half of all human conversations, sharing stories about outliers, sexual improprieties, and strangers in our midst, not to mention juicy secrets. Gossip may have a bad reputation, but it is actually quite helpful to share intelligence, keep people in line, and discuss both prosocial and inappropriate behavior within the group (Beersma & Van Kleef, 2011, 2012; Dunbar, 2004; Feinberg, Willer, Stellar, & Keltner, 2012; McAndrew & Milenkovic, 2002). I came across one interesting theory that women may have invented language primarily as a means to trade gossip about potentially unreliable men since the consequence of mating with a poor choice would have been catastrophic and life threatening for the mother and infant if the partner didn't stick around to help with protection and food gathering.

Add up all the time that the average person spends watching television per day (3 hours), listening to music lyrics (1 hour), watching movies, and using other media, and we can appreciate that our lives are essentially formed through these narratives. Nowadays, even text messages are (very) short stories that are so pervasive that they are simply accepted as standard communication. Emojis are even shorter "stories" represented as a single symbol! And even when we are sleeping the brain effortlessly and automatically converts random fragments of memories and thoughts into the structure of a story. We thus tend to better remember and retrieve information that is coded into narrative form. All this adds up to the realization that if we truly want to be persuasive and influential, the best avenue to do so isn't by giving advice, lecturing, scolding, threatening, interpreting, or explaining, but rather by sharing a story that is specifically designed to have maximum impact.

Stories in Therapy

Sometimes the current political scene reminds me of the wars we used to have in our profession, arguing and fighting about who had cornered "truth," denigrating everyone else who didn't subscribe to the same worldview and beliefs. The legitimate focus of our work, many would say, is coming to terms with the past and revisiting stories during the early years. Others would insist that a far more useful area is to invite clients to talk about stories in the present, what is going on in their lives right now. And still others would urge clients to create stories about their future and what it could be. Likewise, there have been heated debates about keeping conversations centered on feelings—or thoughts—or behavior—or sensations in the body. Even today, there are still rather passionate advocates of experiential therapy versus others that hone in on empirically supported treatments (which are hardly mutually exclusive). Then there are the dozens of popular approaches currently on the scene, all of which have their fans and advocates. The good news is that with the emphasis on integration and pragmatism in today's climate, the debates have been far more civil and mutually respectful. Nevertheless, there are still a lot of disagreements about which approaches are best, for which clients, in which circumstances, each of which is supported by compelling "evidence."

Perhaps one of the features that unifies all forms of therapy, something on which we might all agree, is that therapy is essentially a storied experience, one in which the bulk of our time is spent listening to client's reports, prompting them to consider alternative ways to frame those experiences, and then offer other stories in a variety of different forms (Kottler, 2015b). Given the different conceptual and language systems that various theories favor, it is no surprise that this process is described differently. Most obviously, narrative and constructivist therapists take the lead since so much of their work revolves around the ways that stories are conceived, interpreted, and internalized. So too do feminist and social justice advocates look at the ways that stories have been "colonized" by the cultures within which we live. Almost every other therapeutic system similarly utilizes storytelling as its essence; whether exploring self-talk, utilizing reframing, challenging underlying beliefs, reflecting on disowned and neglected feelings, imagining alternative outcomes, making different choices, or offering different interpretations, they are all interventions that have stories at their heart.

There have, thus, been quite a number of sources that explore the power of storytelling as an agent of change, whether within an individual life (Arana, 2008; Austen, 2012; Bauer & McAdams, 2004; Bucay, 2013), in therapy (Adler, 2013; Bergner, 2007; Bitter & Byrd, 2011; Burns, 2007; Forrest, 2012; Ingemark, 2013; Kottler, 2015b), or even in the larger world (Dunbar, 2004; Gottschall, 2012; Loy, 2010; McAdams, 2006; Strange, 2002). Rachel Carson's *Silent Spring* helped to spark the environmental activist movement.

Upton Sinclair's *The Jungle* was instrumental in creating the workers' rights and union movement. Harriet Beecher Stowe's *Uncle Tom's Cabin* may have actually been one of the sparks that launched the American Civil War just as Thomas Paine's *Common Sense* did the American Revolution. St. Augustine's *Confessions*, Machiavelli's *The Prince*, and Henry David Thoreau's *On Civil Disobedience* were all powerful forces for change within their times. It's pretty clear that particular stories can lead not only to wars, political calamities, and societal destabilizations but also to breakthroughs in therapy and everyday life.

Why is storytelling such a critical part of what we do, and what functions does it serve within the therapeutic process, regardless of the particular approach? Here is a list of features to consider (Kottler, 2015a):

1. Stories capture attention. Immediately. Just hearing the words, "Once upon a time …" puts us into a trance. Stories are entertaining and provocative in ways that mere conversation can't touch.
2. As mentioned earlier, stories naturally follow the structural properties of memory. We tend to be more likely to hold onto ideas or experiences when they are embedded in stories.
3. Therapeutic-type stories such as metaphors offer coded information in a much more efficient package. Just as a picture is worth a thousand words, a metaphor can capture and hold complex ideas that can't be merely described or explained. They also access unconscious processes to enhance their potential for promoting change.
4. Given that vivid storytelling provides a kind of "direct experience" through vicarious imagination, we can lead clients to places they could never otherwise visit on their own.
5. Well-told stories activate strong emotional reactions, the kind that inspire, motivate, or ignite passion. Review any of the greatest speeches ever given, or a list of the most beloved TED talks, and you will find that almost all of them begin with a compelling story that rivets audience interest.
6. Stories can be "hypnotic" in that they can induce altered states of consciousness through immersion in the narrative. When you are reading a great novel or watching an exciting film, hours fly by, and it feels as if you have entered into the action.
7. Stories almost always take place within a particular cultural and historical context, whether within an individual or the larger community. The narrative is understood as representing certain social or environmental values that are critical to the meaning making.

8. Storytelling often bypasses resistance and defensiveness because of its subtlety and visual imagery. You can *explain* something that is threatening, or *tell* clients they need to do something that they don't want to do—or, you can tell a story that contains within it a plot or characters by which clients can position themselves or identify with the action that may parallel their own struggles.
9. Because stories have multiple dimensions of complexity and cognitive processing, they operate on levels we don't thoroughly understand but still have powerful effects.
10. Instead of calling clients "names," in the form of a diagnosis, we can instead provide a much more meaningful representation of their experience and problems in the form of a digestible story.
11. Stories produce overarching, organizing scaffolds that assist with deeper understanding of events and experiences.
12. Much of what we do in therapy is present alternative realities that may be possible as viewed through fantasy stories or fairy tales. They often include creative pathways and options for viewing problems and their solutions.
13. When therapists disclose (appropriate and well-timed) personal stories, they reduce the power imbalance in the relationship as well as model the kind of deep sharing that is desirable for the client.
14. Alternative stories constructed by therapists help to reframe and reconstruct the "victim stories" of trauma survivors into versions that emphasize courage and resilience.

I hope this fairly extensive list is rather persuasive in presenting the case that so much of what we do involves the mutual sharing of stories. Given that this is such a big part of our jobs, I find it interesting that although we receive so much training in various interpersonal and therapeutic skills, one area that has been sorely neglected is the means by which to become better and more effective storytellers.

Harnessing the Power of Storytelling

Throughout the ages, storytelling has been the primary way in which elders have passed along the traditions, values, and rituals of the tribe or people. Whether in the form of myths, legends, sagas, fairy tales, or cave paintings, critical information about hunting grounds, enemies, triumphs and defeats, or historical figures are preserved in collective memories. Values, laws, and moral transgressions are common themes, designed to teach important lessons and warn members of the dire consequences of breaching established norms. As mentioned earlier, gossip, another form of storytelling, is also employed universally to ensure compliance to established norms. That's why people are so curious about sexual improprieties, which represent unsanctioned mating, or individuals who seem strange or mysterious—and therefore potentially dangerous because of their unpredictability.

One purpose of stories, beyond any entertainment value, has always been about passing on wisdom, tolerance, and flexibility in thinking about oneself and others, as well as phenomena within the larger world. It isn't just about the stories themselves either but how they are part of the *relationship* between the storyteller and the listeners/readers. This is as much the case with respect to indigenous storytellers as psychotherapists, since so much of the connection an audience feels isn't just with the characters in the story but also with the narrator. When one village in Africa was presented with a television for the first time, the people were beguiled by this box that told stories from around the world, complete with moving pictures. But after a while, the villagers drifted away and returned to their elder storyteller. When they were asked why they would make such a choice, they agreed that although this box knew many stories, their own storyteller knew *them*.

Prescribing stories in the form of bibliotherapy has long been a tradition within our field, one in which clients are asked to read certain articles or books that directly relate to their presenting problem. Although such action is certainly relevant and appropriate, perhaps even useful at times, it's a rather limiting way to think about this mode of learning and transformation. If fiction is often more impactful than self-help materials, it is because of the emotional valence, total immersion in the experience of the story, vicarious identification with characters who struggle with parallel or similar issues, and the restraint of critical thinking that may keep ideas at arm's length. For instance, in this nonfiction book you would find yourself continuously challenging some of the things I've said, questioning their validity based on your own experience. You disagree with some of my ideas. You skip sections that seem boring or uninteresting. Most of all, whereas you *think* about the ideas, you don't necessarily feel particularly *impacted* by them in such a way that you will remember and use them. It is for this reason that a number of therapists might recommend the kind of stories to their clients with which they might best identify. We are also hardly limited to books, since we might also prescribe films or television shows that resonate with a client's predicament.

Most therapists also reveal stories about themselves that might be instructive. This could involve something rather basic and simple to further make a connection, such as saying, "Yeah, I also have two children, both in college." It could also involve teaching a particular point that is based on prior experiences: "Yes, when I was in a similar situation I recall feeling much the same way, but there was one instance when. . . ." We also share stories that we have collected over time and filed away in our catalogue, each one targeted to a specific purpose.

It's beyond the scope of a single chapter to cover *all* the ways that therapists might improve their storytelling ability to increase their effectiveness, but there are a number of resources available that present the most critical skills (Alexander, 2011; Burns, 2007; Fryer, 2003; Ingemark, 2013; Kottler, 2015b; Murphy, 2012; Pomerantz, 2007; Reese, 2013; Reynolds, 2012; Simmons, 2006; Spaulding, 2011; Yashinsky, 2004; White, 2007; Zipes, 2006). These cover some of the basic ideas, such as the importance of immediately grabbing attention with a "hook," being as dramatic and expressive as possible, using both dialogue and vivid, descriptive details to make the narrative come alive, and, most importantly, customizing the story to fit the client's specific needs to make it personal and most relevant. We don't want clients asking themselves, "So, why are you telling me this?" In addition, it also helps to engage curiosity by presenting a conflict or problem to which the client can relate and including some feature that is novel to catch the client by surprise. Finally, in the best tradition of our profession, it is often recommended *not* to explain the story but to allow clients to find (or create) the meaning and personal relevance to their own lives and presenting problem.

Thinking of Yourself as Professional Storyteller—and Listener

The next chapter delves more deeply into the ways that therapists are influenced and impacted by the work that we do, and especially the stories that we hear in sessions. Many of these vivid and haunting narratives, so infused with strong emotion and suffering, resonate at times with our own experiences, often triggering countertransference reactions, or at least spark powerful memories. At other times, we might inadvertently become so immersed in the telling that we lose our own sense of self in the process.

I have heard stories from clients who demonstrated so much courage and resilience in the face of such suffering that I couldn't help but become affected.

We know that trauma, whether the result of abuse, neglect, or catastrophe, is mostly all about the stories that one tells about the experience, whether as a victim or as a survivor (Cummings, 2011; Hoyt & Yeater, 2011; Kiser, Baumgardner, & Dorado, 2010). In that sense, trauma is often conceived as essentially a "disordered story" that is stuck in active memory with intrusive re-experiencing of the events (van Der Kolk, 2014). Survivors (who feel like helpless victims) are unable to form coherent narratives about what happened (Neimeyer, 2004). During sessions they stop and start, presenting fragmented versions that lack consistency (Stewart & Neimeyer, 2007). Our job in such situations is to help them to reform the memories of what occurred into a far better organized story with considerably less emotional valence. It is as if we are editors, if not contributors, who reframe, restructure, or re-author the version of events as presented, but always within a relational context that makes it safe to do so without retriggering the symptoms (Heineman, 2016).

Therapists invest all kinds of time and energy increasing their knowledge, advancing their skills, attending workshops, and providing supervision, as well as accumulating continuing education credits, most of it focused on hot topics related to mindfulness, technology, attachment issues, and neurobiology. Certainly these are all useful and critical areas, but I am proposing that we could also invest a lot more of ourselves into becoming more effective storytellers that impact our clients in constructive and *enduring* ways. After all, we are all exposed to hundreds, if not thousands of stories every single day—but how many do we actually hold onto?

As far as what it's like to be a therapist, whose job is to tell influential stories, we are saddled with the responsibility for both collecting teaching tales as well as increasing our ability to create them collaboratively with clients. I'd like to end this chapter and transition into the next one on the ways our clients' stories—and behavior—impact us by suggesting that you consider several questions to dig into your own storied life.

1. What is a story that had a powerful influence or impact on your life? This could have been a fairy tale, myth, or legend you encountered as a child. It could have been sparked by a comic book, puppet show, song lyrics, play, opera, documentary film, movie, television show, short story, novel, or a story told to you by someone else. Regardless of its source, this story continues to haunt you to this day, perhaps in some way responsible for who you have become.
2. What is a story that you frequently tell someone new that you meet, someone who you want to truly *know* you?

3. Given that all therapists have developed their own catalogue of favorite teaching tales, designed to reveal important themes or inspire clients, what are some of your favorites that have been consistently most effective over time? How could you further develop them in ways to increase their power and endurance?
4. What is a meaningful and significant experience of your life that you haven't yet formed into a coherent story, one that you can't quite grasp clearly, much less share with others in a way that feels integrated and makes sense?
5. What gets in the way of you becoming more creative, flexible, expressive, dramatic, and accomplished as a storyteller?

Being a therapist means investing in the lifelong mission of collecting and developing just the sort of stories that are likely to resonate most with those we wish to help and inspire. Some of our own muses and mentors have earned their reputations largely as a result of their storytelling prowess, just as some of the most notable and interesting books in the field, such as works by Yalom (1989, 2000, 2015), Haley (1973), Bugental (1990), Lindner (1960), and many others, are compelling precisely *because* they tell engaging and revealing stories in such a way to make the tales both instructive and memorable. Similarly, there are a number of collections devoted to the experience of being a client as well, even though many of them focus on some pretty awful encounters (Bates, 2006; Dinnage, 1989; Fox, 2000; London, 1998; Sands, 2000; Tower, 2005; Yalom & Elkin, 1974).

I've spent much of my life collecting, writing, editing, and sharing the most impactful and influential stories I've encountered, regardless of their origins. Many of us have learned over time that the best way to introduce complex ideas is through an illustrative story. At our core, all of us are storytellers, whether in the role of therapist, teacher, parent, or human being.

5

How Clients Change Their Therapists

SITTING IN A prominent place in my office is a small vial containing an inky mixture of earthen ingredients. It was given to me by a Peruvian witch doctor who believed that clients influence their therapists just as we influence them. He felt that healers, whether in the jungle, suburbs, or cities, need protection against the evil spirits that emanate from people who are suffering.

According to an ancient Incan legend passed on from one generation of healers to the next, all mental and physical illnesses result from an impure soul. The mental spirit of the healer, his or her powers of suggestion and white magic, can purify a sick soul and restore inner control. This purification is always undertaken at great risk—for the destructive energy emanating from a patient also infects the spirit of the healer.

Most therapists understand that they jeopardize their own emotional well-being when they intimately encounter the pain of others. Carl Rogers relates the story of his involvement with a deeply disturbed woman. He vacillated between professional aloofness and the genuine warmth that was to be his trademark.

His client became confused, irrational, and hostile; she even followed him through his relocation from Ohio State to Chicago. As her dissatisfaction with the therapy grew, she became critical and demanding of Rogers, piercing his defenses and triggering his feelings of inadequacy. "I recognized that many of her insights were sounder than mine, and this destroyed my confidence in myself; I somehow gave up my self in the relationship" (Rogers, 1972, p. 57). Continuing this destructive relationship eventually led to a psychotic breakdown for the client and to the borderline of a nervous breakdown for her therapist. Rogers believed he was going insane as a result of the collapsed boundary that occurred with this client. Feeling trapped, helpless, and unable to sort things out on his own, he eventually headed to Atlanta, where he believed that Carl Whitaker was the only therapist who might be able to help him. After several phone consultations with Whitaker on his way south, Rogers eventually returned home, where he began yearlong treatment with a local therapist who eventually helped him come to terms with the toxic effects from this client (Kirschenbaum, 2009).

This leads one to wonder if Freud's admonishment to remain detached in the therapeutic relationship was intended less to promote the client's transference than to preserve the emotional safety of the clinician. Indeed, he suggested his patients lie on the couch, out of range, not just to promote transference reactions but also because he was tired of them looking at them all day.

The experience of any practitioner would attest to the emotional as well as intellectual strains of living constantly with clients' crises, confusion, and intense suffering. We sit in a sacred vault, completely isolated from the rest of the world and all other intrusions, accompanied only by those who have lost hope, who live with excruciating agony, and who sometimes try to make others' lives as miserable as their own. Even with the best defenses and clinical detachment, we are still sometimes polluted by this pain.

Our professional effectiveness, not to mention our personal well-being, is affected by the intimate relationships that have become the trademark of our work. We live with the pressure of trying to meet our own and others' expectations. Despite our best efforts to convince ourselves of our limitations, we feel responsible for clients' lives. We experience repetition and boredom that comes from having an assembly line of people walk through our offices, not to mention the added stress of supervisors and quality review boards looking over our shoulder to monitor our progress. We feel inadequate for not knowing enough, for not being able to help more people, and for not doing it more often. When we do manage to make a significant difference in someone's life, we then struggle with helping make the changes last. And as a result of these close encounters with people in pain, our own issues are constantly touched, our old wounds reopened.

Consider the experience of therapy for *both* participants. Confidentiality, and therefore privacy, are implicit parts of the encounter, as is a level of intimacy that sometimes reaches, if not exceeds, that of parent and child or of husband and wife. We are privy to secrets that the clients are barely willing to share with themselves. We know clients at their best and at their worst. And as a function of spending so many intense hours together, our clients come to know us as well. We aren't nearly as inscrutable as we think. Clients can read the nuances of our behavior, study our most subtle "tells" or micro-expressions, especially those that might reveal any sign of disapproval. They recognize our annoying habits, how we repeat ourselves, when we are bored or irritated. We are indeed partners in a journey together.

The Limits of Continuing Education

There is a myth that therapists learn their craft in graduate school, although this belief is certainly not shared by the majority of practitioners who realize that most of what they learned occurred *after* they graduated. Equally inaccurate is that whatever was deficient in our training could more than be made up for through continuing education workshops. Every state, province, and jurisdiction now requires therapists to accrue dozens of advanced training hours to maintain their license. Although certainly well intended, this policy has created a continuing education industry that is just as intent on making a profit as on delivering a quality education. And let's be honest: it is a game that most of us play.

Many of the workshops we are forced to attend are boring and meaningless, and hardly do more than satisfy our obligation. I say this with full disclosure that I am part of the problem, as I am routinely asked to do such trainings for state or national organizations (although I'd like to believe that some people actually leave with something tangible and useful from the experience). I recently asked an audience how many of them would have chosen to attend the workshop if they had not been required to do so—more than half raised their hands. So maybe it is a good thing that we are mandated to seek additional training that we would not otherwise consider.

In a scathing critique of the continuing education system, Wright (2005) made the point that there isn't much empirical evidence that continuing education workshops actually improve the quality of professional practice, although it is quite clear that they pad the profits of the delivery services. For a fee, therapists can register for online courses, download the tests, and then skim the articles for the answers needed to pass. For clinicians with such a goal in mind, 6 hours of continuing education workshops can be completed in less than an hour.

How many of you have ever left early from a workshop and yet still accepted a certificate saying you attended the whole thing? How many of you sat in the room the whole time but barely paid attention while you completed other tasks to keep you busy? When was the last time you attended a workshop where you left with something significant and useful, or that stuck with you forever after?

Of course, the same thing could be said for books like this one. How many volumes about therapy have you read in your life that really made much of a difference? On such a variable interval reinforcement schedule, it seems as though less than 1% is enough to keep us searching for the Next Great Thing. "Therapy books?" one experienced clinician said with a smirk.

"I stopped reading those damn things years ago. They all seem to reinvent the same things or try to advocate their point of view, which sells more of their books."

"You don't read books in the field anymore?" I repeated in a neutral voice, intrigued but still appalled by what this person was saying.

"Have *you* read any of them lately?" Then he laughed. "Oh yeah, that's right, you write them, don't you?"

I smiled politely and resisted digging back. "What about journals?"

"You're kidding, right?"

I waited, a bit punitively I must admit.

"When is the last time you found something helpful in a journal? They're all about these academics getting tenured, which is directly proportionate to how many statistical tables they include."

"Okay, then, you don't read journals. You don't read books. . . ."

"I didn't say I didn't read books, just not *therapy* books. I've read enough of them to last a lifetime."

It turns out that this therapist read voraciously—philosophy, anthropology, history, literature, contemporary fiction, poetry, and dozens of magazines. He seemed intensely motivated to become better at what he does as a clinician; he was just insistent that this couldn't happen for him in the sanctioned professional literature, which only made him feel more stale.

This may be a rather extreme form of rebellion, rejecting *all* the research and writing in the field, claiming it has no value, but it nevertheless illustrates that something we rarely talk about is the ways our clients can be our best teachers.

So, if we don't learn to be therapists from just our formal or continuing education, how does excellence develop? Certainly from supervision with more experienced mentors who guide us along the path. But just as often, it is our clients who teach us to become better at what we do.

The Enduring Power of Client Relationships

When clients' impact on therapists is discussed at all, it is almost always done so in the context of negative effects. A search of the literature will generate such terms as blurred boundaries, countertransference, co-dependence, projection, overidentification, compassion fatigue, vicarious trauma, secondary trauma, and loss of control, all implying that the therapist must be very wary of the ways that clients can affect us. From the earliest stage of our careers, and throughout much of our supervision, we learn to be very cautious and careful about allowing our clients to touch us or break through the professional barriers that are supposedly in place to protect clients but are really designed as much to protect us.

Because I feel so privileged by the relationships I've had with my clients, and what they have taught me, I have long been curious about the *positive* influence they have on us. I had been seeing one client, a Buddhist nun, who had sought my help to adjust to living back in the "world" after spending many years living in a foreign monastery. Throughout our conversations, I was spellbound by the way she looked at life in contemporary America. She spoke in one session about trying to learn how to function and told a story of taking the bus to work each morning and being so amused by how commuters rush to run across the street to transfer from one bus to the next.

I looked puzzled because this seemed like pretty routine behavior to me.

"Buddhists don't run," she said with a laugh, "because wherever we are is as good as any other place we might be." She then told me that she tried, just as an experiment, to run with the others to catch the bus, but started giggling because it struck her as so funny.

That story stuck with me just long enough that a few days later, when I found myself frustrated and impatient waiting to get somewhere, I felt this lightning bolt of inspiration. I pretended I was my Buddhist client and imagined what she would do. I could feel all the tension drain away and found myself relaxed and even perfectly calm.

I mention this one story not because it is unique, but because, at least in my experience, it is so common. This led a colleague and me (Kottler & Carlson, 2006) to interview prominent clinicians in the field to tell us stories of the ways they were transformed personally and professionally by their clients. As with so many of my books (most of all, this one you are reading), I feel an intensely personal motive to explore a subject that has great relevance to my own struggles. I was looking for validation and affirmation that it really was okay to learn so much from my clients' experiences and our sessions together.

Things did not go well at all at first with our project. Several theoreticians I greatly admired decided to pass, reluctant to talk about such experiences. I didn't find this all that surprising, considering that what we were asking contributors to do was talk honestly and openly about how their clients have had a profound effect on their lives. Then one prominent person in the field said one of the most incredible things I'd ever heard: he said that although he'd very much like to participate in this project, he couldn't think of a single instance in his 50-year career in which a client had *ever* had an impact on him personally. He wondered if he could talk about books that influenced him instead.

Fortunately, we stuck with the question and eventually found two dozen master therapists who were willing to talk about how their clients had transformed them—as professionals, but also on a profoundly personal level. It was interesting the different ways that contributors interpreted the question, which was rather simply stated: tell us about a client who changed you and how this occurred. Whereas some chose to talk about the seminal case that helped them develop their theory or validate their most cherished ideals, others were willing to talk about the ways their lives were altered ever after by their relationship with a particular client.

Consider in your own life the people you have tried to help in some capacity, whether as a therapist or in some other role. Who stands out as the one client who had the most impact on you, personally or professionally or both? These changes you experienced could have been positive or negative, but they occurred as a result of your relationship with this person. Further, the changes still endure to this moment.

When you consider the key dimensions of this helping encounter, what made it so memorable and influential in your life and work?

When asked these questions, some theorists talked about the empathic transcendence they felt in the relationship or the incredibly powerful emotional drama that penetrated them deeply. You would have little difficulty identifying some of your own cases in which the level and intensity of engagement was such that you were left limp and reeling. Perhaps there was even a client who touched your core at such a deep level that you are certain you will never forget him or her.

Other theorists spoke about the ways they were challenged by clients who forced them to go far beyond what they thought they already knew and understood. It was intriguing how some of these groundbreaking thinkers in the field could actually point to one client, sometimes even one session, that was partially responsible for the development of their seminal ideas. Until this point in their career they had been happily following a template that had been firmly established and refined. Then they encountered a client who didn't respond to their favorite methods, who didn't react positively to *anything* they already knew how to do. In light of these setbacks and repeated failures, the therapists were forced to invent something new, something they'd never tried before or even heard of as possible.

Still others were far more personal in talking about how a particular client left a deep impression by teaching them a valuable life lesson. In my own case, I have made a great many profound life-changing decisions as a direct result of my contact with clients. Not all of these have been heroic or desired changes, but I suppose that is one of the prices we pay for allowing clients inside us.

Haunted by Stories

The previous chapter made the case that we tell stories for a living—designed, we hope, to instruct and inspire—but mostly we listen to stories that are so extraordinary, so heart wrenching, that they are sometimes beyond what we can possibly hold. In many cases, we are the only person on the planet who has been privileged (or burdened) to hear stories that are so secret and forbidden that they have never been told before. In each session, we hear another installment in the ongoing saga of a client's life, a narrative that sometimes has as many bizarre twists as anything we could ever find on television or pulp fiction.

Every therapist has collected stories that still leave them shaking their heads—if not shaken in their spirits. Some are life narratives filled with tragedy, abuse, violence, and despair. Some resemble situation comedies or reality shows that rival anything we've ever seen or heard in the media. And others involve dramatic tales so remarkable that if they were ever produced as movies, audiences could only assume that some crazy writer made them up. Yet they are real—or mostly real anyway.

One therapist mentions, without apology or shame, that he finds other people's secrets and perversions to be absolutely fascinating. "I know that everyone has some sort of hidden secret about themselves, things that they may never even share with a spouse, but they may share it with me—and I love that! I love hearing about people's 'dirty laundry' mainly because I am nosy. It's not like I sit around all day collecting these secrets, rather I just happen to find the taboo so interesting, the things that people don't talk about, the things that people do when they are totally by themselves."

Like this therapist, I have also been riveted by people's most private moments and secret selves, what we all do behind closed doors when nobody is watching. For one project (Kottler, 1990), I interviewed more than a thousand people over the course of 10 years, asking them to tell me about the things they do when they're alone. I have always been prone to some rather uninhibited behavior when nobody is watching. I talk to myself in strange voices. I sometimes pretend my house is under attack by aliens and use a squirt gun to fend off the invaders. You know, the usual stuff.

There is a secret world, an alternative universe, that our clients inhabit on a daily basis. When we hear these stories, we are transported to places we could never have imagined, to dark places where people do harmful things and to strange realities with different rules. We hear stories that are so bewildering, so bizarre, so amazing that we can hardly believe they are possible. While we listen with visible casualness, inside our heads we are screaming, "Oh my gosh, you've got to be kidding! That's the weirdest thing I've ever heard!"

You've got your own stories, some revealed in supervision, some shared with colleagues and friends (features disguised of course), and some kept secret. These are not just amusing tales but representative of the kinds of stories we hear from people who are troubled or live unusual lives. They haunt us precisely because of their novelty, because they aren't quite like anything we've heard before.

Things We Learn

Perhaps the greatest benefit of practicing therapy is what we learn on a daily basis. Each client brings with him the sum total of his accumulated knowledge, and his primary job is to share the context of his life, complete with all relevant background information. We are thus offered a glimpse into the most intimate world of humanity. We learn about the customs, language, and culture of diverse ethnic groups. We are exposed to differences in Italian, Persian, Chinese, Mexican, Vietnamese, Jewish, African American, Puerto Rican, American Indian, bi-racial, bi-cultural, blended, single-parent, or multi-generational family structures. We learn about religions, unique foods, and even the most intimate details of sexual and social behavior.

As we immerse ourselves in our clients' lives, we also spend much time learning what people do for work. We learn not only about conventional careers but also about those on the fringe of society, about being on welfare, in foster care, in the juvenile or criminal justice system. In any given week, we may learn about life as a professional athlete, politician, engineer, prostitute, or factory worker. As a by-product of our therapeutic digging, we find out the most interesting details of how corporate decisions are made, how drug deals are consummated, how a poem is created, how clothing is most easily stolen, what waiters secretly do to customers they don't like, how the stock market works, how a tennis player trains, how someone is really elected to office, how an assembly worker copes with boredom on the line, how a seventh grader tries to win friends and influence people, how an advertising writer thinks up ideas, how a policeman controls his aggressive urges, and how another therapist deals with burnout.

We have the privilege of knowing what people really think, feel, and do when their guard is down. And we get paid for it. Not only does the information we gain from clients help us better understand them, such knowledge also helps us better understand ourselves. Indeed, being a therapist allows us to live several hundred or more lives, not as a passive audience to a play or movie but as an active participant in the process of helping others re-create their worlds.

The work of the therapist can be so interesting and so personally relevant as well as professionally satisfying that I sometimes (but not for very long) feel the urge to pay some of my clients for what they teach me. Yet it takes incredible energy to do good therapy. Thus I both resent and feel grateful for the incentive to constantly challenge myself.

Not only do we learn from our clients, but our personal curiosity often complements our professional preparation. The training programs of therapists, whether in medicine, education, psychology, nursing, counseling, family therapy, or social work, emphasize an interdisciplinary perspective to integrate the study of mind and body. Biochemistry is a prerequisite for understanding the organic basis of many emotional disorders as well as the actions of psychopharmacological medication. Neurophysiology is necessary for the differential diagnosis of psychosomatic illnesses. Sociology, social psychology, sociobiology, and social anthropology help explain the social context of symptoms. Educational psychology provides theories of learning and development that we use for facilitating healthy growth. Philosophy and general systems theory help us reason logically, organize knowledge, and formulate coherent explanations for physical and spiritual phenomena.

Freud found the writing of Dostoyevsky, Sophocles, and Shakespeare; the sculpture of Michelangelo and Leonardo; the philosophy of Mill and

Nietzsche to be the inspiration for his theories. It was not his formal medical training as much as his readings of *King Lear, Hamlet, Oedipus Rex*, and *The Brothers Karamazov* that formed the cornerstone of his theories. Freud was first and foremost an integrationist, able to draw on the wisdom of poets, sculptors, neurologists, philosophers, playwrights, and his patients to create a unified vision of the human world.

In the tradition of Freud, many of his followers educated themselves as generalists, with influences from diverse academic disciplines. Jung, for example, was heavily influenced by his Latin and theological studies, as well as by the philosophy of Goethe, Schopenhauer, and Kant and by the practitioners of the new science of psychiatry. Rollo May, the North American champion of existentialism, described perhaps the most pragmatic recipe for a style of therapy that used ingredients from philosophy (Kierkegaard, Nietzsche, Heidegger), psychoanalysis (Freud), phenomenology (Merleau-Ponty, Husserl), art (Cézanne, van Gogh), theology (Marcel, Jaspers), literature (Sartre, Camus, Kafka), and the concentration camps (Frankl). There is, therefore, great historical precedent in our field for learning as much as we can about everything. Ours is a science of experience—not just from formal research and case conferences but from literature—that aids our understanding of the complexities of emotion and behavior. Without Shakespeare's plays, Dostoyevsky's novels, or James's short stories, our knowledge of anguish and conflict would be hollow, our self-revelations one-dimensional.

In examining the experience of doing therapy, especially family sessions, the experience is likened to looking at oneself constantly in the mirror (Heatherington, Friedlander, & Diamond, 2014). Clients are constantly acting, reacting, providing input and feedback to us about how they are responding to our own behavior. They also force us to look more closely at our own families of origin and how they impacted us, as well as better educate us about the ways that loved ones can come together (or pull apart) during crisis or conflict.

When therapists are asked about special or memorable incidents that occur in their work, they often point to new insights that developed, "moments of meaning" that could have been quiet, subtle, hardly noticeable unless you were paying very close attention (Howes, 2015). These are some of the gifts we enjoy as a result of the work we do in that all the while we are talking to clients about their problems we are also speaking to ourselves as a parallel process.

By and large, we are a pretty optimistic group since we prefer to see the best in people and emphasize their strengths and resources whenever possible rather than dwelling only on upsetting experiences. We view the world through benevolent, hopeful lenses. Yet for those who work with trauma, we are tested in ways for which we might not be fully prepared. That is why there is so much discussion in the literature on compassion fatigue, secondary trauma, and vicarious trauma. It is assumed that seeing these kinds of cases would necessarily take a toll on the therapist's emotional being.

Yet just as clients often experience what has been called post-traumatic growth, so too do therapists sometimes enjoy dramatic transformations as a direct or indirect result of delving into a client's suffering (Bartoskova, 2015). I spent several months working in earthquake-ravaged areas in which I not only had to see and treat hundreds of festering wounds, broken bones, infections, and acute trauma, but was also subjected to terrifying quakes every day. I still have flashbacks, startle reflexes to movement or loud sounds, and haunting memories. But I also experienced so much incredible learning and growth as a result of the mission, developing new skills and confidence, bonding among our medical team, and an increased appreciation for the special moments of my life. This is actually not uncommon among members of our profession in that we are afforded so many opportunities to learn from our clients' lives and stories, especially those accounts of heroic resilience and survival that promote our own greater courage. Among those therapists who work with trauma survivors, three-quarters of them consistently report that as a result of this work, they live their lives more fully, treat others with greater kindness and respect, feel more emotionally expressive with loved ones, and feel stronger as a result (Arnold, Calhoun, Tedeschi, & Cann, 2005; Linley & Joseph, 2007). The more deeply we enter into the client's world and allow ourselves to fully resonate with their experiences, the more likely we will be changed by the relationship, for better or worse, depending on how we process it.

Deepening Relationships

"If doing therapy has taught me anything," a therapist explains, "it is how to connect with others. I mean really connect. In my family of origin, I was taught a very restricted, inhibited way of being with others. I always played it safe and mistrusted others. But doing therapy helped me to develop greater sensitivity, intuition, and blunted my fear of judgment."

This therapist owes much of this progress to the work she does. "My clients, many of whom were labeled mentally ill or dysfunctional, were the ones who taught me to be a more empathic parent, a better partner, a kinder daughter, and a more open friend. They are the ones who invited me into a deeper level of engagement with others than I ever imagined possible."

Therapists are relationship specialists, experts at navigating through the most troubled conflicts and turbulent interactions. All day long, people bring us their most intractable problems, their worst nightmares, and we work with them to sort things out and devise alternative ways for them to handle them. We spend our lives learning to become more compassionate, empathic, and loving. We refine our interpersonal skills so that we can communicate more effectively. All of this makes us better therapists but also more responsive human beings in all our other relationships.

A therapist attended a sixtieth birthday party recently and came across a friend he hadn't seen in over 30 years. "Before long we were talking about what really mattered in life. At one point, he paused for a moment and said how surprised he was that we were even talking about things so personal in such a public gathering. He then confided struggles he'd been having, as well as a recent success that brought him a lot of pride." The therapist was surprised by the intimacy and deep disclosures they shared with one another, yet was not really that surprised because this is what we do: we deepen conversations.

In one sense we become accustomed, if not addicted, to deep, intimate relationships because that is where we "live" during the time we spend with clients. Regardless of their age, background, culture, and personality, we learn how to engage them on the most intimate level possible. There is minimal, if any, small talk. The clock is running during the brief intervals we have together, so we spend as much time as possible talking about only the most meaningful, significant subjects. Whenever the conversation drifts toward the mundane or superficial, we gently lead it back (or forward) to more personal engagement. As much as possible, we encourage clients to talk about the taboo and the forbidden, to share their secrets and fantasies. Whenever appropriate and useful, we use our skills to probe and prompt strong emotional responses and help clients to express them more fully. We help people think in symbolic and metaphorical ways about their behavior. We help them look for deeper meaning. We talk about our own relationship with them and ways we might deepen it even further. In other words, we spend much of our work life engaged in the most intense closeness with others that is imaginable.

Then we go home.

As much as being a therapist is a privilege and a gift, an opportunity for us to continuously learn and grow, our clients sometimes touch us in ways that are certainly not enjoyable or desirable. There are hardships associated with the job and lingering effects that sometimes just don't seem to go away.

6

Hardships of Therapeutic Practice

BEING A MEMBER of any profession has certain benefits, as well as liabilities. To make some sweeping generalizations, accountants who spend all their time dealing with numbers may be really good at managing their own finances but somewhat less skilled at dealing with relationship issues. Emergency room nurses may handle their personal crises with calm assurance but have trouble relaxing when the action is dialed down. Forestry rangers may feel perfectly comfortable when working or playing outdoors but struggle when forced to spend prolonged time at home or an office. And then there are therapists, professionals who are trained in the nuances of human behavior, experts in negotiating interpersonal struggles, who also live with the consequences of this career choice.

There is no doubt that we enjoy certain advantages as a result of our chosen work. I have already mentioned how we enjoy a privileged position in our culture as experts in the mysteries of human behavior. Most of us have tremendous latitude in the ways we work; we're able to customize the context, style, and structure of what we do to best fit our preferences and personalities. We have the opportunity—even a mandate—to keep learning, growing, developing, changing, evolving. Yet with these benefits, there are other, darker consequences of this chosen profession. Whereas some of these costs, such as dealing with failures (Chapter 7), difficult clients (Chapter 8), and burnout (Chapter 9), have been well documented, others have not been as acknowledged and deeply explored.

Hardships Within Specialties

The various specialties within therapy present their special stresses and problems. In addition to dealing with the hazards associated with seeing clients and functioning within an organization, each practitioner must confront the identity problems she inherits with training. As we all know, status, power, competence, and expertise are not divided equally among the specialties practicing therapy. Psychiatrists, for example, must contend with their lack of early training in therapy and an orientation toward the medical model that brands them among fellow physicians as quacks who don't do anything and among their nonmedical colleagues as pill doctors who try to do too much.

Many social workers struggle with their obsolete public image as do-gooders who chat with people in their homes. Within the mental health network, they fight for parity with psychologists, who have their own problems trying to prove what they can do best. Psychiatric nurses, family therapists, and mental health counselors quietly go about their therapeutic work, but they are often frustrated by their lack of recognition. All clinicians, regardless of their chosen specialties and work settings, carry a tremendous burden into a therapy session before the client even opens his mouth.

Then there are the special hardships associated with the type of setting where therapy is practiced. A counselor working with child protective services, and another working for the probation department, feel absolutely overwhelmed with the tragic stories they hear—of unremitting violence, hopelessness, abuse, and suffering. Another counselor working for social services assesses eligibility requirements for financial aid among those who are homeless (or claim to be); she encounters not only tragic poverty and despair but also fraud and deceit. An elementary school counselor covers three different schools in the district, with barely enough time to handle even the most pressing cases in the most superficial way. Another therapist leads groups for perpetrators of domestic violence, all of whom are court mandated to attend sessions for a year, and most without remorse or guilt for their actions. A social worker for county social services speaks fluent Spanish but now works in an area with mostly Vietnamese-speaking clients, many of whom understand very little English (and no Spanish!). Other practitioners work in halfway houses, refugee camps, crisis intervention clinics, state mental health systems, veterans hospitals, prisons, jails, juvenile detention centers, battered women's shelters—all with shrinking budgets, increasing caseloads, and more severe disorders.

Even private practice is not what it once was during the golden years. Competition is fierce in the community. Managed care restricts both the fees that can be charged and the length of treatment. Quality assurance boards (what a name, huh?) micromanage treatment plans and require ever-increasing documentation of services. What had once been considered a relatively plush professional life, catering to the worried well—the neurotic privileged class—is now both far more diverse and interesting in its clientele. There is a greater need for private practitioners who are prepared to work in minority and marginalized communities and to encounter greater challenges and hardships.

Special Problems of Beginners

I hesitate to talk in much detail about the hardships of therapeutic practice. After all, why scare beginners away when they are often so filled with optimism, enthusiasm, and excitement for their new profession? Yet it is ignorance about the challenges you will face that most contributes to the feeling of being ambushed when these challenges do occur. Without meaning to temper any exuberance regarding your choice to be a member of our esteemed guild, I would be negligent not to offer the same informed consent that you are ethically mandated to provide for your own clients.

The truth is that being a therapist changes *all* your relationships, and many friends and family will get left behind. You will face your own most terrifying demons every week, and this takes its toll. You will be underpaid and unappreciated. You will see people when they are at their worst, and you will be expected to present yourself at your best. Every time.

Therapists in training shoulder additional burdens related to their fears of inadequacy and avoidance of failure. They are under competitive academic pressure at the same time that they are struggling to develop a professional identity and to reconcile some of the paradoxes of their profession—to get close but not too close to clients, to be caring yet detached, to provide support without fostering dependency, and to unravel the ultimate mystery: How it is possible for so many of their professors and supervisors to be equally effective in their work even though they appear to be doing such different things.

Perhaps most stressful of all for neophytes is reconciling the discrepant feedback they receive. Present a case—any case—to a collection of peers, and watch the heated debates begin.

I was completely stuck with a young woman who had been deteriorating after showing an initial surge of progress. A crucial point in our work together centered on the ambivalence she felt toward men. She had as yet been unable to consummate sexual intercourse because of an inability to lubricate sufficiently, perhaps even because of vaginismus, or tightening of the vaginal muscles. "Why," she asked me at a critical juncture, "if I am so afraid of penetration, is my most frequent fantasy of being raped?"

A good question. Actually a brilliant question. Unfortunately, I had no earthly idea as to the answer. Because I could not think of what else to do, I did what any self-respecting therapist in my position would do: I stalled and put the focus back on her until I could get some help. "That's a good question," I responded after a long a pause. "What do *you* think it means?"

We hemmed and hawed for a while. The session ended with the resolve that we would explore the issue in greater depth next time. The moment she walked out the door, I cornered a tribunal of my peers. "Okay, folks, here is the situation. What the heck does this mean?"

Another issue involved here was my feeling of inadequacy: if I were really a good therapist, I would know what this means. My uneasiness was only reinforced by my colleagues' easy assurance that they understood this phenomenon. What confounds me to this day is that each of their interpretations was different!

"She was obviously sexually abused. You checked this out, didn't you?"

Before I could reply, another chimed in, "I would think she has fears of intimacy. I would reframe this as a relationship problem rather than a sexual issue."

I took notes furiously. That last one sounded good, until the next suggestion, and the next one, and the one after that. I heard five different suggestions for the same case. I wondered how a doctor would proceed if he or she asked five colleagues to examine a patient and they came up with five different diagnoses and treatments.

This discrepant feedback we get from superiors, colleagues, and books we read only adds to the confusion, uncertainty, and stress we live with. We face people every day who want answers, and we do our best to appease their needs for certainty. But all the while, we have our own doubts: feelings of uneasiness that are often made worse by the sheer diversity of ideas—all with a devoted following—that flourish in our field.

Occupational Hazards

It was Freud who first suggested that therapists submit themselves for further treatment every 5 years because of the regressive effects caused by constant contact with clients' emotionally charged issues.

In the face of incredible emotional arousal—anger, sadness, panic, despondency, conflict—the therapist is expected to maintain neutrality, detachment, tolerance for frustration, empathy, alertness, interest, and impulse control, all without feeling depleted, deprived, and isolated. Further, being a therapist requires us to be contemplative, self-analytic, and self-reflective, continually self-monitoring our inner states, our motives and desires, our behavior and interpersonal patterns. Although this continual focus on our own internal states is great for promoting increased self-awareness, it can also lead to a degree of self-absorption, and this is one of the major symptoms of depression. Indeed one of the things we hear a lot from friends and family outside our esteemed guild is that we think too damn much.

As if such demands were not enough, we are also supposed to be charming and invigorated by the time we get home. Because our friends and family know what we do for a living, they have greater expectations that we will be superhumanly patient, forgiving, and compromising during those instances when they have us locked in battle. If we should slip up in some way or lose composure, some people will throw it back in our faces: "And you say you're a psychotherapist?"

One social worker has worked for the county department of social services for 12 years. She is completely entrenched in the system—politically, emotionally, and financially. She is also cynical, aloof, and sarcastic. Her job description as senior clinician sounds as though it were written by a naïve, altruistic academic. There is little time to spend with her clients because most of her energy is devoted to keeping her position in the ever-changing power hierarchy. She is afraid of the abused women she must treat—they seem so pathetic and remind her too much of the way she feels. She commutes an hour into the city each day and is patiently waiting for 18 more years to pass so she can retire. She feels old at 34. She has seen too much of human misery. She has nightmares about broken people without hope; she sees the faces of children dotted with cigarette burns. She cannot leave the system because she has a vested interest in the retirement plan. Besides, where would she go?

A psychologist in private practice appears to have the best of all worlds—a full caseload, freedom, self-employment, self-direction, status, and relative financial security. What is there not to envy? But he is trapped by his own success. He conducts 45 sessions per week, neglecting his health, family, and leisure pursuits in order to maintain his expenses and lifestyle. He has virtually no discretionary time. He hasn't taken a vacation in years because he can't justify the cost of losing 2 weeks' income in addition to the cost of the trip. He finds it difficult even to meet a friend for lunch because he figures in the cost of 2 hours he could have billed for his time.

A marriage and family therapist who splits her time between contract work for a community agency and a part-time private practice feels as if she is always looking for more work. A single parent with complete financial responsibility for her children, she can never quite get on a solid footing. Most of the families and couples she works with cannot afford her full fees, so her sliding scale has slid below what she can afford to live on. There was a time when she loved doing family therapy, but now it feels to her as if she is grossly underpaid for the quality and quantity of work she does. She feels torn when a couple cancels—finally an hour to recover from her previous sessions of the day—yet when she does not work, she is not paid for her time. She thinks seriously about taking on a third part-time job, just for a little while to make ends meet.

The preceding examples of how a few professionals experience the hardships of therapy portray only a minority of therapists and certainly very few of those readers who would ever purchase and read a book on the personal consequences of practicing therapy. Nevertheless, we all know practitioners who have let the side effects of therapeutic work really get to them. We shudder at the thought that it could be happening to us at this very moment. And what is the "it" that infects the nervous systems of people who try to help others for a living? How do our clients get to us, unravel our precious control, haunt us with their fears?

Sleepless Nights

Clients bring us their nightmares, drop them in our laps, and then leave us to sort them out for ourselves. They have been enduring sleepless nights for years; now the challenge for us is to keep their demons away. Especially at night, when we are relaxed and our defenses are down, images creep into our dreams, or, if we are lying awake, they invade our peace. We toss and turn, probably in synchrony with the very client who infected us.

Any client's story could be the trigger, but there is usually one particularly sad or terrifying tale that returns to haunt us when we are alone in the dark. We tell ourselves it was someone else's misery, but by then it is too late: the chain reaction has started, and we are probing deeply into our own failures.

One image brought to me by a client will haunt me until I die. Even though I had read stories and seen movies about this sort of thing, I could never have been prepared for the intensity that I would feel from being so close to someone who had been really terrorized.

One day, when the client was living in a faraway city, she ran into an old high school friend who was on vacation. Although he was more of an acquaintance than a good friend, she nevertheless knew him quite well because he had been her senior class president. They were delighted to run into each other after so much time and in such a large city. They stopped to have coffee, chat, and catch up on their lives. Then they parted ways. She went back to her apartment, and as was her habit, she read stories to her little girl until the child fell asleep. Then she began studying at her desk.

Several hours later, there was a knock at the door. She asked who it was and heard her high school acquaintance's voice say that he had brought something she had forgotten. As her hand hovered over the handle, she saw her daughter standing in her bedroom doorway. She was momentarily distracted as she swung open the door and turned to see her friend with a disfigured, hideous grin on his face and a butcher knife raised in each hand.

Although she eventually recovered from her wounds, she would never again open a door without taking some evasive action. And she has never since had a peaceful night.

It has been a while since I heard this story. I still hesitate before I open doors to strangers. And late at night, I see those with hideous faces from my past coming at me with big knives.

Every therapist has heard similar stories from their clients—people terrorized and horribly abused; people subjected to the most awful injustices and miseries; victims of rape, mutilation, attempted murder, satanic cults, genocide, or disaster. You meet people who sexually or physically assault their own children and people who have been subjected to such actions. You even meet parents who accidentally or deliberately killed their children. Each of these stories, told through the tears of ongoing anguish, penetrates you to your core. You weren't actually there to witness the crimes against humanity, but it feels as if you were. And rather than having to come to terms with only one such atrocity, you must metabolize dozens or even hundreds of them. This is but one source of ongoing stress in the life of a therapist.

Sources of Stress

Many therapists are heard to say that if only they could be left alone to do their real work—the business of seeing clients—and insulated from the politics of their organizations, their lives would be greatly enriched. The sad fact is that many staff groups are like extremely dysfunctional families. Power struggles and economic competition go on behind the scenes. You may be constantly triangulated into conflicts with peers and supervisors that drain your energy and demoralize you. All too often, what is best for clients takes a back seat to the posturing of your most insecure colleagues. The demands of insurance companies and managed care policies pressure you to compromise treatment planning for the sake of economic realities.

Whereas our working environments ought to be a source of support, nurturance, and growth, too often we attempt to function effectively in spite of daily frustrations. In one private practice setting, the therapists spend more time discussing how to beat the system and keep up their billings than they do planning ways to help their clients. In a community mental health center, staff members spend their free time griping about budget cuts, supervisors' ineptitude, and nonsensical rules. A substance abuse treatment center lost a huge grant as a funding source, sparking a civil war among the staff fighting over the meager resources. A group of school counselors and social workers lament to one another that they never help kids anymore because they are so locked into their scheduling and administrative duties. Staff members at a university counseling center complain that they cannot do their jobs properly because of a lack of support among administrators who view their services as "nonessential."

In each of these cases, the professionals spend almost as much time dealing with bureaucratic annoyances as they do getting on with their clinical responsibilities. The usual pressures that they experience as a result of their clinical work are exacerbated by additional obstacles. The result is an alarming burnout rate and distress level within our profession. Time pressures are often cited as the most frequently occurring precipitant of strain, although organizational politics, excessive workload, and conflicts with colleagues are also mentioned frequently.

On the basis of several studies (Mathieu, 2012; Norcross & Guy, 2007; Riggar, 2016; Sussman, 1995; Wicks, 2008), as well as my own interviews with practitioners in the field, it would appear as if sources of stress can be grouped according to four categories. The one we talk about the most includes *client-induced stress*, such as those times when they display angry outbursts, intense anxiety, worsening depression, suicidal threats, or attempt to triangulate us into family dysfunction. Also frequently cited are sources of *work environment stress* such as political infighting, nonsupportive colleagues, overbearing supervisor, excessive paperwork, time pressures, or restrictions on freedom. Third are those unforeseen things that happen in our lives, *event-related stressors*. These could include health problems, money problems, major life transitions, change in job or responsibilities, legal actions, or family difficulties. Finally there is *self-induced stress* that represents our own inability to take care of ourselves. Typical of this last category are excessive rumination and worry, self-doubt, need for approval, feelings of perfectionism, and poor lifestyle choices.

A pattern of distress emerges from each of these sources, one that includes psychological symptoms (boredom, isolation, frustration, irritability, depression), behavioral symptoms (procrastination, substance abuse, lowered productivity, recklessness), and physical symptoms (sleep disruption, appetite gain or loss, headaches, respiratory problems, muscular tension). It appears as if the restraint and concentration that we continually must exercise take their toll on our mental and physical health. We develop many of the same symptoms that plague our clients, only we are better than they are at denial. Not only do our bodies and minds suffer, so do our relationships.

One-Way Intimacy

Kovacs (1976) considered the tragic flaw of most therapists to be not the need for intimacy but its avoidance. Only within the sterile, ritualized context of a therapeutic session, where a clinician is both boss and observer, can he or she feel safe. There the therapist can experience loving relationships but also avoid the risks associated with real family conflict. Whether we actually got started in the helping profession to save the world, to save our families, or to save ourselves, we enjoy getting close to others and helping them solve their problems. Yet the intimacy a therapist experiences with clients is strange—there are rules and structures, even payment, for attention.

One major source of complaints to professional ethics committees and state licensing boards involves alleged sexual intimacies between clients and therapists. Researching the patterns of these incidents, Pope and Bouhoutsos (1986) identified a number of common types, including the "Svengali" scenario, in which the therapist creates and exploits client dependencies. Others include "as if," wherein the therapist confuses transference with infatuation; "it just got out of hand," in which emotional closeness grew beyond manageable limits; "true love," or its rationalization as a justification for abandoning professional boundaries; "time out," in which the therapist makes an arbitrary distinction that what occurs outside the office does not count; and "hold me," in which erotic contact escalates from comfort gestures. In all these cases, sexual involvement results from the high level of intimacy that makes both participants more vulnerable to counterproductive entanglements.

We become for our clients not only objects of transference but living, breathing, loving, attractive people. Our clients' friends and spouses pale in comparison to the ways they see us with unconditional acceptance and professional relationship-building skills. We are rarely angry, irritable, short-tempered, or demanding (at least when on duty). Instead we demonstrate limitless compassion, patience, wisdom, and control. Our clients feel attraction and gratitude. Some people, especially those who may find themselves in therapy, want to show their affection with their genitals.

So we understand how a client might be motivated to seduce a powerful, attractive model who also may be a reminder of prior unresolved relationships. What then of the temptations felt by the therapist? We also have unfulfilled needs. Our hormones do not differentiate which individuals are off-limits. So we try to ignore our own needs for intimacy or friendship with clients. Many of our clients not only look good to us but also feel good to know. They are people not unlike ourselves—motivated to grow. They have been dedicated learners. Some have worked very hard to turn themselves into our Galateas (as we are their Pygmalions). They can express feelings fluently, use the language and terms we favor. They have been completely open, sharing, and honest with us. They have disclosed their histories, fantasies, dreams, and desires. And for this dedicated effort, we like many of them a lot.

The consequences of acting on our impulses are obvious. We lose our objectivity and jeopardize the trust and therapeutic work that have been accomplished. Sexual contact with clients or ex-clients represents an abuse of trust and power and is always self-indulgent and anti-therapeutic. Many of the victims of "therapeutic incest" experience lowered self-esteem; sexual dysfunctions; feelings of exploitation, anger, and betrayal; and a feeling of mistrust toward other helping professionals that makes them reluctant to seek treatment for their now-compounded problems. We know all of this. And that is why we work so hard to restrain our natural (and unnatural) desires.

It is especially important that therapists at greatest risk—those in the midst of divorce or separation—recognize their vulnerability to the temptations of acting inappropriately. Those clinicians who have been victims of sexual abuse, who have frequent sexual fantasies about their clients, who are in the midst of personal crisis, who don't maintain clear boundaries in their client relationships, and who are isolated professionally are particularly at risk of acting out.

And then there are gray areas in the restraint of intimacy. Some practitioners restrict their therapeutic activities to their offices, whereas others work wonders in the outside world making house calls, doing community interventions, escorting therapeutic field trips to practice new skills. The difficulty of maintaining intimacy boundaries increases during field trips and in sessions conducted in restaurants, at picnic tables, or on walks. The temptation to become involved with clients beyond appropriate limits is more severe. The therapist must exercise incredible self-monitoring, self-control, self-deprivation. The pressure builds.

Restraint

The cumulative pressures from maintaining prolonged one-way intimacy are hardship enough for a professional who also requires liberal doses of approval and affirmation. The tension is compounded by other ways in which a therapist exhibits restraint. From training onward, we are often told what things we must not do during sessions with clients. Most of all, we are warned not to do too much (even when practicing action-oriented, directive approaches); it is the client's responsibility to do the work, choose the content, pace the progress, develop insight, and change behavior. Embedded in the admonishment to avoid doing too much to rescue the client is an unwieldy list of more specific negative imperatives. Don't express personal opinions. Don't take sides. Don't be too passive—or too directive and controlling either. Don't moralize and impose your values. Don't let your attention wander. Don't meet your own needs in session. Don't share too much of yourself, but don't be extremely withholding. Be genuine but not too transparent. Be honest but don't say everything you're thinking. Find your own path and clinical style, and don't pay too much attention to lists like this.

Depending on your training, theoretical allegiances, and supervisors, this personal list of precautions will vary. Regardless of the context, there is often a theme of "Stifle yourself" juxtaposed with encouragement to be authentic. We know what happens to children who deliberately withhold their true feelings and repress their unsatisfied needs: they become neurotic, well-disciplined adults. We know what happens to children in a double-bind family where they get mixed messages: they become confused or even crazy. What happens to therapists who experience these same contradictory and paradoxical messages?

Self-deprivation comes with the territory. We are trained and paid well to put others' welfare before our own. We are disciplined to stifle our own desires. By dispassionately acknowledging our personal needs, we lessen their grip on our actions. More and more we simply observe rather than identify with our motives. It's not so much that we are trying to push them away; denial buys us no peace. Rather, we are loosening our attachment to our motives by letting them slumber.

In our drive to be therapeutic, we harness self-centered urges. Yet it is hard to tread water with someone on our back without drowning. We can only give so much without needing support in return. And just when we have achieved that miracle of therapeutic love, when we feel comfortable and safe, when we even look forward to the meetings with clients we have grown attached to, it is time to say good-bye.

It is during the closure of therapy that we must often restrain our own feelings of loss and mourning each time a relationship ends. There could be lingering insecurity and doubts about what transpired during the process as well as ongoing shame that result from four interconnected factors, the first of which is that we don't really know what we are doing, nor have a clear understanding of what happened and why. "Like Adam and Eve," observes Buechler (2012, p. 110), "we have eaten from the tree of knowledge and are aware of our nakedness." In other words, we know all the things we don't know. Second, we are often asked to do things we don't know how to do. Clients tell us their problems, expect immediate relief, and anticipate that we have some magical formula or technique to create an instant cure. This is related to the third factor, that we don't have many definitive answers to the questions most often posed to us. Finally, "all our gods are dead" (Buechler, 2012, p. 110), meaning that we have no higher power or absolute authority to provide us the direction and answers that we—and our clients—most desperately desire.

Narcissism—in the Therapist, Not the Client

Many years ago, before the days of mobile phones, I was standing in a movie theater lobby. There was a long line of people waiting to use the only pay phone in sight. I recognized a well-known psychiatrist striding across the room toward the phone. He ignored the people who were waiting and approached the woman who was currently speaking on the phone. She promptly turned her back on him and continued her conversation.

"Ahem," the psychiatrist said, clearly his throat loudly. "Excuse me please." His booming voice immediately drew the attention of everyone else in the vicinity, but the woman just ignored him and kept talking.

The psychiatrist impatiently tapped the woman on the back. "Excuse me," he said once again.

The woman cupped her hand over the phone. "Yes?" she said, looking over her shoulder, more than a little annoyed by the interruption.

"Excuse me," the psychiatrist repeated, "but I'm a doctor." As he said this, he pointed to the phone in her hand.

"Your mother must be very proud," she answered, then turned around to continue her phone conversation.

Everyone in the lobby started applauding wildly. The good doctor turned with a harrumph and slinked away.

The arrogance of this psychiatrist is, unfortunately, not especially unusual within the therapist (and medical) community. Sometimes we take ourselves so seriously that we really do think we are special and entitled to special privileges. We are used to people deferring to us, paying homage to our position. After all, we get paid to talk for a living and dispense wisdom. Our clients treat us as sages. Strangers treat us with a certain reverence because of fears that we can see through them to their core. Yet it is our own illusions of being perfectly empathic beings, of infallibility, that most feed our narcissism.

A particular kind of narcissistic yearning in therapists can manifest itself in several different forms. The same interpersonal sensitivity that makes us ideally suited to the profession also creates problems for us. This relational attunement may have been nurtured through our professional training, but in many cases, its roots lie in our families of origin, in which we developed a kind of "audience sensitivity" to win approval and validation. Many therapists report taking on caretaker roles as children, equating love as a transactional reward for service.

After my father moved out of the house when I was 12, I was stuck taking care of my two younger brothers, as well as my depressed, alcoholic, suicidal mother. I remember more than a few times calling her therapist on the phone when she locked herself in the room, drunk and despondent, threatening to kill herself. During a time when I was struggling with my own adolescent insecurities, I was forced to take on the role of the ultimate parentified child who was required to be a caretaker—never feeling adequate or prepared for that role and always striving harder to do a better job. I've been working toward that perfection ever since.

One of the dangers of unresolved narcissism in the therapist is a much greater propensity for stress and burnout because she has little inclination toward, or practice of, self-care. Clinically, the therapist strongly desires to rescue clients because there is so much at stake for her own self-worth. Does any of this sound familiar? It does to me.

I can't quite claim that now my own secret is out, because I've been writing about this exact struggle for decades. It is just startling to discover that I am one of so many who were first attracted to this profession because it was part of my training in childhood. To this day, before I go to sleep at night, I ask myself what good I've done and how many people I've helped, and I measure my success in terms of the quality and quantity of such goodness. Along with this perhaps laudable but neurotic desire comes the drive toward perfection along with the avoidance of feeling like a fraud. Who would need to write three to four books each year if he were not attempting to prove his worth? Who would choose to study failure and imperfection in the profession if he were not investigating his own struggles? Who would write a book such as this if he were not trying to finally come to terms with his own secret failings?

Restraining our egos is a challenge that many of us will never quite meet. What with our diplomas, titles, and carefully appointed chambers, it is hard for us not to take ourselves seriously. Such self-centered preoccupation with the image we project to the world is hazardous to our mental health. We become disembodied selves, separated from our feelings and from those of the people we try to help.

Honestly consider for a moment the real kick you get out of being a therapist—besides all the benefits you enjoy. I suspect that deep within my own heart is the desperate need to influence others. I am afraid of dying and, worse, of being forgotten. I feel as though I am in the process of immortalizing myself with every disciple who goes out into the world with a part of me inside him or her. It is as if I can cheat death, if only I can keep a part of me alive. Does this motive affect what I do in my sessions? Naturally. Does this grandiose self-involvement limit the quality of my work? Of course. Do I feel impaired in my capacity for empathy because of this narcissism? Unfortunately, yes. But I stay safe.

To give up our narcissistic stance is to risk a deeper, more terrifying form of self-involvement: confronting the feelings we fear most. Like most obsessives, we successfully distract ourselves from those things we least wish to understand. We can avoid real intimacy even in our sacred chambers by keeping clients at a distance. We can glorify the influence we have had on clients while denying their influence on us. We can distance ourselves from pain by retreating deep inside our chair-side manner—a few strokes of the chin, a blank stare, a delusion that we have the power to heal.

Enter a woman in her mid-thirties who is far from composed. Suffering oozes from her pores; even her tears have tears. She feels hopeless, despondent, deeply depressed. This is her third attempt to seek help in as many months. She saw the last therapist for six sessions.

"What did he say?"

"I don't know."

"You don't remember?"

"I remember quite well. He didn't say anything."

"He said nothing?"

"No."

"What, then, did he do during the time you spent together?"

"He took notes."

"Uh-huh."

"He said thank you when I paid him at the end."

"Why did you go back if you didn't feel he helped you?"

"He seemed so important. He came highly recommended. And he seemed so awfully busy. He had to arrange things to fit me into his schedule, and several times he was interrupted by calls from people who needed him. I thought maybe if I waited long enough, he might notice me. But he only seemed to notice himself. It's like he looked right through me, as if I wasn't there. I felt like a bug he was inspecting. All he did was take notes. Even when I broke down sobbing, he just looked at me across his desk and kept writing in his pad."

The woman stopped abruptly, peeked out from behind her anguish. I asked her if she would give me a chance to help her. She said she was tired of seeing therapists, but she would think about it and let me know. She drove straight home, drew a bath, swallowed 12 antidepressants, drank a pint of bourbon, and slit both her wrists. She died from the chronic indifference and narcissism of the therapists who refused to see her as a human being.

There is a danger in using anecdotal material such as this to support assumptions about therapist characteristics and experiences. We all know individuals in our profession who believe themselves to be godlings and demand homage from their disciples. "The field of psychotherapy inevitably attracts people with god complexes, and it is custom designed to exacerbate the condition when it exists" (Maeder, 1989, p. 45). Nevertheless, in a study designed to test the notion that therapists are more narcissistic than others, Clark (1991) found no evidence for this idea. Although this investigation is quite old, and based on a very small sample, it does remind us to be careful of exaggerating a problem that although perhaps not widespread, is at least something that we should monitor in ourselves. Therapists in our society are, after all, treated as if we have special powers that allow us to see inside people's hearts and souls, predict the future, and heal suffering. It is indeed difficult for us not to come to believe in our specialness.

I have long felt that I hold superpowers. After all, it seems at times (to others if not to myself) that I can read minds, predict the future, and hear, see, feel, and sense things beyond the powers of mere mortal beings. I have worked hard to develop my capacities for intuition, sensitivity, and verbal fluency far beyond the levels of those without my training and skills. It is no wonder, then, that I take myself far too seriously and inflate my sense of self-importance. Moreover, I know that I am not the only one among my brethren who does so.

Knowing Too Much

There is something to be said for a certain degree of ignorance, or at least being shielded from the dark side. But we have nowhere to hide. Every day, every hour, people disclose to us the most disturbing and dysfunctional behaviors imaginable. After a while we lose the ability to be shocked by the weird, creepy, sick, hurtful things that people do to themselves and others. People tell us secrets that have never been shared before—of abuse, trauma, suffering, addiction, compulsion, perversity, anger—and we are expected to hold all that and tell no one. People confide their worst instincts, fantasies, hallucinations, delusions, and obsessions, and we are required to listen and take it all in. Nothing we see on television or the media can touch the realities that we encounter in our offices. We see people at their absolute worst, when they are on the verge of cracking. We are subjected to onslaughts of rage, shame, indignation, seduction, and manipulation during times when people are most powerless and out of control. We talk to people about the forbidden, about that which is not said.

Forget about peering inside someone's mind or heart: we see inside their *souls*. And what are the effects of being so close to people who are struggling with the ultimate questions of existence, meaning, and survival?

Graham, an ex-priest who later became a therapist, talked about the transition from hearing one kind of confession and offering God's forgiveness to quite another in which people must learn to forgive themselves. "Now I struggle alongside people trying to make some sense of their lives. I try to help them find some kind of meaning. It feels like I am an oasis in their lives, a place for them to rest and recover during times when they are lost. When I was a priest, I was expected to know the answers. As a therapist I now accept that as much as I know, I don't have any answers. I just know that we can't do it alone. It is all pretty frustrating knowing that peace or satisfaction will never be achieved."

Like this therapist, we are often forced to surrender our illusions. We can't pretend that things are simple. We know too much about what happens when people deceive themselves. And all day long we listen to people lying to us, lying to themselves, and trying to find a way to cope; our job is to confront this deceit. When the day ends, we are left to face our own self-deceit.

Pathologizing of Self and Others

It is both amusing, and potentially dangerous, when a trainee first studies the *DSM* and learns the diagnostic process. At first, there is power in this knowledge, the feeling that finally we have the means by which to classify and label the bewildering variety of disorders that we may be asked to treat. There is almost a mathematical precision in learning the coding system, complete with the numbers associated with each possible variety of any given category: "dementia with Alzheimer's," "dementia due to Creutzfeld-Jacob disease," "dementia, late onset, with delusions," "dementia, early onset, with depression." It's about the time we delve into personality disorders that we begin to see florid examples everywhere among our friends, family, and coworkers and in the media. We start using the new language we've acquired, delighted with the symptoms we recognize in people all around us. In our heads, if not out loud, we start calling people histrionic, narcissistic, avoidant, OCD, or—when we're really angry—borderline. This pathologizing lens has been referred to as the "therapist's disease" in which we tend to constantly look for what is wrong in others, what is dysfunctional, maladjusted, disturbing, abnormal, self-destructive, crazy, obsessive-compulsive. The more familiar we become with the nomenclature and diagnostic labels, the more fluently we incorporate the terms in our everyday thinking. Although this thinking is a natural and important part of becoming a competent therapist, it also shapes the way we look at the world, at other people, and ourselves.

In spite of influences from the positive psychology movement in which the research and writing has refocused attention on human strengths and resources, therapists remain firmly embedded in a psychopathological worldview. We are specialists in figuring out what is wrong with people. Our clients only come to us when they are desperately in the throes of dysfunctional behavior. We constantly sort through the presenting complaints, narratives, life histories, and presentations of clients in order to identify problems and disorders in need of attention. Moreover, it is very, very difficult to turn off this pathological filter when we aren't in session.

It is all too easy for us to become psychological hypochondriacs, constantly aware of every nuance of possible problems in our own functioning. We are taught to become increasingly self-aware for purposes of honing our clinical skills and working through countertransference reactions. We are admonished to continually work on our own stuff so that it doesn't pollute our work. As I've discussed, this is a gift, but it is also a terrible burden.

Mya, a therapist intern, freely admits that she entered the field as much to work on her own growth as to help others. She is delighted with the personal gains she has already made—improved communication, deeper intimacy in relationships, increased empathy, greater knowledge and self-awareness—but she also feels raw and vulnerable. "We get so much encouragement from supervisors to be open, honest, and authentic, yet often it isn't safe. Am I really accepted for who I am? How am I being judged as not good enough? There are such conflicting messages. We are told to open up and be trusting and share ourselves, yet also don't be too self-indulgent. Our performance is always being evaluated, and we are told to evaluate ourselves after every session. I have to tell you: it all gives me a headache. I feel weak and vulnerable. And oh so tired."

Fatigue

In an article on his lifestyle, one prominent therapist describes a typical day as being so rigidly scheduled from 7:00 a.m. to 2:00 a.m. the following morning that each 15-minute segment of time is meticulously accounted for. He runs 25-minute sessions back to back without a break. He inhales his meals between administrative, lecturing, writing, and consulting chores, and even must schedule conversations in advance. Although he defends this inhumane regimen as an "affair of the heart," it could more accurately be described as a case of neurotic workaholism that is part of a maladaptive vicious circle. Even 30 years after this report on his working habits, and over 90 years of age, this theoretician still worked from dawn to dusk.

As noted earlier, time pressures head the list of therapist stressors. There are never enough hours to see all the people we need to see, return phone calls, attend meetings, complete paperwork, do outreach, keep up with the literature, eat, sleep, and have a life outside the office. We often run behind schedule. For those who work in the public sector, there are often people waiting, yet there is always pressure to see just one more client.

For those in private practice, there is a different set of time pressures and fears, mostly related to maintaining one's tenuous hold on financial stability in the face of increasing competition and economic realities. I could never quite get over the terror that one day the phone would stop ringing or that the referrals would stop coming. I could never quite turn down a new client for fear that the lean times would hit soon, and inevitably they would. So it was often a matter of feast or famine, and the feast times brought with them different challenges of balancing excessive work with a healthy lifestyle.

One would think that once the door closes and we immerse ourselves in a session, the narrowed focus on a single life and task would provide some relief from the exhausting pace. With distractions and intrusions kept at bay, the rhythm of the day slowed down to that of the client's heartbeat, we can feel our profound weariness. It is so hard to sit still. Our knees ache; our eyes burn. After the eighth, ninth, tenth, or eleventh session in a row, there is little left beyond an empty shell.

We get so tired of sitting, of listening, of talking, of thinking. This fatigue comes upon us when we take on too much work out of pride, greed, habit, escape, fear, or taking the path of least resistance. One therapist notices that the times he feels weary are those when he is blocking some other feeling: "In one session with a client where tiredness tugged at my sleeve, I found a resentment I had pushed aside about his call at the last minute to cancel our previous session. In another, I looked under the feelings of tiredness and got in touch with some sexual feelings I wasn't acknowledging to myself. With another the feelings were ones of danger and the client volunteered that she was feeling self-destructive and not telling me" (Griswell, 1979, pp. 50–51).

Much of the time, we urge clients to avoid the excesses of overwork. We caution moderation to reduce stress, fatigue, and mental exhaustion. We teach people to better appreciate their present moments, to live a tranquil existence. We warn them of the dangers of continuous multi-tasking, constant interruptions from messages, calls, texts, emails, all while we engage in the same behavior. Until we can create balance in our own lives between work and play, abandoning the search for perfection, it is very difficult to teach clients to lead more moderate lifestyles.

I know therapists (and so do you) who specialize in wellness and stress reduction in their practices, and all the while they are seeing 50 clients each week on top of other professional responsibilities. I know therapists who run busy private practices on top of their regular 40-hour-per-week jobs. I know therapists who work until 9 or 10 each night and most of their weekends. I know a therapist who writes for a few hours every day beginning at 6 in the morning and then heads off to his university job. He can't sleep well at night unless he has completed his creative output, often juggling work on four, five, or even six books at the same time. (Yeah, that one is me.)

We show symptoms of overwork when we skip meals or refuse to decline work when we are already overloaded. We neglect family, friends, and most of all ourselves. There is so little time to be alone, to think, to feel, to relax, to do absolutely nothing. Some of us are reluctant to take more than a few days off work because we fear losing income or losing power in the organizational structure. It doesn't take others very long to realize that we are replaceable—even if we nurture the illusion that we must do everything ourselves because nobody else would do as good a job.

When we are not working, we mull over our cases. We consider the direction our clients will head next, the things we did that we wish we had not done, and our plans for the following week. At odd moments, we wonder how clients are getting along. Why did they never return? What did we do to chase them away? These people populate our world. We see them more frequently than we see most of our friends. No matter how much we work to preserve our professional detachment, no matter how hard we discipline ourselves to push them out of our minds when they walk out the door, we still carry them around inside us. How could these people not be significant in our lives and loom in our minds when we spend week after week discussing the sacred details of their lives?

I feel exhausted; my energy is depleted just thinking about the burdens we routinely carry. It is strange to think that we work so hard while sitting still. Maybe it is because we must remain immobile and attentive that the job is so tiring. If only we could separate ourselves from the chair. If only our existence outside the chair could be as meaningful as the time we spend enveloped within it.

Isolation

Therapy exists to provide a safe and private haven for people to resolve their underlying problems. Without a guarantee to the client that communications will be held in strictest confidence, it is unlikely that we can accomplish much effective helping. To protect the client's right to privacy, secrecy, and dignity, we swear allegiance to our profession's code of conduct with regard to privileged communication. If we do nothing else in treatment, our primary obligation is to respect and protect the confidentiality of information received during sessions.

Naturally, clients appreciate our integrity and sense of honor. For us, it is second nature after years of training. We would no sooner commit an indiscretion that might compromise a client's safety than we would neglect to guard our own shameful secrets. When talking about our work in any context—with colleagues, client families, friends, and even spouses—we routinely monitor what we say so that client identities are disguised and their secrets protected. This shield serves our clients well, as presumably our prudence protects their privacy. However, like all barriers, it not only prevents things from getting out but also ensures that other things do not get in.

One of the most meaningful, interesting, and fulfilling parts of a therapist's life is the time spent with clients. At times, we may be practically bursting at the seams to tell friends about some prominent citizen we are working with. Yet we can tell no one about the people we work with or about the details of what we do.

If we run into a client at a social gathering, etiquette requires us to fade into the background unless the client chooses to recognize us. If a client's name comes up in conversation, we must pretend indifference so as not to give away our involvement. It is as if we were conducting secret affairs with 50 people simultaneously! We even arrange our schedules and offices so that clients do not accidentally meet one another. All of this results in a kind of sanctuary for the people we help and a kind of prison for us.

Physically, we are separated from the outside world, ensconced in a soundproof chamber. We (hopefully) don't answer the phone, open the door, or otherwise tolerate interruptions during sessions; in the intervals in between, we are so busy doing paperwork or going to the bathroom that there is little time for interaction with anyone. Visitors rarely stop by because we are continually unavailable or in session. It is as if we cease to exist in the outside world.

What are the effects of this compartmentalized isolation? Maybe it contributes to therapists' feeling of specialness and sainthood: we suffer in silence so that others may be released from pain. We also may become secretive, mysterious, aloof, and evasive when we are not at work, while we continue to struggle to be authentic, transparent, and genuine with clients. We retreat inside ourselves for comfort and pat ourselves on the back for being so professional. Actually, we feel like martyrs.

All over town, there are restaurants and bars that we can't visit because clients or ex-clients work there. At parties, we have to monitor closely how much we drink, knowing that losing control would sully our reputation. We have to carefully scrutinize anything we might post on social media, or else opt out altogether. Neighbors watch our children for signs of emotional disturbance, so they can substantiate the myth of the crazy shrink down the block. People constantly ask for advice on what to do about their lives. Others feel intimidated by their own perception of therapists as mind readers. They will not get too close for fear we will expose their insecurities with a casual glance. "Oh, you're a therapist. I suppose I should be careful around you (giggle)."

So we live on display in glass houses. If clients or prospective clients research our reputations in the community, we hope they will discover that we are not only competent professionals but also nice people. Because we are being watched, we stay in line and cultivate a consistent image. We watch, listen, speak when we are spoken to, and keep our mouths shut.

Money Issues

It might seem peculiar that money is discussed in the context of therapist hardships, but many of us do have an awkward relationship with it. On one level, it sometimes feels that we are *way* undercompensated for the hard work we devote to our craft; on the other hand, it can feel quite awkward accepting payment for what can seem like just a supportive conversation between two old friends.

Of course therapy is practiced differently in various settings, with fees for service a big part of the negotiation in private practice or else completely irrelevant in a county agency. The therapy approach chosen, the length of treatment, and the methodologies employed will depend, to a large extent, on certain economic realities. In a community mental health center with a 2-week waiting list and funding contingent on the number of new patients enrolled, it is unlikely that psychoanalytic treatment will be all that popular. And in private practice, where a therapist's livelihood depends on being able to consistently sell one's time by the hour, it is unusual to find someone exclusively practicing brief therapy interventions. A therapist with a large turnover might require more than 400 new referrals every year just to survive, whereas another clinician could get by quite comfortably with 10 or 12 if she specializes in long-term, more severe cases.

We belong to a profession whose members cannot decide whether they are scientists or philosophers, technicians or artists. We cannot agree on whether therapists should be trained in schools of medicine, health, education, human development, family studies, liberal arts, social work, or the seminary. We cannot agree on whether therapy takes a short time or a long time, whether it ought to focus on the past, present, or future, whether the therapist or the client should define the problem we are to work on, or even whether the therapist should talk a lot or a little. And perhaps more important, we cannot decide whether therapy is essentially a profession or a business or a calling. And the reality is that we may often spend a small portion of every session calculating how much we earned while listening to someone tell his or her story.

We have a tangled relationship with money, often creating guilt and conflict in our lives (Berger & Newman, 2012; Trachtman, 2011). Some therapists identify with the role of monk, in which they believe that having too much money will corrupt them; they experience a tremendous amount of anxiety and conflict over the business aspects of their work. Others feel like prostitutes—they are providing intimacy to strangers for a fee. And quite a number of practitioners in private practice may feel guilty about being paid to do work that they love.

When we splice into this picture the feelings among some clinicians that they are not really doing much in their work anyway, that they are frauds who are just paid to listen, guilt can lead to a vicious circle. Because these therapists may feel that they haven't really earned the money, they want to get rid of it as quickly as possible, ensnaring themselves in a consumerist lifestyle: work, spend, work, spend (Schor, 1992). One therapist of my acquaintance was incredibly busy, seeing 50 to 60 clients per week and making more money than any reasonable person could hope to spend. With no leisure time to shop in person, she shopped online between sessions, eventually ordering so much merchandise that she worked herself into unrecoverable debt.

To complicate money matters further, even while we are dealing with the guilt of being paid for doing what sometimes seems like so little, marveling at the salary we are paid to do what we most love, we struggle with the corresponding feeling that there is not enough money in the world to compensate us for the tedium and abuse we must put up with. Nobody works as hard as we do mediating battles between family members, dealing with surly adolescents whom nobody else can handle, and seeing people in anguish and suffering.

Further, each of us has a personal relationship with money, a circumstance that creates additional hardships in our work. We see couples who argue about money or who will not talk about the subject at all. We see disadvantaged clients who have no money, sparking guilt that we have too much. We see wealthy individuals who fritter away their funds in a search for fulfillment. Envy, resentment, and pity get in the way of our compassion. And when it comes to managing our own resources, each of us has issues that impinge on our work and can muddle things quite a bit.

Once upon a time, the practice of therapy was a calling. It was less a job or a career than it was a commitment to helping. There was passion and single-minded devotion to a simpler world with simpler ideals. Then the image of the therapist was transformed from that of a kindly country doctor dispensing advice to that of a consummate professional with computer and psychometric support. Legislators began regulating the field. Professional organizations mandated appropriate conduct. Insurance companies got into the act, followed by health maintenance organizations and preferred-provider plans. Now competition for customers is the name of the game for many therapists and mental health organizations. Some of the most popular programs at conferences and workshops have titles that euphemistically (but misleadingly) imply how you can get rich marketing your practice.

Clinicians are caught between an image of themselves as missionaries and behavior that is more characteristic of manufacturers' representatives. We feel frustrated about being unappreciated and underpaid. Sometimes it seems that no amount of money could fairly compensate us for the aggravation, intensity, emotional turmoil, conflict, and frustration. Other times, we feel guilty about being overpaid for seemingly doing nothing, simply listening to someone ramble on for an hour. In exchange for spending 45 minutes listening to someone talk and then telling him what we think about what he said, we receive enough money to buy 10 books or a whole night on vacation. It would almost seem that even with the hardships of being a therapist, we have a great thing going.

Yet there are also those nagging doubts that weigh on our conscience. We try our best, but sometimes it's not nearly enough. Among the most challenging hardships we face are the limits of our own ability to make a difference. There are disappointments. And failures.

7

Being Imperfect, Living with Failure

WHEN YOU THINK ABOUT IT, the prospect of spending 10, 20, or even 100 hours with someone trying to get him to change his behavior, when he is alive close to a million hours, is pretty futile. No matter what we do, how hard we work, how skilled we are, how much experience we have, or how many workshops we attend and books we read, it is inevitable that some of our clients are not going to improve; some will even become worse while under our care. And when clients do make significant progress in therapy, most of the time we have no idea if the changes will last over time.

Even what I am doing with you in this book is mostly doomed to fail. What are the chances that anything I say to you on these pages is going to have a significant impact on you, let alone produce the kind of profound impact that would make some idea memorable enough that it would actually lead you to think and act differently? You have dozens, hundreds of books sitting on your shelves or on tablets that represent all your previous attempts to hold on to what you've learned. If you're honest, you'll have to admit that most of the time this stuff just doesn't stay with you.

What Is Bad Therapy Anyway?

Although the client plays a huge role in the eventual outcome of treatment, and there are certainly other factors that enter into the picture, we also have responsibility for what happens. Most of the time we may do really fine work, but it is hard for us to talk about our mistakes, misjudgments, disappointments, and failures. All of us mess up on occasion, miscalculate what we believe a client can handle, push too hard or not enough, or make some blunder about which we can only cringe with regret.

Various studies of therapy dropouts estimate that roughly one-third of clients don't return after their initial interview, and close to half don't come back after the first two sessions; most therapists don't know why (Goldberg, 2012; Schwartz & Flowers, 2006). Those clients who do keep returning to sessions but without any observable or reported gains will typically continue treatment for an average of a dozen more sessions before concluding that things aren't working out (Stewart & Chambless, 2008). This doesn't include the estimated 10 to 20% of clients who actually deteriorate in therapy, with percentages significantly higher for those therapists who do grief work, traumatic stress debriefing, or work with dissociative disorders. To comfort ourselves in these and other cases, we deploy a variety of tactics and excuses:

- *Externalize responsibility for the outcome:* "The client wasn't motivated."
- *Rationalize the lack of progress:* "Sometimes you have to get worse to get better."
- *Find solace in colleagues' support when they say:* "This is all part of the resistance."
- *Define failure as success:* "The reason he did not return after the first session is that he was cured."
- *Subscribe to minimal expectations:* "As long as she keeps coming back, she must be getting something out of therapy."
- *Pretend we are succeeding:* "He is really improving but he just won't admit it."
- *Blame factors outside our control:* "How can I make much of a difference when this client has such severe disturbances?"
- *Insist that the client isn't ready to change:* "My job is simply to wait until the client decides to take charge of her life."

The fact of the matter is that sometimes we just do lousy work. It hurts to admit when we fail our clients, and we do take it personally.

If it makes you feel any better to hear about them, there have been some spectacular cases of really bad therapy with some well-known figures (Kottler, 2006). Judy Garland's therapist used to see her twice per day for sessions and prescribed all kinds of drugs to help her sleep, stay awake, and reduce depression, anxiety, and loneliness. (She died of an overdose.) Beach Boy Brian Wilson's therapist actually moved in with him for a year, insisted that all music composed during that time credit the therapist as a coauthor, and charged Wilson $1 million. My personal favorite was Marilyn Monroe's therapist, who may have actually been the one who killed her with a barbiturate suppository.

(He was the last one to be seen with her alive.) He also made the depressed actress run errands for him, gave her unlimited supplies of Nembutal, Seconal, and chloral hydrate, and required that she purchase her house within walking distance so he could have easier access to her.

Although these are clearly cases of bad therapy and treatment failures, there is much disagreement about what exactly constitutes such negative outcomes. We asked prominent therapists to define what they thought was bad therapy and were surprised by the variety of answers we received (Kottler & Carlson, 2002). Some of the theorists focused primarily on clients' behavior and responsiveness, whether they were acting differently outside of sessions, whether they felt understood, whether they improved or got worse. Interestingly, other prominent figures looked more at their own experience of clients, whether they felt in control or not, to what extent they demonstrated compassion and empathy, their degree of flexibility and freedom within the relationship, the accuracy of their assumptions and diagnosis about the case, as well as the amount of their own arrogance and overconfidence. It was also intriguing the way some of the theorists were quite forgiving of their mistakes, refusing to call that bad therapy as much as reliable data that should be taken into account before changing direction. According to this perspective, miscalculations, errors of judgment, awkward timing, poorly executed interventions don't necessarily imply consistent and chronic ineptitude unless the therapist fails to make adjustments.

Interesting, isn't it, that experienced practitioners have such radically different notions of what constitutes bad therapy? Whereas some theorists based the assessment totally on the client's ultimate opinion or actions, others considered such possibilities as their own feelings about what happened. Is a case a success if the client leaves a happy, satisfied customer, even if nothing fundamental has changed in her behavior? What about the case of a client who claims there has been no progress whatsoever, but about whom others report dramatic improvement?

We might conclude, therefore, that bad therapy involves some kind of assessment by *both* parties that the results have been less than satisfactory.

Keeping Failure at a Distance

Negative outcomes are not only disappointing to the client but often threatening to us. Being bright, perceptive, and psychologically sophisticated folks, if we are going to find excuses to explain negative outcomes, they will be very good ones. Certainly, these explanations do have merit.

Methods of warding off the confrontation with failure, and of subsequent stress reduction, do not take into consideration what many practitioners believe: that it is the client who succeeds or fails, not the therapist. Nevertheless, whether we admit it or not, we cannot help but be affected by a client who is deteriorating before our eyes and for whom there is nothing we can do to stop the downward slide. These are the cases that haunt us the most, invade our sleep, occupy our idle time, dominate our conversations with colleagues. In some instances, they are the most influential individuals we will ever know—shaping our theories and whole style of practice.

During my own training years, I watched videos of the masters in the field with awe and admiration. I got the distinct impression that this was what my own psychotherapy was supposed to look like, these magical single sessions in which the clinician produces an amazing breakthrough. Attending workshops only made things worse because presenters are so often interested in selling their approaches, demonstrating how efficiently and effectively they produce changes we can only dream about. It has been one of my most closely guarded secrets that my own sessions looked nothing like what I had seen on these films; they were often chaotic, confusing, and awkward, and they sometimes required considerable time to produce desired effects. This led me to spend the past two decades talking to therapists about their own experiences with failure in order to feel better about my own (Kottler, 1993; Kottler & Blau, 1989; Kottler & Carlson, 2002).

When I was eventually invited to do my own demonstration video, I was determined to try something different. I was sick of all the masters in the field showing what wizards they were, so apparently self-assured and effortlessly working their magic. I wanted to do a session that really looked like therapy in the trenches with all the awkward negotiations that take place in the beginning.

I was surprised to learn when I showed up for the taping that there were actually three different clients I was scheduled to see. When I inquired why this was necessary, considering that the way I do therapy is different with each person I worked with and that I was perfectly content to show any example, I was told by the producer that many of the masters in the field whom we see on videos can't do therapy very well, so they need at least three tries to get an acceptable session. I thought that was hilarious (and affirming).

It turned out that the session with the first client I saw did turn out surprisingly well, and I happen to know why. Before we went onstage and faced the lights, cameras, and studio audience, I turned to the client and asked her if she was feeling as nervous as I was. When she grabbed my hand for reassurance, I just knew that everything would be okay: we had bonded in that moment, before the cameras ever started rolling. There was an implicit contract between us: "Look, I'll watch your back if you'll watch mine. It's us against them."

If the first session went incredibly well, the second one was only fair. It was the third one that was absolutely awful. I mean it was so bad that I almost got up and walked off the production set. The adolescent client wouldn't talk. He said he had nothing to work on. The more I pushed him, the more reticent he became. I violated everything that I hold most scared in my work; most of all, I didn't respect his pace and needs, instead pursuing my own hapless agenda. At one point in the session, you can actually see me lean over and physically poke the guy in the arm, daring him to take a risk with me. It is humiliating for me to watch the video, yet it accurately demonstrated what therapy looks like with a resistant adolescent boy during a first session (especially in front of an audience).

Once the ordeal was over, I argued that this was the case we should use in the video. I wanted the world to see what therapy looks like when I am failing miserably. It seemed to me that this would be so much more instructive. The producer disagreed with my preference. We selected the best session after all, the one that makes me look as if I really know what I'm doing. But this spawned an idea about how much fun it would be to ask the most famous therapists to talk about their most stunning failures.

The main themes that emerged from these and other studies are that failures are absolutely critical to our continued development—if, that is, we are willing to acknowledge them. In most of the cases, the negative outcomes helped us develop greater flexibility, creativity, resilience, humility, and openness. It is when things go wrong that we are forced to think about the ways we work and the things we can change. When things merely go well, we move on to the next challenge without a further thought.

Causes of Failure

Failure in any enterprise, especially one as complex as therapy, involves a variety of factors. Clearly some are related to the client's characteristics and what he or she brings to sessions in terms of motivation, unrealistic expectations, and hidden agendas. When clients are referred against their will (as many are), blackmailed into treatment by significant others, or ambivalent about changing (as almost all are), impeded progress is more likely. Then there are the personal characteristics and attitudes that influence outcomes, not to mention certain counterproductive attitudes and beliefs, such as "I know this won't help, and there's nothing you can do." There are also particular personality styles (borderline, narcissistic, histrionic) that could signal trouble ahead, as well as organic factors that might impair the client's capability for insight and processing information.

Next there are variables contributing to failure that are outside our control. These are extraneous factors that are part of the client's reality and situation, including an enmeshed or sabotaging family, lack of a support system, ongoing substance abuse, poverty and deprivation, and lack of reliable transportation to attend sessions. If the client can't get to therapy on a regular basis, then obviously results will be compromised. If the family or friends are actively involved in sabotaging and undoing any progress, that also makes things more difficult. When the client doesn't have solid supports in place to reinforce new behaviors, then it is challenging to maintain progress outside of sessions and make the effects last.

Third, there are factors related to the therapy process and relationship itself. Sometimes there is a basic incompatibility between clinician and client—things just don't mesh because of a clash in personalities, values, or styles. The pace of sessions could be too fast or slow, causing the client to drop out prematurely. There is an inadequate alliance, with a corresponding lack of commitment, trust, and perceived understanding. There could be dependency issues operating or transference processes that are all part of the relationship.

Last but hardly least are therapist characteristics that get in the way of success, not just with a given client but with our work in general. Practitioners who communicate negative attitudes, who are perceived as rigid and arrogant, or who display blatant narcissism and self-centeredness can drive clients away. Practitioners can also be deficient in certain skills, struggling, for example, with confrontation or other interventions that are awkwardly timed or poorly executed.

If you do your own honest self-assessment of your weaknesses, lapses, and most consistent mistakes, such an exercise is both disconcerting and clearly enlightening. One of the most valuable contributions we make to clients' lives is when we are able to tell them things about themselves about which they are apparently unaware—the things they do that are off-putting and push others way, their annoying habits, their self-sabotaging behaviors that consistently get them in trouble. Given how useful such feedback can be, it is absolutely crucial that we subject ourselves to the same kind of self-scrutiny to improve our own performance and effectiveness. Take a few moments to consider the kinds of things you have most frequently heard from former and current clients, as well as colleagues and supervisors, about the things you do that are less than ideal. I've been told repeatedly, especially by students but also by clients, that I have an inscrutable blank face when I'm concentrating, which is often interpreted by them as critical judgment; I've been told repeatedly to show more authentic reactions. I have struggled with my own internal critical voice most of my life, frequently forming judgments about people that are less than kind. I pout when I don't get the approval I feel I deserve. I have this burning need for recognition that has fueled my unrelenting ambition. I self-disclose too freely and sometimes self-indulgently. But my biggest problem of all is my impatience, pushing clients too fast, too hard, because *I'm* the one who wants or needs to see some action.

What about *you*?

Processing Failures Effectively

Failure can be conceived simply as useful information that what we are doing is not working. Admitting this requires a degree of honest assessment, as well as recruiting the client's help as to what is working most and least effectively. In fact, one of the best predictors of a positive outcome and a turning around of disappointing results is the therapist's systematic attempt to solicit feedback from clients after every session. Even when things aren't going well, clients still report greater satisfaction when they are allowed to provide their input on what they like and what they don't (Duncan, 2010; Miller & Rousmaniere, 2014).

It is critical not only to acknowledge and own our failures but also to be forgiving of these lapses. What distinguished the master therapists I've interviewed from others I have known is their resilience and acceptance of themselves as fallible people who sometimes miss something important. It is also useful to be able to reframe failure as constructive feedback, as this permits a greater level of flexibility to make needed adjustments when things are going well.

Failure is useful to us in many ways, teaching us to be more creative and experimental, to try out new strategies when familiar ones are not working. It teaches us humility and patience and promotes greater reflection about what we do and what impact our behavior has on others, for better or worse. Failure is at the growth edge in our work and in our lives.

Last night I led a therapy group that was one of the most frustrating professional experiences of my life. Nothing seemed to work. There were long silences. Nobody would volunteer or agree to work on key issues that they brought up during the check-in. When I attempted to confront the resistance that was going on, most of the members denied such feelings. When I attempted to stir things up through immediacy and talking about my own feelings of frustration, a few members used it as an opportunity to express their anger in indirect, manipulative ways. I tried breaking the group up into smaller units to talk about what wasn't being said. I deputized a few other members to take over and lead the group. Nothing worked, and we remained at a stalemate. Of the groups I'd led in the past, I had never encountered anything quite like this before. I felt lost, confused, and clueless about what to do next.

Okay, I didn't sleep much last night while I was trying to sort out what was going on and what I might do next with this "failing" group. I reviewed my own leadership interventions carefully. I played back critical issues that had occurred in the session, making links to previous content. I wrote down some possible hypotheses to explore in future sessions (if the group stays together). Most of all, I have been doing some hard thinking about what I know, what I think I know, and what I don't understand at all. This is painful work that is both disorienting and quite exciting. And all the new learning and growth taking place for me this minute as I write these words is the direct result of perceived failure. Regardless of what happens next group session, being and feeling blocked have led me to consider alternative ways to work in the future. Although I can't honestly say I'm grateful for this opportunity, I am trying to make the most of it.

Talking to Ourselves About Failure

Albert Ellis (1984) claimed that it was rash, if not downright irrational, for therapists to believe that they can be successful with all their clients. I am certain he was right. We understand that it is beyond our means to help everybody. Yet this realization does not protect us from the beliefs that "All my interpretations must be profound," "I must always make brilliant judgments," "My clients must appreciate my work and be grateful as hell," and "They should work as hard between sessions as I do when I'm with them."

One of the most illuminating interviews I did with a prominent therapist about attitudes toward failure was with psychiatrist Frank Pittman, who responded to the question by saying, "You want an example of failure? Do you want one that happened today? I've got so many I don't know where to begin."

"Well," I prompted him further, "how about your favorite one?"

Pittman then began to tell the story of the time he was doing a demonstration with a family onstage in front of a large audience. He pushed the identified patient, a young man, hard enough that the boy indignantly walked offstage in anger. The boy's mother and sisters were so furious at the way he had been treated that they gave Pittman a piece of their mind and then walked offstage and out the door, never to be seen again. Then the audience protested the treatment of the family by getting up and walking out, leaving Pittman sitting onstage alone. The organizer of the workshop was so upset by this that she immediately drove Pittman to the airport without speaking to him; it wasn't even the airport he was supposed to leave from, just the one closest to the venue.

"How can you live with yourself after that?" I asked Pittman. "How can you show your face in public again?"

Pittman just shrugged. "You win a few; you lose a few."

"That's it? That's the way you dealt with blowing the session like that?"

"Hey, it's like this. You can't do good therapy unless you take some risks. Sometimes they work out, and sometimes they don't."

I still don't know how he could shrug off the incident so easily, but I found great wisdom in his reminder that living with mistakes and failures is just part of being a therapist, and there is no sense in denying it. The important thing is what we learn from these experiences.

Living with Futility

There is no surprise more devastating than receiving a Release of Information form from another therapist who is now working with an ex-client of ours. First feelings of anger and betrayal emerge; then self-doubt sneaks up and builds to a thundering crescendo. If we have a colleague available to complain to, it is likely that we will hear a comforting pronouncement: "You were so effective with that client that he is afraid to come back to you, knowing he will have to change." Sure.

The truth is that there are times when each of us feels lost. We just cannot get through to some people because of our (or their) deficiencies and limitations. Most of the time, we never find out what really went wrong. The client stops coming and does not return calls. In some ways, it feels even worse when a client keeps coming but will not let you get through to her; she feels strong enough and safe enough to continue therapy without the fear of having to change. It is no consolation to remind ourselves that we get paid whether the client appears to change or not. We still have to deal with that stony, determined face. We still have to put up with the games, defensive reactions, and stubborn resistance and not take them personally.

There are those clients who will seemingly come forever: the passive, dependent personalities who need someone to dish out approval; the narcissistic people who need an audience; the borderline clients who, when they are not bouncing off the ceiling, need someone they can pay to abuse. It sometimes seems futile to work with these people because they will often improve slowly and will rarely be cured. We measure progress among the severely disturbed population in terms that are less than spectacular. We have the audacity to believe that we can change the tide of a person's genetic structure, a family's rigid hierarchy, or stable personality traits that have been in place since birth. It is a miracle that we ever make a difference in these clients' lives. And it is not unusual for us to encounter a force greater than we are capable of counteracting. Even when we do manage to play some significant role in helping a person change, that does not mean the effects will last for very long.

It seems futile to try to convince a 17-year-old that we can offer him an antidote to his lust for excitement that can compete with marijuana, beer, Ecstasy, or meth. It feels hopeless to try to help a child who has been the victim of physical and sexual abuse, living in a temporary care facility because she can't be returned to her parents and there is nobody who will take her into foster care, much less adopt her. It feels similarly hopeless to try to lure an alcoholic away from bourbon with the mere promise of greener pastures. It is futile to try to help an enraged adolescent when his parents sabotage treatment. When an individual jumps right back into his peer group after leaving our office, it is unrealistic to think we can alter his values. We experience futility when we attempt to cure anybody of anything. Nobody wants what we are selling until they find they have no other choice. And even then, they will settle for cosmetic changes if they can just buy some time. We can give them what they want—a little relief—but we know that is futile, too.

Tentative Conclusions

So what is to be concluded from this discussion of failure in therapy? For one thing, it isn't just when you do something terribly stupid or graceless that you do lousy work, but also when you demonstrate benign neglect. Laziness, complacency, and functioning on autopilot all contribute to mediocre work.

Second, reflecting on your failures and disappointing results can serve to considerably improve your skills in the future, teaching you to be more flexible and inventive in your interventions and more responsive to each client's needs. Yet excessive self-reflection also has its side effects in contributing to greater self-absorption, self-doubt, and feelings of perfectionism, for you can never measure up to the ideal you have in mind.

Third, the key to processing failures effectively begins with owning them, acknowledging your mistakes, and talking about them honestly with colleagues whom you trust. This doesn't mean just complaining about client resistance and noncompliance but talking about your own behavior and ways you can improve. Related to this point is the importance of not only accepting your limitations but also forgiving yourself for being imperfect, flawed, and human. No matter how hard you try, no matter how much you study and learn and practice, you'll do good therapy, and you'll do bad therapy.

Just hope you can tell the difference.

8

Patients Who Test Our Patience

I HAD BEEN working as a full-time therapist for 10 years when most of my clients started to sound the same to me. It got to the point that I was teetering on depression myself because it seemed that my work was becoming so routine, if not futile. I started to think about my clients in the most derogatory terms, resenting some of them, celebrating when they canceled appointments, dreading the prospect of enduring some of the sessions. It was during this time that I conceived of a book idea that was certain to be a raging success: I would call it *Clients from Hell*, and each chapter would be about a different kind of client who had been sent to make my life miserable.

I don't know whom you might nominate for inclusion in such a book, but I had no trouble making a long list of prospects (many of those in my caseload at the time). There was the surly adolescent who wouldn't talk—I mean never. He would make hand gestures and sulk; that's about it. The only thing he'd agree to do in therapy was play the card game War, which is just about the most boring game in the world and requires no skills whatsoever. Then there was the elderly woman who wouldn't stop talking at all, never letting me get a word in. She would ramble on, repeat the same stories over and over, and refuse to respond to any meager thing I offered. There was another client who would tell me each week that I was the greatest therapist in the world, but never changed a single thing about her dysfunctional life and was still involved in the most abusive relationship I could imagine. There was the guy who kept coming back, week after week, to complain about how incompetent I was and how nothing I was doing helped him, but he refused to go away until I fixed him. There was . . . well, you get the point and could perhaps construct a list of your own.

I was very excited about this project about difficult clients who test our patience and drive us crazy. I had little problem getting other therapists to talk about their own most difficult clients, nor finding tons of material in the literature about so-called resistant, reluctant, ungrateful, noncompliant, nonresponsive, defiant, challenging, rebellious, uncooperative, obstinate, hateful clients. I had discovered a gold mine and couldn't wait to excavate it further. I was feeling better already about how unappreciated I was by many of my clients who had the audacity to resist my best efforts to help them.

The manuscript was sent out for review; one reviewer offered the following feedback: "I think Kottler has a problem because he thinks all of his clients are sent from hell to make his life miserable." As I read these words, I found myself immediately nodding my head in agreement. "Further," the reviewer added, "it seems to me he has lost his compassion."

Yikes—that hit me square where it hurt the most. This reviewer was absolutely on target: I *had* lost my compassion and empathy for my clients. I *did* see them as enemies to be defeated. I did feel embroiled in conflict with many of them, fighting a losing battle. And I was impatient because clients weren't moving as quickly as I wanted them to; in fact, they weren't moving as fast as I *needed* them to because my own life felt stale and stuck. I realized, then and there, that it wasn't that my clients were being all that obstructive as much as that my own attitudes led me to be the one who was being difficult.

I made several important decisions once I digested that single, incisive comment. First I switched the name of the book from *Clients from Hell* to *Compassionate Therapy.* I changed the whole focus of the project to look not only at the ways that clients were being resistant but also at the ways that therapists were making things so much worse for themselves and those they were trying to help. The second consequence of this realization was that it was time to get another job because I recognized that I was not functioning very well in my current work situation.

Oh, by the way, who was that reviewer who pointed out the importance of compassion, understanding, and empathy in working with those who don't cooperate in ways we would prefer? Who was this scholar who reminded me about how important it was to be patient and accepting of where my clients were at? Perhaps you've heard of him: his name was Albert Ellis.

Preferred and Nonpreferred Clients

Some of the perils that a therapist encounters are an implicit part of the job. Just as a construction worker would hardly complain about the heights at which he must work and a soldier would not be surprised to find people shooting at him during a war, a therapist accepts the challenges of spending time with people who are troubled and often interpersonally challenged. Unfortunately, there is increasing evidence that conditions like depression really are contagious, especially within the intimate context of families or therapy relationships. Furthermore, certain clients present extreme disturbances of personality or behavior that not only drive us a little crazy but penetrate our souls.

That clinicians have strong preferences concerning whom they prefer to work with is well known. Most everyone prefers clients who are bright, eager, verbal, perceptive, and attractive. These clients not only grow quickly but also can be patient, polite, prompt, and grateful, and they pay their bills on time.

What is often left unsaid is how much more comfortable a therapist (or anyone) feels working with people who are most similar to her in terms of religion, race, socioeconomic background, and core values. A young Japanese American female therapist tells me in supervision that she fears working with the inner-city African American youths who make up part of her caseload. A Latino school counselor from a homogeneous community struggles with some of the Asian girls in his elementary school, who seem so quiet and passive compared with the other children. An African American pastor and family counselor finds himself resenting some of the whites who are attending his congregation and finds himself guiltily wishing they would stay away. And a middle-class so-called liberal therapist likes the idea of helping at-risk populations but fails to make the kinds of deep connections with these clients that she does with those who are more similar to her in background. The conclusion, hardly surprising even if rarely talked about in public settings, is that we tend to feel more comfortable working with people who are most like us (however that is conceived).

Therapists may express preferences based mostly on the similarity of cases to those others that have turned well, whether the case falls within their spectrum of expertise, or whether it involves issues that are not very personally threatening. Therapists would also have expressed preferences for those clients who are more flexible in scheduling sessions and who either have good insurance or pay their bills on time without having to remind or beg them. We also all form first impressions and initial assessments regarding how challenging we think a client might be for us to help or handle, especially when we encounter someone who seems either overly compliant or aggressive.

Part of being a therapist involves working with those individuals who, for a variety of reasons, will test your patience, flexibility, and resourcefulness in ways you've never imagined were possible. In some cases, they push your buttons and ignite a whole host of strong personal reactions that may or may not be related to the client's own issues.

Countertransference Reactions

Perhaps the most thoroughly discussed hazard of therapeutic work is the classical countertransference reactions to problem clients. The term *countertransference* is used in several different ways, depending on the context and theoretical orientation. It has been described most generally as the therapist's personal feelings toward a client, which may or may not represent some degree of distortion, bias, or projection. It can involve the way the therapist responds to the client's transferential feelings, triggering strong reactions to being treated as a parent, or authority figure, or some other ghost from the past. Like so many other processes in therapy, countertransference can be classified in terms of whether the reactions are essentially reactive, induced, displaced, or projected (Rowan & Jacobs, 2002). In each case, there is the likelihood of some degree of distortion that can lead to treatment difficulties as well as the possibility that such feelings will have either beneficial or detrimental effects.

In reviewing the anecdotal and empirical literature that has been presented in both psychoanalytic and generic psychotherapy literature, it is evident that these personal reactions can be used as significant turning points in the therapy, a means by which the therapist can offer feedback and impressions that might otherwise be withheld (Aleksandrowicz & Aleksandrowicz, 2016; Gelso & Hayes, 2007; Hayes, Nelson, & Fauth, 2015; Masterson, 2014; Strean, 2002).

Any interpretation that a therapist offers contains a statement not only about the client but also about the therapist himself. Any clinical decision to choose one course of action over another is based on more than objective analysis of what is best for the client; it also represents the subjective inner world of the practitioner, including our moods, responses in the moment, and whatever else is going on in our lives at the time.

It is within the context of our relationship with clients that we are most likely to see evidence of our overinvolvement in some way. Treadway laments the case of his most memorable failure: "I can still see Amy sitting there, cross-legged, with her arms folded across her chest. She was perched on the hood of my car. Our therapy session had ended five hours earlier" (2000, p. 34). He had lost control of the case, mostly by failing to manage his own feelings for the overly dependent young woman. He wanted to save her, and by distorting his own power, he got caught up in his grandiose beliefs in his power to heal.

The manifestations of therapist distortion—overidentification and overinvolvement—may take a number of different forms that have been most commonly mentioned:

- The arousal of guilt from unresolved personal struggles that parallel those impulses and emotions of the client
- Impaired empathy, whereby the therapist finds it difficult to feel loving and respectful toward the client
- Strong attraction to or repulsion for a client that may result from the therapist's own unsatisfied needs
- Erotic feelings toward a client
- Inaccurate interpretations of the client's feelings due to the therapist's identification and projection
- Feelings of being generally blocked, helpless, and frustrated with a particular client
- Evidence of boredom or impatience in the therapist's inner world during work with a client
- Unusual memory lapses regarding the details of a case
- Mutual acting out in which the client begins living out the therapist's values and the therapist begins acting out the client's pathology
- A tendency to speak about a client in derogatory terms
- An awareness that the therapist is working harder than the client

Countertransference was first uncovered by Freud in his relationships with patients (such as Dora) and colleagues (such as Fleiss and Jung) that sometimes inexplicably spun out of control. In 1910, in a letter to his friend Sandor Ferenczi during a period of conflict, Freud (1955) revealed that he was not the psychoanalytic superman that Ferenczi imagined him to be, nor had he overcome his strong reactions. He would develop these ideas in a paper published a few years later in which he stated that the therapist's personal feelings toward the client are both the greatest tool in treatment and the greatest obstacle (Freud, 1912). This belief was later echoed in greater detail by others who thought countertransference feelings were not simply undesirable complications in the therapeutic process but, rather, real assets in the promotion of a true human encounter. Such psychodynamic theorists as Frieda Fromm-Reichmann, Franz Alexander, and Therese Benedek felt that although the analyst's personal reactions to patients could be seriously disturbing to both parties, the dangers were minimal if the analyst had undergone intensive treatment and supervision in his own analysis (Alexander & Selesnick, 1966).

There have been many refinements in therapeutic technique since Freud's day, yet clinicians still struggle with their feelings, distortions, unconscious reactions, unresolved conflicts, misperceptions, antagonism, and subjective experiences in relation to certain clients. At best, unraveling these personal reactions can be seen as a creative act of personal discovery, not to mention a therapeutic breakthrough. At worst, such experiences can provoke a personal crisis for the therapist in ways that may not have been anticipated. One therapist describes a case in which her strong feelings toward a particularly difficult client didn't crop up until 14 years later (Khair Badawi, 2015)!

Whether we catch ourselves being overprotective, overly solicitous, aloof, or downright hostile, it is evident that we have very different feelings and reactions to certain clients. A brief glimpse at the appointment calendar reminds us of those people we eagerly await and those we dread. We are friendlier with some clients than with others. Some of them are greeted cordially with an open smile and an offer of a beverage, whereas others are coolly directed to their place with a reminder of their delinquent bill.

Of course, we are supposed to treat all our clients with an equal degree of respect, solicitousness, and caring, regardless of their background, race, religion, socioeconomic class, sexual orientation, personality, or presenting complaints. It even says so in our ethical codes! But we know that is not nearly the case. We genuinely like some clients better than others—we are drawn to them (or even overly drawn to them) because they share our most cherished values. We also have strong personal reactions to those who are from backgrounds foreign to our experience. Our socially liberal, politically correct sensibilities may lead us to find such individuals exotic or interesting, but sometimes we are frightened and put off by this differentness.

A Chinese immigrant tells his sad tale of leaving his family behind to make a new life in an adopted country, but it is hard to concentrate on the story because he keeps spitting phlegm in his handkerchief, in keeping with his custom back home.

An adolescent girl from the inner city talks about her troubles fighting with her boyfriend, but all the therapist can do is focus on the dozens of piercings that protrude from her nostrils, ears, lips, tongue, and eyebrows.

A school counselor with strong feminist convictions sits in a family session appalled at what is unfolding before her. The family is of Persian origins. The mother is dressed in a chador, the traditional Islamic head cover. While she and her son sit obediently and quietly, the father speaks with authority and condescension about how the school is at fault for not doing a better job of tolerating their son's "creativity." Each time the counselor addresses a question to the mother, the father answers for her and does so in a manner that suggests that if only she would be more obedient, then perhaps they wouldn't be having such difficulties in the first place. The counselor tries her best not to leap across the room and slap the guy for his insolence. But the truth of the matter is that she has lost her composure, lost her ability to understand the cultural context for what is going on, because her own buttons are being pushed.

Such inadvertent, unconscious, utterly understandable reactions abound even though we are supposed to be feeling compassion and a certain neutrality. In reality, there are times when we feel slightly put off, if not totally repulsed, by some clients we see. Some of this may be the result of their antisocial or annoying behavior, but other times the strong feelings of aversion arise from our own prejudices, racism, biases, and lack of experience with people of some backgrounds.

Many therapists consider their intense personal reactions, when recognized, to be crucial in diagnosing how others might respond to the client in the outside world. Such reactions can be valuable clues in making sense of chronically dysfunctional patterns.

One client speaks in a general, abstract way about what is bothering him, but I've been able to narrow it down to a communication problem with his girlfriend. Every time I encourage him to elaborate and say more about the issue, he announces with finality that he'd rather not. I struggle to respect his right to go at his own speed, but I can feel my frustration start to build. I now have a sense of what I think his girlfriend must be feeling every time she tries to get him to open up.

There is no shame associated with admitting we have strong personal reactions to our clients. It is when they remain unacknowledged and unchecked that the feelings not only ferment within us but also compromise the quality of work we can do in sessions. One interesting place to explore this territory is within our own internal world.

Some Therapist Fantasies

When reactive feelings are ignored, denied, distorted, and projected, both the client's treatment and the therapist's mental health can often suffer. One obvious place to uncover possible clues to countertransference reactions is in the texture and content of our fantasy life. Whether these fantasies are primarily rescue-oriented, erotic in nature, or expressive of rage, frustration, and anger, we can't help but think about and daydream about some of their clients, especially those who are most vexing, uncooperative, or manipulative.

The following descriptions of reactions toward clients come from a mixed group of social workers, family therapists, counselors, and psychologists that highlight some of the fantasy landscape in which we might sometimes reside.

> I genuinely love a few of my patients. I mean, I love them as much as I love my sister, my best friend, or my husband. I suppose, in a way, a few of my patients have become my closest friends. I think about them during the day, and when I do, I feel warm inside. I have known this one patient for about seven years and I like her so much. I feel sad sometimes that I can only know her as her therapist because I would very much enjoy meeting her for lunch and telling her about my own life.

> This guy I've been treating for a few months is the president of a major corporation. He's got a tremendous amount of power and responsibility. He hires and fires people at whim, and he's let me know that I'm under his scrutiny as well. I think about how great it would be if I help this guy, that maybe he would invite me into his company to work with his people. He's got offices all over the world, and I think about traveling from Bangkok to Rio putting out fires.

> I see this adorable Mexican kid who has no stable home. His mother is hardly ever around doing who-knows-what. His father is back in Mexico trying to keep things together. And this poor kid is lost and alone most of the time. There are times when I think about adopting him, taking him home with me, giving him a proper home rather than just the Band-Aids I apply once a week.

> I work with this one incredibly attractive woman. She has a crush on me and we both know it. She wears these outrageously revealing outfits and acts quite seductively. Naturally, I interpreted her obvious attempts to sabotage the sessions, and she has toned down quite a lot. But sometimes I feel this almost uncontrollable urge to get down on my knees and stick my head underneath her dress.

> I could strangle this guy he's so whiny and complaining. He exhibits everything I despise in other people and myself: passivity, external control, helplessness, incompetence. I know he knows that I don't really like him much. But he's so used to having people not like him that my relationship with him seems normal. I end up feeling like he does—helpless—because he refuses to change. As I listen to him talk in his

> high-pitched monotone, I idly wonder what creative things I could do to break through his inhibited exterior. I picture myself slapping his face or laughing at him. Then I feel such guilt because I lose my compassion.
>
> I sometimes imagine what it would be like to be married to a few of my clients. This one guy is just a doll, and he's trying so hard to improve himself. He's just my type—strong but self-reflective. There are times during the week I wonder what he's doing. I also wonder what he'd look like without his clothes on.

These and other fantasies represent only one narrow aspect of the therapist's phenomenological world, and they are certainly not typical of the way we think about our clients all, or even most, of the time. Occasionally, however, such fantasies give us clues to how we are reacting to our clients. Only when we are willing to identify and explore how we feel about our clients and how such feelings affect our clinical judgment can we ever hope to harness this energy constructively.

In processing strong countertransference reactions toward some clients, there are several questions to be considered:

- What is it that first brought the strong feelings to your attention?
- How are you overreacting to what is going on between you and this client?
- How might you be attempting to disown the problem by blaming the client for being resistant?
- What might you be expecting from the client that he or she is unwilling or unable to do?
- How could you alter or reframe your working diagnosis in such a way that you feel less frustration and futility?
- Who does this person remind you of?
- How might you own projected feelings be distorting the way your client appears to you?
- What needs of yours (to be appreciated, respected, validated, loved, empowered, and so forth) are not being met in this relationship?
- How is your competence being challenged by this person?
- Which buttons of yours are constantly being pushed by this client?
- What is the conflict between the two of you *really* about?

Because these questions require a high degree of frankness and honesty, it is often challenging to consider them productively without the assistance of a colleague or supervisor to confront your attempts to disown your own role in therapeutic impasses, or at least a self-supervision structure or workbook that leads you through a systematic process (Davis, Eshelman, & McKay, 2012; Kottler, 2012). It is just so tempting to blame the client as the problem, the one whose resistance, defensiveness, and plain orneriness makes your life so unnecessarily difficult.

Difficult Cases

Among experienced therapists, there is some consensus concerning clients who most consistently present special challenges. Borderline personalities, sociopathic personalities, and those with conduct disorders test a therapist's patience and defenses like few others. The prognoses are poor; progress, if any, is slow; and the therapist is likely to be on the receiving end of manipulation, dramatic and painful transference, and projective identification.

A number of studies on the client behaviors that therapists experience as most stressful create a consistent portrait of most frequently mentioned occurrences: threats of suicide, expressions of anger, demonstrations of hostility, severe depression, abject apathy, and premature termination. In addition, characteristics and behaviors of clients are frequently mentioned, such as those who:

- Suffer from physiological disorders (strokes, closed head injuries)
- Experience extreme psychotic symptoms (major hallucinations, delusions)
- Have hidden agendas (workers' compensation or court referrals)
- Violate boundaries (chronic lateness or missed appointments)
- Externalize blame ("It's not my fault")
- Refuse to accept responsibility ("You fix me")
- Are argumentative (hostile, skeptical, aggressive)
- Fear intimacy (avoidant or seductive behavior)
- Are flooded with emotion and overwhelmed
- Push your buttons (bring up your own unresolved issues)
- Are impatient ("Fix me quick")
- Are literal and concrete (unable to access or express internal states)
- Are actively suicidal
- Have poor impulse control (offenders, substance abusers)
- Are in life circumstances (homelessness, poverty) that make therapy seem useless when compared with what is really needed most
- Have limited command of your favored language (literally and figuratively)

This list might make it appear as if *all* our clients are difficult. As therapists, we see the most perverse, bizarre, sometimes even the most evil parts of human existence. We are constantly exposed to cruelty, conflict, deception, manipulation, cynicism, mistrust, and betrayal. We see people at their absolute worst. We are privy to their most secret, hidden selves. We are the folks delegated to pick up the pieces after disappointment, divorce, or death.

There are clients we encounter whose main purpose in life seems to be making others miserable. They are schooled in the intricacies of sociopathic, narcissistic, hysterical, or borderline behavior. They know just how to get under our skin, and they feel most fulfilled when they succeed. Through all the rage and despondency and conflict, we are supposed to remain unperturbed. The sheer energy it takes to stay calm and in control in the face of such behavior is a major drain on our resources.

It is interesting, however, that not everyone agrees on which cases are most troublesome. For every therapist who dreads working with dissociative or borderline disorders, there are others who absolutely love the drama and challenge of such cases. The really intriguing part of this exploration is to examine carefully those clients whom you enjoy seeing most and least and what that says about you.

Examples of Clients Some Therapists Find Most Challenging

As mentioned, some clinicians thrive on the challenge of personality disorders. Others are remarkably patient and effective with people who are manifesting psychotic symptoms or with drug abusers or with the intellectually impaired. But for most therapists, several patterns of client behavior are often difficult to deal with.

"I Got Held Up in Traffic."

Resistance, in all its manifestations, is hardly the nuisance and obstruction to treatment that Freud once believed. Whether clients are overly compliant or dramatically hostile, we now understand that they are doing the very best they can to keep themselves together. We also remind ourselves constantly that missed or chronically late appointments are not part of a conspiracy to make us miserable, but rather may be the client's attempt to retain some control in a threatening situation. Ideally, clients will stick around long enough, and we will exercise sufficient patience and set firm enough limits, to allow the resistance to be worked through.

Noncompliance by playing with space and time arrangements in therapy is one of those things that beginners are taught to expect but nevertheless may not be prepared to handle effectively. No one likes to be stood up (flashback to adolescent rejection), even if you are being paid for the idle time. Some therapists protect themselves by keeping a favorite novel available, so that if a client is "held up in traffic" or "the car broke down" or "the meeting ran over," the gap can be happily filled. And it *is* irritating to wait for someone, even if it is part of the treatment.

"I Want to Die."

Death is the ultimate failure. It is especially tragic when someone takes his own life—not just for the victim but for those who are left behind. Family, friends, and those who tried to help, experience guilt, responsibility, and regret. For any therapist who has ever lost a client through suicide, there is a special sadness, a vulnerability, and a fear that it could happen again. Furthermore, there are few socially acceptable ways that therapists are permitted to mourn their loss in any public way.

Suicidal clients present a challenge on multiple levels. Looming foremost in our souls is the pure emotional terror of being close to someone who is so despondent and desperate that nothingness seems like a viable option. There was a time in all our lives when we flirted with hopelessness; it was a time we would like to forget.

Second, we feel an incredible burden of responsibility in trying to help a suicidal client. There are, of course, risks of legal repercussions if things go awry. There are also moral obligations to push ourselves beyond our usual limits, to do everything in our power to remain vigilant. A mistake or miscalculation may have lethal consequences. We must make ourselves available for genuine crises or lambs crying wolf. Every threat must be taken seriously.

Third, once a risk of suicide is assessed, a different therapeutic machinery is set in motion. Records are documented meticulously. All clinical staff move cautiously, covering themselves, doing everything by the book. But it is hard to be all that therapeutic when handling a client with kid gloves. Confrontation and deep interpretations are tabled in favor of mild explorations of feeling. Until the client is once again on stable ground, most efforts are devoted to simply maintaining basic life functions while rekindling the will to survive. There is a tightrope to walk between pushing the client hard enough to get him off the fence and not pushing him over the brink. The margin for error is small, and the pressure on the therapist is profound.

A fourth challenge is in being able to leave the problems of the potentially suicidal client at work. Needless worry will not prevent a tragedy. Therapists who spend their time excessively preoccupied with clients who are at risk may do so more for their own benefit, as a distraction and inflation of power, than for any useful purpose. We can feel important running around with our phones beeping the siren of despair. We can feel needed when we are interrupted at the most inopportune moments by a nagging voice that asks, "Did you do everything you could?"

"How Do You Feel About Me?"

At one time or another, most clients troll for our affection. They do so as part of the transference, to get out of us what they have always wanted from another, or they do so because in our role as a model we have the power to dispense approval for those actions that are desirable. Another possibility is quite simply that we are their confidants, the keepers of their secrets, and they have a natural curiosity to know what we think and how we feel about them. Although we may use evasive tactics to deny that we feel anything at all, or choose to withhold such opinions as irrelevant, clients well understand the rules of the game.

With seductive clients, we find our powers of restraint pushed to the limit. Some of them are determined to have their way. Conquering a therapist is the ultimate victory, proof that anyone can be corrupted. It is a way in which the client can regain control of the relationship and win power and approval. It satisfies the desire to flirt with the forbidden, and it gives the client a means to frustrate the therapist just as she has been frustrated by the therapeutic experience. It is also the best way for a client to confound the relationship, sidetrack the treatment, and prevent further therapeutic assaults.

The therapist's efforts to confront the client about the seductive behavior often lead to frustration. If the feelings are discussed directly and the therapist gently yet firmly rejects the overtures, the client may feel humiliated and rejected. If transference feelings are interpreted, the client may fall back on denial. Yet if the therapist attempts to back off and let things ride for a while, the seductive efforts may escalate. There is no easy solution.

One other part of this problem deserves attention: clients may behave seductively for other than sexual reasons. Often sexuality becomes confused with intimacy, especially when the two people in the room feel an attraction to one another. Many seductive clients do not have the slightest interest in a physical relationship but would like to establish an emotional one. This problem is just as common when the client and the therapist are of the same sex. The client feels that she is giving, giving, giving, and getting precious little of a personal nature in return. This perception is accurate and part of the grand design of things. The client therefore must exercise considerable ingenuity to find out what her therapist really thinks of her. Clients may measure the time it takes for us to return their phone calls, how many minutes we will allow the session to run over, or the frequency of smiles as indications of our true regard.

The therapeutic relationship is a unique and asymmetrical contractual arrangement in which the therapist reveals about herself only what she wishes. For people who are already insecure about where they stand in relation to others' esteem, the therapist's detachment can drive them even further away. The clients who get better eventually work through all of this insecurity and become more autonomous for having done so. But a few clients consider it their personal mission in life to get to the therapist—if not physically, then emotionally.

"This Isn't Helping, but I'm Coming Back."

There are less obvious ways to resist treatment, such as by being overly compliant ("This is so much fun") or using the classical defenses of repression and denial ("Of course I had a happy childhood"), but a direct challenge to our competence is the most difficult to stomach. Sometimes these resistant clients are the most diligent as far as keeping appointments, showing up on time, and at least pretending to do what they are supposed to do to get better. But they keep getting worse, and we may not know why. Oh, we have ready responses to give them, saying things like, "You'll get better when you're ready to," "You really are much improved, but you just don't recognize it yet," or "This is really frustrating for you that you can't see the changes you have made."

Deep down inside, we are afraid to admit the naked truth: we don't know what we are doing with this client, and we can't figure out why the he keeps coming back to remind us of our ineptitude. Certainly, the key to the puzzle is what the client *does* get out of returning to the sessions without any apparent gain. Beneath the surface lies the client's hidden agenda.

For 90 consecutive sessions, Brenda entered the office just as the second hand crossed the 12. She always paid in cash, crisp $20 bills, which she insisted that I count. Each week, she took her place, looked up, and sneered. Her opening remark, cutting and cynical, usually sent shivers up and down my neck: "Well, as you probably expect, I'm still not feeling any better.

I know I'm a fool for coming here every week, paying you my good money to listen to you pretend you care if I live or die. We both know you're in it for the bucks, but God do you look foolish sitting there acting like you know all about me. You don't know shit. When are you going to give up and give me the boot?"

Suddenly one day, just as I had dreamed it would happen, her facade came tumbling down, exposing a quivering, vulnerable human being. I honestly don't think it was because of anything specific I did—unless you count 90 consecutive sessions of waiting for her to make the first move. She later explained that all that time she was just waiting until she felt she could trust me.

As long as these clients can keep us off balance, we will not be able to get close to them. Because they are used to functioning in antagonistic relationships, even our disdain does not disturb them much. Their goal is to keep us in line until they decide they are ready to give up the verbal combat. In the meantime, it is kind of fun for them to ridicule this symbol of authority and wisdom.

Sometimes client resistance is a figment of our imagination. The problem lies not with what the client is doing to avoid our well-meaning help but with something in us that is interfering with our being more patient, forgiving, and accepting.

"Um. Uh. No."

One of the basic rules of therapy is that the client talks. When that convention is broken, all else becomes uncertain. Occasionally, we do work with people, often children, who are not all that verbal, who answer questions in monosyllables if they answer at all, who are uncertain and indecisive, and who can outwait us. We can try any trick in the book—staring contests, interrogations, monologues, card tricks—and we will still end up with virtual silence. It is easier with children because there are still many nonverbal options in the ways time can be spent constructively.

With overly passive or withdrawn adults, a single hour can last weeks. I think the clock actually slows down—if not downright stops—when these people enter the room. Something in their hormones must impede time. We feel, at first, like vaudeville entertainers trying to get a laugh. We could sing, dance, probably do a striptease, and the silent client would merely watch indulgently.

"So what brings you here?"

"Not sure."

(Kick in active listening.) "You're feeling uncertain and confused."

"Uh-huh."

(Wait him out. Silence for 4 minutes.)

(Active listening again.) "It's difficult for you to talk here."

"Uh-huh."

(Try again. Reassurance.) "I, uh, mean with a complete stranger most people find it hard to get started."

"Yes."

(Probing questioning.) "Can you tell me a little bit about what is bothering you?"

"My mother."

(Persistence.) "That *is* a little bit. How about some details?"

"She doesn't understand."

Finally. A breakthrough! The session will drag along at its own interminable pace. Once there is a hint of feeling, an opinion, a concern, we slowly and determinedly explore its shape and form, build on it and connect it with previous disclosures. Eventually, we help these people open up more. But it takes so much work.

Equally difficult is the client who talks incessantly but rarely says much and never listens. These clients also have the power to slow down the clock. They have been compulsive talkers for so long that they are virtually impervious to interruptions, confrontations, snoring, gags—everything but fire alarms. Some of these folks eventually find their way into Congress, but the rest end up in therapy because nobody else can stand to listen to them.

Occasionally, when they draw a breath, take a drink, or pause to write a check, they will let us talk for a minute—even a few minutes if we can talk fast—but they will continue with the monologue after this interruption. Amazingly enough, at the start of the next session, the client will remember exactly where she left off and will continue as if the week had lasted but a moment. Naturally, the client's intent is to prevent hearing anything that might be unpleasant. Eventually, with patience and persistence and once trust is established, we can try to alter this pattern.

With either the silent or the excessively verbal client, the therapist is required to do more, which is to do less. The more we attempt to manage and control the sessions, the longer the obstructive behavior will continue. We can well understand this intellectually, but still may be unable or unwilling to restrain our impulse to control. To sit with someone hour after hour after hour and really be with him while he is off in his own world is a difficult task indeed.

"But I Don't Really Have a Drug Problem."

Substance abusers are among those clients who improve only as long as they are in the office. Once they leave, they often resort to past habits of getting high to avoid their pain. We face an uphill battle, because therapy can never compete with the instantaneous pleasure that a drug can provide, or even entrenched habitual patterns grooved into the brain. It is hard enough to counteract the effects of past trauma and the usual defensive reactions. Once the ploys of a skilled alcoholic or addict are added to the scene, the therapist who really thinks he can make a difference before the client is ready to change may end up an addict himself. In addition to the abuser's denial that he has a problem, and added on to all his manipulation, deceit, and sneaking around, are the physiological effects. This client is physically addicted and psychologically dependent, and he may be experiencing some deterioration and memory loss. The need to escape is much stronger than the need to understand. Avoidance wins over confrontation.

Substance abuse counseling and Alcoholics Anonymous emerged as specialties largely because traditional therapy was not working with the chemically dependent client. As long as she has her Xanax, vodka, Vicodin, or wine to ease the emotional discomfort and pain, she has very little incentive to work on the underlying problems.

Clients with drug and alcohol problems who are unwilling to admit their dependency typify the kind of work that can be incredibly frustrating for the therapist. Then there is the likelihood of relapses on the way to eventual recovery. In many cases the therapist's own feeling of impotence may reflect the client's powerlessness.

"Sorry to Bother You at Home."

The fastest way to get any therapist's attention is with a panicky 3 a.m. phone call or text. It is hard to say what actually precipitates the late-night call because by the time we are fully awake, we are already 5 minutes into the conversation. The gist of it is this: (1) Did I wake you up? (2) Sorry to bother you; (3) You said I could call if I needed to; (4) This is kind of an emergency.

Phone calls or messages at home, one of an array of devious ploys common to the manipulative or desperate client, are irritating but unavoidable. Those who are severely depressed or prone to panic need to have the reassurance that they can call if they absolutely have to. And simply instructing them to call 911 won't usually take care of things because they not only wanted help but also attention and sympathy. Two or three calls annually are probably not a nuisance. Anything more than a few per year may be considered a form of cruel and unusual punishment.

Success with Difficult Cases

Many therapists may be underpaid, overworked, and unappreciated, but there is no doubt that the greatest benefit of our work is the pure unadulterated joy we feel when we can see the results of our efforts, particularly in difficult cases. We become great explorers and guides, midwives to deliver greater freedom.

Francine, a seriously disturbed woman, was prone to an assortment of self-destructive, manipulative behaviors that easily qualified her for the dreaded borderline diagnosis. She called her therapist at home, threatening suicide, at regular intervals. She relied on an assortment of means to sabotage her own progress just to get under the therapist's skin.

The clinician stayed with the case for several years. She gnashed her teeth, sought the counsel of her colleagues, attended conferences, and read innumerable books, trying anything and everything to find the key that might prove helpful. On two separate occasions, she referred the woman to other specialists, only to find that, like a boomerang, Francine sailed back into her office with a completely new set of symptoms.

I lost touch with this therapist for a few years. When we resumed contact, I asked how Francine was doing. I expected the therapist to roll her eyes skyward or to begin a litany of complaints that I had heard many times in the past. I was, therefore, quite surprised when she broke out into an angelic smile and her eyes sparkled with pride. There had been no single breakthrough, but gradually, ever so slowly and painfully, Francine had made steady if not dramatic progress. It had taken more than 4 years of patient, excruciatingly difficult work, but now both the therapist and Francine could see an amazing difference.

"She still drives me to distraction sometimes. But it has been worth it! I stayed with her. I hung in there when nobody else would or could. I don't mean to be grandiose, but I know I saved her life. And by doing so, I saved a part of my own."

Responding to Problem Patients

A significant number of us entered the profession because we like to be needed, to have people depend on us. It is therefore ridiculous for us to complain when clients exhibit exactly those qualities of neediness, dependency, helplessness, and manipulation that they came to us to cure. We must expect a certain amount of intrusion, of having people smother us with their demands and even invade our lives with their late-night cries of anguish. We should not be surprised at the lengths to which a disturbed person will go to get the attention he or she equates with love.

Most of us have learned over time several principles that should be followed in dealing with any problem client:

1. Determine whether the problem is with the client or with you. In many cases, it is your own impatience and need for control that lead to unnecessary struggles and conflict.
2. Respect the purpose and function of resistance and client defenses. It is safe to assume that the client's irritating or manipulative behavior has served him well for quite some time. The fact that you are feeling annoyed and off balance is evidence that this behavior is working with you as well.
3. When feeling trapped, follow the principles of the *reflective practitioner*, which allow a professional to restructure a problem in such a way that a different set of actions is possible.
4. Do not try to cure the incurable. It is necessary for you to accept your own limits and share with the client the responsibility for the success of treatment.
5. Acknowledge to yourself that the client is operating under a different set of rules than the one you would prefer. Do not retaliate in anger. Retain your compassion and caring at the same time that you enforce appropriate boundaries.
6. Remain as flexible as possible. Patients test our patience precisely because they require treatment that is more innovative than we are used to. Allow so-called difficult clients to help stimulate your own creative capacities. It is highly likely that such a case will require you to develop, adapt, or invent something altogether new.
7. Educate yourself about clients who come from backgrounds that are beyond your experience or comfort level. I know this is the standard advice that is mentioned repeatedly, but for good reason: all too often, biases, prejudices, blind spots, and overreactions occur because of ignorance about the cultural context for behavior.
8. When all else fails, allow the clients to keep their dysfunctional behavior. It is theirs to keep or lose as they see fit. When they are ready to change, they will do so. Our job is to help them get ready—on their schedule.

When expert therapists were asked how they dealt with their most challenging cases, first of all they found their particular theoretical orientation useful in terms of interpreting and making sense of the impasses. Second, and just as important, they doubled down on their level and depth of empathy to the point it became an embodied state that created a "relational space" for mutual growth (Moltu & Binder, 2013). Yet much of the challenge with such cases isn't only related to what we do (or not do) with challenging clients but also how we manage our own anxiety between sessions (Karakurt et al., 2014). Whether we are talking about clients who are suicidal, decompensating, traumatized, or otherwise nonresponsive or spinning out of control, one key to these cases is related to confronting our own needs and feelings of incompetence.

Perhaps the last and most important principle is to practice a high degree of self-compassion because we are often so critical and hard on ourselves, especially when we encounter clients who don't seem to be cooperating with our best efforts. Schwartz (2015) echoes a point made in an earlier chapter that sometimes our most challenging clients become our best teachers. He suggests that our clients become our mentors by the ways they "torment" us, helping to make us more aware of the parts of ourselves that are most in need of self-compassion.

All the client patterns presented in this chapter make our lives more difficult but also more interesting and challenging. The key to preventing boredom and burnout, to surviving in the field with the minimum of negative personal consequences, is to do only what we can—no more and no less.

9

Boredom and Burnout

OF ALL THE problems a therapist encounters—from someone who wants to jump out of a window to someone who is trying to jump out of his skin—none is more difficult than the challenge of staying energized about one's work. If burnout is caused by an overload of stimulation, then boredom is caused by its absence—at least in terms of subjectively perceived experience. Both involve a discrepancy between what one is giving and what one is receiving.

The first part of this chapter will discuss the phenomenon of therapist ennui and tedium; the second will cover overstimulation, emotional exhaustion, and a broken spirit. In both boredom and burnout, the clinician experiences a loss of motivation, energy, control, and direction. These conditions, if left untreated, can become chronic and incurable.

I realize that beginners in the field might find it hard to imagine that someday they would ever become bored with the job considering all the complexities and overwhelming challenges and stimulation. But like everything else we do in life, autopilot takes over when we become complacent and stale. Thus in some ways experienced therapists are far more at risk if they don't remain committed to continual vigilance and a sense of renewal that channels "the beginner's mind" so filled with enthusiasm and excitement for helping others.

I also wonder what it says about me that this is one of the longest chapters in the book? I suppose my excuse is that I decided to combine both boredom and burnout as different manifestations of the same phenomenon instead of separating them into individual chapters. In both cases, the therapist has developed a loss of engagement and passion for this work, a condition that becomes increasingly challenging without initiating some changes in what we do and how we do it.

About Boredom

Boredom involves a loss of interest and momentum, either temporarily or chronically. Although it is usually experienced as uncomfortable, it also serves to rest the mind and spirit and to give them time to rejuvenate. Boredom thus does have its functions and purposes as a transitional period between what you have been doing and what you may do in the future.

People have died of boredom, and perhaps an intolerance for sameness leads others to the fireworks of madness. Boredom is nature's way of saying, "Get back to work!" If people felt content with staleness and with doing nothing productive, our species would die out. We have instinctual urges to procreate and preserve our gene pool, to protect and provide for our offspring. And we have urges and ambition to have more, more, more of what we already have—not because we need new things, but because of that voice within us that protests against contentment.

When work becomes routine and predictable, when stimulation is minimal, when a person dislikes her own company and that of others, boredom will seep in to motivate some action. It is less a condition than a way of viewing the world, especially by experienced therapists who, as mentioned, are far more prone to boredom and inertia than are novices because of predictable routines.

Boredom can be precipitated by a collapse of meaning in what we do and a sense of futility that it doesn't matter nearly as much as we once believed. Once upon a time, there was a therapist who wished to save the world. He had a diploma, a jacket with patches on the elbows, a leather chair, and the best of intentions. Then he discovered that most of his clients did not want his help and that the rest of the people in the world went to someone else. Day after day, he said the same things to his clients, and they said the same things to him in return. He said, "If you're so miserable, why don't you change?" They said, "I can't." So time went on. His elbow patches became frayed. And so did his patience.

He began to feel more and more confined by his leather chair; by this time, it had lost most of its stuffing. The diploma had yellowed. And his clients stopped saying "I can't" and started saying "I won't." This didn't seem to him to be much progress. His prison walls grew closer.

Boredom has its benefits, as sensory deprivation experiments will attest. Those athletes who run or swim or bike in ultramarathons for 8 hours at a time can also testify to what endless repetition can teach in terms of focus and self-discipline. While we are bored, there is time "to strip away our character armor, shed layer after layer of imposed motivations and values, and circle closer to our unique essence" (Keen, 1977, p. 80). It is a time to stand naked and confront one's pain without distractions or diversions. World-class runners are able to simulate a perfect state of boredom in their quest for optimal performance. They refuse to retreat into fantasy when the pain becomes intense, but instead stay with the discomfort and pain: "I not only pay attention to my body as I run, but I also constantly remind myself to relax, hang loose, not tie up" (Morgan, 1978, p. 45). Pounding the pavement mile after mile, hour after hour, they concentrate only on the nothingness of where they are—the placement of the foot, the pace of breathing, the swing of arms. Such athletes excel because they are willing to put themselves in that place where there is nowhere else to escape to, no matter how much discomfort or pain they might feel, they stubbornly cling to the belief that the more focused they remain on each moment the more likely they reach optimal performance.

Therapist Vulnerability to Boredom

The experience of boredom is, in part, affected by a person's conception of time. Those who are clock-watchers (as therapists tend to be), who are constantly aware of how time progresses, find themselves waiting more often for things to happen. Our involvement in life is regulated by what the clock dictates. The nature of a job that requires the precise timing of a conversation to the minute, with frequent checks of the clock (5 to 10 times per hour), makes therapists much more vulnerable to the subjective flow of time. As boredom is most likely to occur when time seems to slow down, clock-watchers, by inclination and training, are more aware of this phenomenon.

Where people have a radically different conception of time—in Latin American cultures, for example—boredom is experienced with less frequency. Ask a person on the street what time it is, and rather than hearing the precise voice of a person with a digital device say, "8:48," you will hear a gravelly and unconcerned "about 9:00," with an accompanying shrug to indicate "What's the difference?" In Latin cultures, there is a great respect for the present and less concern for the future. Nothing is more important than what you are doing now—talking to a dog, finishing a conversation, watching one of the frequent car accidents. Therefore, regardless of what the clock says, whatever you are currently involved in should not be rushed. Time will wait; and if it will not, who cares?

Some of the best therapy sessions we've ever experienced are those when we have reached a state of *flow*, of effortless and heightened concentration in which time seems irrelevant (Csikszentmihalyi, 1975, 1998). Boredom is impossible for those who are so totally involved in what they are doing that they even lose their sense of self; they become what they are doing. For veterans this means stopping internal and external distractions to remain in the flow state; for beginners it means stopping self-critical talk. These distractions can take many forms: intrusive thoughts ("Must remember to pick up the mail"), distractions in the environment (phone, email, noise), body urgings (indigestion, hunger, bladder, discomfort, fatigue), time constraints, or ongoing issues in your life that require attention.

It is when we lose the sense of challenge in what we're doing, when we think we know where things are going, that boredom can most easily infect us. Time seems to stand still. We feel embarrassed by the number of times we have looked at the clock. After planning your dinner menu in your head, figuring which ingredients you have on hand, calculating which bills to pay, and going off into fantasy land, you notice with a start that someone is talking to you. You think, "What are you doing here? Why don't you go home already?" It is the repetition that is so difficult to tolerate, not only in the similarity of client complaints but in the therapeutic messages we relay. Certain styles of therapy, for example, can become repetitive in their execution, as Ellis (1972, p. 119) admitted: "I have seen myself at times doing the same thing over and over with clients and have recognized that this is a pain in the ass, this is something I don't greatly like." Whereas some clinicians might feel "stuck" with their chosen orientation, many others keep evolving their style to practice to keep things fresh.

Burton (1972) points out that therapists have a particularly difficult time dealing with boredom and so chose a lifestyle that permits a variety of tasks, allows them to get to the heart of problems quickly, and grants them the opportunity to work with very interesting and very strange people. He claims that therapists seldom feel bored because they get to hear titillating secrets from clients who try very hard to be entertaining. The people who march through our offices are indeed unique and individual, yet after years of practice many of the voices sound the same.

A couples counselor: "If I hear another husband say he'll do anything to save his marriage, but he doesn't have time this week to schedule an appointment. . . ."

A psychiatrist: "They all want drugs. They come in prepared to do a song and dance showing how sick they are and hoping for relief from some magic pill they think I'm hoarding."

A psychologist: "I've done over 4,000 child assessments in the last several years. I do them in my sleep. Sure every kid is different, but the damn questions never change."

A social worker: "I don't know how many visits I've made to the homes of abused children. It's always the same. I go in and interview the parents, who swear the kid slipped in the bathtub, then admit maybe they did try to teach her a lesson but they'll never do it again. 'You've got to teach these kids they can't walk all over you.' 'Yes, Mr. Walker, but your daughter is 18 months old. What did she do, *crawl* all over you?' They never get the point and they'll never change. The kid will go to a foster home and probably get beaten by someone else. Maybe a long time ago I found this interesting. Now it's just frustrating and boring."

English (1972, p. 95) recounts his experiences with boredom in therapy work: "There have been patients I liked to see and treat and some I dreaded to see, some who amused me, some who bored me to distraction. Some could put me to sleep, and I use the word *put* rather than say I went to sleep on them. Because I would find myself thinking, 'How sleepy I am. When the patient leaves I'll take a nap for sure!' But when he departed the office I couldn't go to sleep for the life of me."

One therapist commented that when she felt bored in therapy, it was usually because she wanted to cut herself off from issues that were threatening. I like that premise because it assumes a degree of control on our part. When a session or a meeting becomes tedious and drags on endlessly, we can look first toward ourselves—what are we hiding from inside this cloak of disinterest? It is far more common, however, to just check and respond to messages when things drag on. Mobile devices have become the antidote to even a few seconds of stillness, always beckoning, always distracting, always providing instant diversion whenever there is a moment's downtime.

A second possible explanation for our boredom is that there are people walking around who are objectively, intrinsically, completely devoid of spirit and energy. Some clients come to our offices because they cannot find anyone else who will listen to them. They speak in monotones. They may be alexithymic, incapable of describing internal thoughts and feelings. They are concrete, repetitive, utterly predictable in what they do and how they do it. Each session they cover the same ground and repeat the same stories.

These people are thankfully rare. They will test the patience and compassion of any therapist because they do not respond very well to either subtle nudges or more dramatic confrontations intended to move them toward being more expressive. There is even some question as to whether, neurologically, they have the capacity to be so. They drone on and on about topics so pedestrian and disconnected from their own experience we can hardly pay attention.

The third possibility when we encounter boredom in our work has less to do with the client or with the particular issues that are present than with our own narcissistic demands for stimulation. Although we may be reluctant to admit it, many of us selected this kind of work because we are entertained by the voyeuristic delights of being privy to people's private lives. It is like television, each channel a window into a different life. But then one channel gives us identical programming each time we tune in—maybe a fishing show—and we feel cheated: "You aren't doing your job! Don't you know you're supposed to go out there in the world and do fun stuff and then come back and tell me about it?"

Boredom, in this third case, results from our own expectations for how clients should perform for us. It is also the situation we can do the most about. People who appear chronically boring believe they are essentially unlovable and have discovered a very effective way to keep others at a distance. Our job, then, is to love them in spite of their attempts to keep us at a distance. This is easier said than done, however, for to do so we must stretch ourselves beyond the limits of our patience and concentration.

Boredom and the Avoidance of Risks

On one end of the continuum is a therapist steeped in boredom—demoralized, dissatisfied, restless, and weary. On the other end is someone who has become timid, irresolute, and fearful of taking risks. Change in some clients is stymied by a reluctance to act differently or to experiment with new modes of being. In much the same way, some therapists tend toward safety, security, and predictability at the expense of their own growth.

Therapists can avoid constructive risk taking in a number of ways. I'm not talking about reckless thrill seeking but rather about those occasional opportunities to take an unknown route and end up in a very different place. Reluctance to expose oneself to hazard and danger, unless the perceived gain seems worth the potential loss, is sensible. But much more than the desire to protect ourselves from needless jeopardy is a determined avoidance of risk. When someone is secure and comfortable, it takes some real incentive to convince her to venture out into the cold. We may therefore be just as guilty as anyone else of postponing action until it becomes absolutely necessary and of avoiding the unknown when it is at all possible.

Therapists who play it safe in their work may remain basically satisfied with their moderate gains. They will do just enough to get the job done but not enough to produce dramatic results. Under the guise of protecting their client's welfare, they will avoid confrontation and conflict, preferring instead to move at a pace consistent with the client's own tolerance for boredom. They will wait and wait, knowing that waiting has its therapeutic value and that most clients will get better on their own, or in spite of what the therapists do. They will say only what they have said before. They will do only what has been tried before. Any departure from the formula must be preceded by a consultation of the works of their favorite authority.

Certainly, it is neither appropriate nor helpful to advocate risky therapeutic interventions to appease some restless spirit in the therapist. On the contrary, those who are able to satisfy their needs for stimulation and excitement in their personal lives have no interest in using their clients as guinea pigs in experimentation for its own sake. Therapists, in fact, have an obligation to protect people at risk from exposure to unnecessary dangers. But there are many ways that a clinician may safely and responsibly try new intervention strategies without jeopardizing the client's safety.

Antidotes to Boredom

Although boredom is an inevitable if uninvited guest, it need not stay long. Yet when the clinician feels apathetic and helpless, boredom may become a permanent resident. Sometimes, despite a therapist's fervent desire for renewal, boredom nevertheless hangs on.

Excitement and stimulation result from the perception of challenge matched to our abilities. This is one of the main messages we send our clients: any emotional state, boredom most of all, is the logical consequence of our chosen cognitive activity. The primary cure for boredom in therapy is thus to focus on the uniqueness of each case, the individuality of each client, and the opportunity for growth in every encounter. When our minds function routinely and interventions have become mechanical, we experience tedium.

What truly distinguishes master therapists is their passion and commitment for avoiding complacency in the search for new and more effective ways of helping people (Goh, 2005; Kottler & Carlson, 2008, 2015; Miller & Hubble, 2011; Skovholt, 2012). It isn't just that they work harder or practice their craft for a longer period of time, but that they engage in "deep practice" to improve their identified weaknesses (Colvin, 2010; Ericsson, 2014). They attain extraordinary levels of excellence in their work because it is so important to them.

When I catch myself feeling blasé about the real magic that is transpiring in my involvement with a client, I make a deliberate shift in my perception. If I first change my position in the chair and concentrate on my breathing and on my posture, if I go back to the basics I learned as a student, I find that something wonderful takes place. The client becomes more special, her words carry more power, the whole experience becomes energized. I can feel the new energy, and so can the client. As she notices my renewed interest, she begins to feel and act more interestingly, not to entertain me and release me from my boredom, but because I value our time together more. She begins to believe that she is more exciting. The changes are, at first, very subtle: I forget to watch the clock and the session runs over.

One practitioner relates his strategy for avoiding staleness in his work: "I have never been bored. . . . I consider myself very fortunate to be doing such interesting work, particularly when I can experience a degree of falling in love with a patient. This is not a threat to my marital commitment but rather is a further installment on the resolving of my romance with my parents and my siblings. When I can no longer fall in love with patients to some degree, I will be approaching the end of my vitality as a therapist" (Warkentin, 1972, pp. 258–259).

When I hear statements like this, I feel instant admiration, followed by a certain shame because it is so unlike my own experience. I have to reinvent myself at least every few years because I get so bored with myself. I'm tired of listening to myself, of hearing my own stories, or reliving the same things over and over. How often do any of us repeat ourselves in sessions, tell many of our clients the same things, even the same way? It is really about being lazy: it is so much easier to pull familiar interventions off the shelf than to invent something altogether new.

One of the reasons I have revised this book every several years is that I am no longer the person who existed at the time of its previous edition. I have changed, moved on, learned new things. I read what I've written 5 years ago and realize I don't believe that anymore or don't work that way any longer. I have this fantasy that if any two of my clients were to meet and describe their therapy, they would think they were seeing someone completely different, because I try to keep changing what I do and how I do it. This is one of the keys that keeps me energized and loving my work, even after three decades.

It also helps to bring feelings of boredom out in the open in sessions, at least with those clients who are ready for more authenticity and honesty in the relationship. Preferring to work in the present moment in most circumstances, Yalom (2002, p. 66) describes how he might bring this up: "For the last several minutes I notice that I've been feeling disconnected from you, somewhat distanced. . . . I wonder what is your level of connection to me today? Is your feeling similar to mine? Let's try to understand what's happening."

Wiseman and Scott (2003) summarize much of the literature related to therapist boredom and conclude that although there is no single solution to the challenge of remaining energized and focused, it is wise to try an assortment of things: becoming more active and involved in the relationship, finding meaning in the experience, using the feelings as a diagnostic tool, or realizing that it is time to diversify your life and change the ways you work. It also helps to be more playful and find the humor in things that might otherwise drag us down (Malinowski, 2013). Other therapists successfully immunize themselves against boredom by taking on challenging cases that do not permit a lax attitude. Also useful is to be under the supervision of someone who helps keep you off balance, humble, and comfortably confused. Boredom thus can be kept at bay by your working consciously and deliberately to keep things fresh, and especially by looking for meaning in the things you do.

About Burnout

No matter how skilled a practitioner is at avoiding other occupational hazards (including boredom), there will be some period of time—a day, a week, a month, or all eternity—in which serious consideration will be given to leaving the field. Perhaps it will be one of those days when successive no-shows combine with an irate phone call from an irrational parent. Or maybe one of those weeks in which you discover that the supervisor you liked has moved on and the colleague you do not like has just been promoted (over you) to that position. Or one of those months in which your tires are slashed by an ex-client you thought you had helped and your ego is repeatedly slashed by peers who are trying to undermine your authority, referral sources who have lost confidence, a supervisor who feels threatened by your superior intellect, and clients who will no longer return your phone calls.

The question, then, is not *who* will experience burnout but *how long* the next episode will last.

In fact, burnout may not be the best term to describe the kind of insidious neglect and deterioration that takes place when professionals lose interest and effectiveness—perhaps *rustout* is a better description because it better represents the kind of slow, gradual process that eats away at a therapist's spirit (Gmelch, 1983). After all, you will hardly wake up one morning and discover that your fire, like a burst of flame, is burned out all of a sudden; rather, hundreds of such mornings have elapsed over time, each one contributing to your overall disillusionment.

It is the nature of the human condition in general, and the therapist condition in particular, to experience ebbs and flows in life satisfaction. This is a very emotional business, with many highs and lows. Sometimes we feel as close to being a god as any mortal can—powerful, elegant, graceful, wise—and other times we feel so totally inept that we wonder how we can be allowed to continue to practice. No matter how many people we have helped, deep inside there is a sickening feeling that we will never be able to do it again. For the life of me, I do not really know what I did the last time. And when a new client comes in, sits down, presents his case, and then waits expectantly for my assessment, there is always a minute of panic in which I stall and think to myself, "I don't have any idea what's going on, nor do I have the foggiest notion of what is going to help this gentleman." Then I take a deep breath, jump in, and say something, anything, even if it's only, "I don't know yet what is happening, but I'm sure we'll figure it out together."

Burnout, or rustout, is taking place when you realize that you neither know what is going on with your clients nor really care. Conversely, these conditions can be just as prevalent when you are a little too certain about what is going on and what is best for everyone else and you feel frustrated because others won't listen to you.

For those newcomers to the field who are reading (or skimming) this chapter because boredom or burnout are the least of your concerns as you begin your career, consider this fair warning that *all* therapists started out with optimism, enthusiasm, and incredible excitement about their work. You may vow never to become victim of the emotional erosion that you observe in some older veterans, but trust me when I tell you that years of work in the trenches do indeed take a toll. The best way to prevent such negative effects is to develop an early warning system to recognize initial symptoms as they emerge.

Signs and Symptoms of Burnout

Burnout is commonly described as having several features: (1) emotional depletion or exhaustion, (2) negative attitudes toward clients (depersonalization, cynicism, critical judgment), and (3) a perception of diminished personal and professional accomplishment (frustration, pessimism, futility). Although a number of sources (Farber, 1990; Maslach, 2003; Orlinsky & Ronnestad, 2005; Polman, 2010; Riggar, 2016) seem clear about the symptoms of this condition, there is considerably less consensus about the causes, which have been ascribed to any number of factors, such as work environment, client load, compensation, self-image, and lack of collegial and family support (Rupert & Morgan, 2005). It makes sense that those practitioners who tend to become emotionally overinvolved with their clients, as well as those who display low energy because of chronic fatigue, would be at greatest risk (Rzeszutek & Schier, 2014). It's also interesting how the environment and cultural context in which therapists operate also influence the ways they metabolize stress and experience burnout. Whereas in the United States burnout is most often attributed to mental and physical exhaustions from the demands of doing (too much?) therapy, therapists in Japan most often mention perceptions of inefficiency or feelings of failure as a primary cause, and those in Korea say that it is influenced more by problems in their personal lives. Also interesting in this study is that therapists in the Philippines didn't report experiencing much burnout at all (Puig, Yoon, Callueng, An, & Lee, 2014).

I am discussing burnout not as simply a problem that interferes with the therapist's enjoyment and satisfaction with work but as a condition that can lead to significant deterioration in professional effectiveness and an increased probability of ethical misconduct (Corey, Corey, & Callanan, 2015; Remley & Herlihy, 2015; Welfel, 2015). We risk greater vulnerability to sexual improprieties: feeling sexually aroused by a client, discussing sexual issues based on our own interest rather than on client needs, meeting clients outside the office for supposedly legitimate reasons, or asking clients to engage in certain sexual behaviors so that we may enjoy them vicariously (Pope & Bouhoutsos, 1986). The vast majority of therapists admit to knowing a colleague who is seriously burned out, and fully one-third of practitioners acknowledge that they have personally experienced this condition (Mahoney, 1997; Wood, Klein, Cross, Lammes, & Elliot, 1985).

Burnout, or therapist impairment, looks like plain old depression at first glance. There is a loss of energy and motivation, feelings of helplessness and futility—and it most certainly is depressing. "It is the rising tide of disillusionment, hopelessness and exhaustion that gradually swamps all the good intentions, enthusiasm and sense of meaning that once-dedicated people brought to their work" (Wylie & Markowitz, 1992, p. 20). Yet whereas depression is an all-pervasive state, burnout is centered around and sparked by our work.

A number of fairly specific behavioral indices of acute burnout have been described by several authors. The following discussion of the symptoms, causes, and cures for burnout was inspired by input from several sources (Brems, 2000; Edelwich & Brodsky, 1980; Freudenberger, 1975; Kottler, 2012; Maslach & Leiter, 1997; Mathieu, 2012 Norcross & Guy, 2007; Rupert, Stevanovic, & Hunley, 2009; Wicks, 2008). The symptoms that follow are the clearest indications of an incipient problem:

1. There is a general unwillingness to discuss work in social and family circles. When queried by friends about what is new at the office, the therapist's eyebrows rise, shoulders shrug, but nothing comes out. In fact, the therapist, if she makes any response at all, may snort and then use all her therapeutic skills to deftly change the focus to someone or something else.
2. There is a reluctance to check voicemail and email or call the office for messages and a resistance to returning calls. It is as if there could not possibly be any message that is worth getting excited about. In their most pessimistic states, burned-out therapists may think that a message can bring only one of three possibilities: (1) someone is canceling an appointment at the last minute, leaving a gaping hole in the therapist's schedule during the middle of the day; (2) a new referral has called and wants to be squeezed into an already overloaded week; or (3) a life insurance agent has called to talk to the therapist about his inevitable death.
3. When a client does call or text to cancel, the therapist celebrates with a bit too much enthusiasm. Dancing and singing in the hallway is a dangerous sign of advanced deterioration. Whispers under one's breath such as "Thank God!" and other expressions of relief are certainly more socially appropriate, but they are equally indicative of professional dread.
4. One of the clearest signs of burnout in a therapist is when several clients complain of similar symptoms. When there is a rash of complaints about hopelessness, frustration, pessimism, and doubt in the therapeutic process, the clinician may silently be in agreement. Because clients resonate

our faith and beliefs, they also sense and imitate our despair. Frustrated and unmotivated therapists do little to promote growth in their clients. If clients improve, it will be largely in spite of their therapist rather than because of her help. In fact, some clients will get better just to escape the punitive drudgery of their sessions.

5. The alarm clock is less a signal to begin the day than an order to resume one's sentence. There is reluctance to get out of bed; excuses to avoid getting started abound. During the day, the therapist functions at half speed and is lethargic, apathetic, disconnected. Much time is devoted to coffee breaks and ploys to stall action.
6. As in all instances of prolonged stress, therapists are prone to anesthetizing themselves with self-prescribed medications. In some cases, legal prescription drugs are used with regularity. Just as frequently, stressed therapists resort to abusing the recreational substance of their choice. Just as with the general population, therapists may also be prone to medicating themselves with other coping strategies: overeating, compulsive shopping, gambling, overexercising, sexual acting out, addictions, destructive risk taking.
7. Cynicism is manifested in a number of ways. To colleagues and friends, the therapist may make a number of deprecating remarks about clients, ridiculing them for their weaknesses, joking about their helplessness. And the therapist may find a commentary running through his head during sessions: "If you only knew what a fool you look like," "You are so boring, no wonder your wife left you," "I don't care what you do. What are you asking me for?"
8. Sessions lose their spark, their excitement, their zest and spontaneity. There is very little laughter, little movement. The room feels stagnant. Voices become monotones. There are lots of yawns and uncomfortable silences. Sessions end early.
9. The therapist falls behind in completing paperwork and billings. Progress notes, fee sheets, treatment plans, and quarterly summaries pile up. During the best of times, such chores are handled with less than joy; the burned-out therapist may spend more time complaining about the forms to be completed than actually finishing them. Management intervenes to slap the therapist's hand, often with other punitive measures to enforce compliance with organizational rules.
10. During leisure time, there is a distinct preference for passive entertainment. Losing yourself in videos, television, or the Internet is easier than getting out in the world to do something. One therapist commented about this: "I'm so tired of having to be responsible for other people's

lives that I want someone else to take charge of mine. I just don't have the energy for anything else."

11. The therapist is so emotionally tied to work that an active social life is completely precluded. He has difficulty relinquishing control, feeling he must do everything himself. He experiences excessive internal pressure to succeed and an overidentification with his clients to the point of losing his own identity.
12. The therapist is reluctant to explore the causes and cures of her burned-out condition. Rather than making needed changes or confronting the emotional difficulties that are blocking satisfaction, she prefers to make excuses and criticize others for the problem. Much of what a therapist does involves interrupting this destructive cycle in others; thus one symptom of burnout is an inability or unwillingness to apply one's therapeutic wisdom to oneself. There is probably some ironic justice in creating so devastating a punishment for those who practice therapy in a spirit of hypocrisy and self-neglect.

To bring this discussion to a far more personal level, ask yourself at the end of the day the extent to which you feel: (a) mentally and physically exhausted, (b) signs of somatic distress (headaches, muscle tension, stomach problems), (c) overwhelmed and flooded because of all the things that are still left to do, and (d) hopeless that you can somehow possibly catch up and complete all the tasks that require your attention.

Fantasy Trips as Clues

One reliable measure of disengagement would be the frequency of daydreaming and escapist fantasy. During sessions, the therapist's eyes are inadvertently drawn to the window or door. It takes constant vigilance to stay with the client. Yet in spite of these good intentions, the mind drifts away to some other place and time. During idle periods, the escapist thinking continues as the therapist imagines herself rescuing princes in distress or lying on a beach in Tahiti.

The content and pattern of your fantasy life, both during sessions and elsewhere, offer rich clues as to the relative prevalence of burnout-impairment symptoms. I think it is interesting to ask any practitioner two questions:

1. During your typical sessions, about what percentage of the time do you spend fully engaged and completely focused? In other words, how often

are you listening intently to what your clients are saying, as opposed to drifting off, fantasizing, and thinking about other things?
2. When you do leave the sessions in your head, where do you go?

As to the first question, I have heard estimates of anywhere from 20% to 75%, meaning that practitioners confess that they are actually paying attention to their clients anywhere from one-fifth to three-quarters of the time. Personally, I think we are all doing quite well to actually listen about half the time, considering there are so many things going on inside us. A client says something, and that triggers a whole range of internal fireworks in which we make connections to our own lives, drift off for a minute, lapse into fantasy, and plan what we intend to do later in the session—or later in the day. Then we tune in once again for a few minutes until something else sets us off, and we leave the room for a little while. Some of this may be boredom, of course, but a lot of these mind trips are the inevitable result of processing everything that we hear and experience during such an intense conversation.

My point is that how often you remain focused in sessions— and how often you leave the room to go off into your own world—are indications of your relative engagement with your work. This will vary from client to client, day to day, and therapist to therapist. Some clinicians report phenomenal powers of concentration in which they claim that they are actually listening to their clients 80 to 90% of the time. (I find this hard to believe only because I don't even listen to myself that much of the time.) Others among us can do excellent clinical work tuning in half the time or less; we might even find a lot of creative energy during those reflective journeys.

Apart from frequency of fantasies, the more interesting question is the second one: When you do leave the session to go into a favorite fantasy, where do you go?

For a period of time when I was in my twenties, intense, vivid, incredibly detailed sexual fantasies dominated my inner world, both during sessions and outside them. I am not speaking of sexual fantasies about my clients (although I had a few of those as well), but about past romances or imagined encounters with attractive strangers. Then, when my hormones settled down, I left my sessions to entertain rather descriptive images of some future world that I wanted to create. I pictured myself in some ideal job different from the present employment situation. I relived conversations with someone with whom I had been in conflict, rehearsing what I wanted to say. By my late thirties, settled and successful in practice, I next had a binge of materialistic fantasies, thinking about all the things I wanted to buy and trips I wanted to take. Well, you get the picture . . . and have one of your own.

So back to the question: Where do you go when you leave your sessions and journey places in your mind? And what does that tell you?

Causes of Burnout

Depending on your immunological system, recuperative powers, and work environment, therapist stagnation can be either a temporary nuisance or a tragic flaw that requires a career change. Several influences determine the extent and duration of this occupational and personal crisis.

Predisposing Factors

It is the nature of the human life cycle to experience periods of relative calm alternating with spurts of disorientation and subsequent growth. Developmental theorists have documented how growth and evolution proceed according to an orderly sequence of stages that build on prior adaptive experiences. During the career of a therapist, as well, there are predetermined stages of growth that are facilitated by such variables as formal training, critical incidents, and exposure to theories, mentors, and experiences. According to a developmental conception of occupational growth, certain predictable hot spots will emerge. Therapists are most vulnerable during life cycle transitions, during periods of accelerated metabolic changes, and after decades-long intervals between theoretical changes. Those who are most at risk for burnout are likely to have some preexisting conditions that make them more vulnerable. Therapists who have experienced previous trauma, are dealing with major personal conflicts, employ avoidant coping styles, and hold pessimistic attitudes are in greatest jeopardy (Gil, 2015).

Some therapists are at risk not only because of developmental transitions but because of certain personality characteristics. Those with a low tolerance for frustration and ambiguity, a high need for approval and for mandatory control, and rigid patterns of thought are going to be in for greater turbulence. One social worker, for example, has been practicing orthodox psychoanalysis for 20 years. He subscribes to all the appropriate journals, attends conventions religiously, and is proud of the fact that he has not changed his style since he completed his own analysis decades previously. He resists change even within his sheltered professional circles and scoffs at ego psychology or Jungian analysis as too revisionist. He actually does very little in his sessions, although he can talk to a colleague for hours about all the fascinating things that are happening. He is often frustrated because he sees little progress in his clients and receives so little feedback from them concerning how they feel toward him.

Although I use the example of a psychoanalytic practitioner, I could just have easily selected a professional who subscribes to any rigid orthodoxy that mandates specific, repetitive conduct. Some cognitive therapists are known to become bored, dispirited, and burned out from disputing the same old irrational beliefs over and over, just as reality therapists may get tired of asking people about the consequences of their choices, and narrative practitioners may find that looking for unique outcomes has lost its original kick. We thus struggle with trying to develop a well-constructed, reliable, and comfortable style of practice that is consistent with current theory and research and yet allows sufficient flexibility and creativity that we can keep things new and fresh.

The seeds of disillusionment may first be sown, if not fertilized as well, in graduate school. Therapists get themselves in trouble with unrealistic expectations and unreasonable goals. No matter what the textbooks and professors say, you are not going to cure schizophrenia by reflecting feelings, and you are not going to wipe out chronic depression by disputing a few irrational beliefs. Naïve beginners enter the field prepared to conduct neat, elegant, organized therapy in 10 sessions or less with people who will change fast, pay on time, and be exceedingly grateful. It takes several years for them to realize that some clients will always be much the same no matter what you do, that you will never get the recognition you deserve, and that most of the time you will be unappreciated and overworked.

Bureaucratic Constraints

There are factors within most organizational structures that may make for efficient operations, happy boards of directors, and balanced budgets but that are hardly conducive to staff morale. Paperwork is just one example of a product that pleases funding and accreditation agencies but drives clinical personnel up the wall. For every session of therapy that she conducts, the therapist may spend 15 minutes describing in sickening detail what the client talked about, what interventions were used, how that particular session contributed to the overall treatment goals, and how the client felt after he left. In some settings, all this material must be repeated again and again for summaries, insurance forms, case reports, and departmental files.

Some mental health agencies, hospitals, social service departments, universities, and clinics are notorious for their political wars. Power struggles are waged not only among department heads and within the administrative hierarchy but especially among the different professional groups. Psychiatrists, social workers, family therapists, counselors, psychologists, psychiatric nurses, and mental health technicians often stick together in their respective groups, each with its own biases toward others. The result of this often intense competition is an environment in which staff vie for control, status, recognition, and power. In such a setting, it is not surprising that people choose to drop out.

Even the most dedicated and well-meaning practitioner who has successfully avoided all the previously mentioned traps may find it difficult to resist the contagious effects of others' disillusionment. When the institutional norm is to complain about the food, it is difficult to enjoy a meal. When other staff members complain about how they have been abused by the administration, it is hard to go about one's business as if others care for your welfare. In the worst of circumstances, it takes a new recruit but a few weeks to lose her initial surge of enthusiasm.

Emotional Distress

Most of the problems contributing to burnout are centered less around the actual daily work than around the therapist's unresolved emotional difficulties. Several different clinicians can be exposed to exactly the same clients or presenting complaints; whereas some will internalize the despair, others can easily shrug it off. This relates not only to clinical style, cognitive activity, and coping mechanisms but also to preexisting stress levels and stressors in the therapist's life.

Some professionals invest their egos too intensely in the outcome of their work, a result that depends very much on the client's motivation and behavior. They may therefore attempt to do too much in the sessions, taking excessive responsibility for filling silences, providing immediate relief of symptoms, and generating insight. The more control the therapist takes, the less the client assumes. The more the therapist does, the less there is for the client to do.

One of my own greatest problems is that I attribute way too much power and control to my own abilities and skills in sessions (and in life). This means that I take more credit for outcomes than I justifiably should and also accept more than my fair share of responsibility for failures. I have known this for a long time and have worked on it repeatedly in therapy, supervision, and peer consultations, yet I still refuse to change this behavior (and it is a deliberate choice). I know the right things to say to my own supervisees and students—that they need to let the client do the work, that there are limits to what we can do, and that the rest is up to factors outside our control—yet I enjoy the illusion of power that comes with the belief that I can control certain things that are really beyond my grasp. I also like the continued growth that accompanies this self-critical style, even if it does predispose me to burn out faster if I don't carefully monitor what is happening.

Therapists who are more highly evolved than I am in this area are hardly justified in assuming a passive, detached, observatory role that allows their clients to flounder aimlessly. Certainly, we share some responsibility with the client for planning the content of sessions, providing some input into choices, and gently helping the client generate a degree of self-understanding and subsequent action. The problem arises when, out of a personal sense of importance, the therapist feels a genuine, gut-level stake in what the client does and how fast she does it.

Emotional factors enter the picture not only for the therapist who tries too hard but also for the one who overidentifies with a client's situation. No matter how many times I hear a young client cry out in anger and frustration at being teased by his peers, I feel the pain every time. As the little guy goes on to relate the incident of striking out for the third time in front of his heckling teammates, I can feel myself actually shaking. I was one of those kids sent into exile in right field while playing baseball.

Often the sutures closing up an old wound fail to hold against the onslaught of emotional issues presented by clients. Sometimes the best we can hope for is constant vigilance: "This client is not me. This client is not me. I am sitting over here in the more comfortable chair. I am being paid to sit here, to listen, to react, but not to get into my own stuff."

A final emotional issue worth mentioning concerns those therapists who lack family support for their work. Helping professionals require much nurturance, understanding, and demonstrations of affection. After giving and giving all day long, a therapist can come home with a short fuse and a long list of demands. Tender loving care is indicated until he or she returns to the land of the living. This is especially true for women in the field, who often must contend with more than their fair share of family and household chores in addition to a full work schedule. Single parents also shoulder a disproportionate burden of financial hardships, carpooling, laundry, and late nights spent cleaning house.

Cures for Burnout

First of all, as you'd guess, there's no permanent cure for burnout as some degree of ongoing stress is part of what it means to be a therapist. Even more discouraging is that there are few consistently reliable and effective strategies for counteracting the effects of secondary trauma or compassion fatigue (Bercier & Maynard, 2015). But if this distress reaches the point of impairment, where symptoms begin to affect daily functioning and compromise professional effectiveness, then some sort of intervention is necessary, usually in the form of mandated supervision or personal therapy. The major problem for burned-out professionals is the attitude they bring to their work and life priorities, which at some point has slipped into a condiciton of self-neglect.

For us, just as for our clients, denial is the major impediment to successful treatment of burnout. In the face of dwindling caseloads, client or colleague complaints, family concerns, or obviously dysfunctional behavior (substance abuse, depression, sexual problems, financial irresponsibility, psychosomatic complaints), some clinicians refuse to admit there is a problem, hoping things will improve on their own. As we know only too well, they rarely do.

The result of many of these factors that contribute to burnout is increased isolation and withdrawal on the part of the therapist. As much as any other solution, recruiting family and friends for support has been found to be absolutely critical in mediating the effects of burnout (Rupert et al., 2009). Because it often is difficult for professional helpers to ask for help, the self-destructive patterns become more entrenched and more resistant to treatment. Several self-administered preventions and cures can nevertheless be useful.

Recognize Burnout When You See It or Experience It

It isn't that difficult to notice when a colleague has lost energy and focus. You see the signs so clearly—the professional is acting out, displaying classic signs of depression or anxiety, drinking too much, not honoring commitments, appearing frazzled, making mistakes, and, most of all, denying that there is any problem whatsoever. It is much more difficult to recognize the signs and symptoms of burnout in yourself.

We are all human. We are all struggling to keep ourselves afloat. We are all wrestling with our demons. We all have our issues that continue to plague us. And in the arena of being a therapist, there is no place to hide (try as we might).

Here are some questions to consider. Before you skip this section and move on to the next one, humor me (and yourself) and just read through these queries, attending to what comes up for you. You might find it helpful to talk to someone or to write in your journal afterward in order to process whatever is activated by these questions. Remember that this is a privilege of our job: we are not only permitted but encouraged to be reflective and brutally honest with ourselves (and others).

- What haunts you the most, especially when you are feeling raw or vulnerable?
- In what ways are you not functioning as fully and effectively as you could?
- What are some aspects of your lifestyle that are especially unhealthy?
- What are your most conflicted or chronically dysfunctional relationships?
- Where do you hold your pain?
- In what ways do you medicate yourself (whether with substances or with particular behaviors)?
- What are the lies you tell yourself?
- What do you most spend your time avoiding or hiding from?
- Who is it who most easily gets to you, and what does that mean?
- What are the unresolved issues that have plagued you throughout your life?
- How does all of this affect your work with clients?
- What is it about these questions that you find most threatening?

Because self-identification of the issues stirred up by these questions is difficult, it is advisable to discuss them with a trusted colleague or friend or, better yet, bring them to supervision or your personal therapy. This last option is rarely exercised, though: less than 1% of therapists ever seek personal therapy for issues that crop up in their caseload (Norcross & Connor, 2005).

Do Therapy Differently

The simplest and most direct way to breathe life into unsatisfying work is either to do something else or to do what you are already doing a little (or a lot) differently. The booming business of presenting workshops and seminars attests to the popularity of this particular strategy, even if the effects are short-lived. After an initial surge of enthusiasm upon returning from a workshop or conference, many therapists slip back into the doldrums. A good speaker can be infectious in her spirit, but just as in therapy, unless the participant continues to apply the ideas on a daily basis, regression is likely.

After many years of struggling to sort through the vast array of theoretical orientations, therapeutic technology, and conflicting claims, you may feel more secure sticking with a proven and familiar recipe. Even if you have no particular objection to learning new concepts, new rules, a new vocabulary, and a new set of skills, trying something new seems to mean condemning the old ways to obsolescence. This is hardly the case, as we always retain those ideas that are still helpful. Nevertheless, until therapists encounter discomfort of sufficient magnitude, they may exhibit considerable resistance to radical change. The key, therefore, is to give yourself permission to change a little at a time, to experiment, and to be more creative.

One psychologist had been giving his clients relaxation exercises with great success for years. He had found a proven formula for creating effective and efficient induction procedures, vivid images, and positive results. His clients were still improving (though less so in recent months), but he was feeling much worse. With all the complaints he made about how stale and boring his work felt, with all the options he considered in giving up behavioral strategies, it never occurred to him to simply change his exercise instructions. He did not really need to read them anymore, but he did so because he did not trust himself to work spontaneously. An unusual example of rigidity, this case highlights the point that a psychoanalyst need not become a Rolfing specialist, nor does a Gestalt therapist need to adopt behavior modification, to reenergize her work.

Doing therapy differently means forcing yourself to venture off into uncharted territory where the destination is less well defined. It means joining the client as a partner in the spiritual odyssey. Most of all, it means, paradoxically, conquering burnout by initially working even harder until it no longer is work at all.

Teach Others

There is a very good reason why so many professors do counseling as an avocation and why so many therapists teach, and it has less to do with generating pocket money than with rejuvenating one's enthusiasm. Therapists teach not only as a way of spreading the gospel and increasing referrals and their reputation but also as a way of giving greater meaning to their clinical work. When you explain to others what you do, how you do it, and why you do it a particular way, you are forced to think through the rationale for every intervention.

An ex-therapist, ex-professor, and now university administrator still works with a few clients just to keep her skills honed and her perspective fresh. She still fights for the opportunity to teach one clinical course each semester, even though it means extra work. She does not receive extra compensation, nor do her superiors approve, as it means time away from her office. She does it for her own mental health: "Teaching helps me to be more honest and self-critical. When I talk about what it means to be a good therapist, it helps me to be more that way myself."

Another therapist teaches a graduate-level course even though it means another night away from home each week and only a token honorarium: "I usually get stuck with the classes none of the full-time staff want to teach. But I don't mind. It's a way to get to talk to people in the field who are still eager and fresh. It's a privilege and an honor to work with the really good students. I'd do it for free. I teach this one techniques class that nobody ever likes—not the professors or the students—because it involves making and analyzing verbatim transcripts. My therapy has changed so much since I started studying the work of beginners who know next to nothing. They use low-level and awkward active listening, and yet they are still effective. Since I started going back to the basics in my own work, I'm surprised to find I enjoy it all over again."

A full-time professor relates the impact of teaching on his clinical work: "Questions drive me nuts! The questions some students ask. . . . Like one wiseass asked me how I know that any of my clients ever really get better. Maybe they're just pretending. Now this guy had no intention of being profound; he was just being silly. I put him off with some appropriate remark. But then I started thinking, really thinking, about the reasons I know for sure that clients really change, not just fake it. The more I thought about it, the better I felt about doing therapy."

Clinicians who do research, give public lectures, publish articles, and write books report similar experiences. To teach is to magnify our influence. To teach is to continually evaluate what we do from the perspective of an innocent. We derive greater meaning not only from the single lives that we help improve but in how those lives help us understand and improve the process of change.

Take Personal Responsibility

In every institution in every city of the world, there are therapists who are relatively immune to burnout. They get a tremendous kick out of making a crying child smile or an adult with a plastic smile cry. They stand aloof from the backstabbing, yet they retain their power through their expertise, dependability, and tremendous competence. They take care of themselves and of the people around them. They expect honesty and respect from others. Even in a closed environment, we can choose such colleagues as friends. We can also find ways to exercise more personal control over how we work, as it is precisely a perceived lack of control that most often leads to burnout.

Seeking out enthusiastic colleagues is only one of several practical strategies, which might include any or all of the following:

- Assume as much responsibility for your own growth as you try to assume with your clients.
- Use multiple measures of success in your work, not just the client's explicit gratitude.
- Set limits with demanding clients and colleagues concerning what you are willing to do and what you are not able to do.
- Develop outside interests as a form of renewal—especially activities that exercise parts of your body and mind that go unused during work.

Create Work Breaks

Some therapists are great advocates of work breaks that are used as buffers against stress, as emotional breathers providing time and space to unwind, and as safety valves to blow off steam. For some practitioners, this simply means not scheduling so many appointments consecutively. Other clinicians are more systematic in their efforts. As one therapist relates, "Since I normally start to drag in the early afternoon and begin asking myself why I am still doing this kind of work after all these years, I have learned to program the hours from 2:00 to 4:00 for my own mental health. I read somewhere that this is the time when most mammals take naps and when most industrial accidents take place. I can believe it. Anyway, I take time out from my day to go for a walk, to work out, or to read a novel."

As an example of a therapist who is working in a school or agency, and therefore has less flexibility than in private practice regarding how he structures his time, one professional explains how he keeps burnout at bay: "I build rest periods into my day whenever I can. I might steal a few minutes here and there to meditate or read a magazine. Sometimes when I have an unexpected cancellation—at this place, that happens every day—I force myself to not use the time productively. I like to just close the door of my office and play online games."

Examining the Influences of Technology as a Source of Stress

In many cases, job stress results from a specific, identifiable source. The physical environment may be a factor—for instance, sharing space with a coworker. The relationship that you have with your immediate supervisor is another definite possibility. Nothing is more frustrating than an incompetent boss who enjoys having others under his thumb; demands stringent accountability; likes paperwork; sends conflicting orders; invites honest feedback, but only if it is pleasant; and understands very little about therapy.

In his first job out of graduate school, a man reports that while he counseled young adolescents in a cubicle without a door or ceiling, his supervisor would listen with her ear to the wall. Every time he said anything to a client that she did not agree with, the supervisor would bang on the wall and yell out, "Don't tell him that!" When the startled child and fledgling counselor then continued their conversation in a hushed whisper, another bang would ensue, followed by the words, "If you two have to be so secretive, you shouldn't be talking about whatever you are talking about." The counselor now works as a salesman.

Another major source of stress in contemporary life is the *dis*connection that results from being so continuously connected through technology. We are always accessible and available through mobile devices, phones, text messages, social media, and—coming soon—communication implants. You can't help but notice how much relationships have changed as result of the technological advances of the past several years. Some of these breakthroughs have been remarkably useful and exciting, whereas other experiences—such as someone in a movie theater who insists on checking his messages every few minutes, or someone on a cell phone talking in a booming voice—are downright annoying. No matter where you are these days—in a theater, mall, or airport, standing in line or sitting in any public space—you notice practically everyone engaged with his or her mobile device. It is not unusual to see a family of four sitting at a restaurant having dinner, each person talking or texting someone else while they sit in one another's company. It is not that rare that clients want to answer their mobile phones or messages while sitting in session (and we often wish we could do the same!).

Turkle (2015) makes the case that with people constantly tethered to their devices there's no downtime anymore to relax; we've lost the art of daydreaming because we are constantly occupied with distractions—or more demands for our time. Turkle also makes the point that people are losing their capacity for empathy and deep conversations, valuing convenience, efficiency, and what she calls "the illusion of friendship without the demands of intimacy" (2015, p. 7). At least this bodes well for the future of our profession because people will inevitably become more hungry for meaningful conversation that is actually spontaneous and uncontrolled.

It is as if practically nobody is fully present anymore. In recent years there has been an erosion of attention and an addiction to technology that keeps us connected to news, networks, information, and friends, but that also disconnects us from those who are in the room. It is rare nowadays to have anyone's undivided attention. There is even a high probability that as you are reading these words, you are doing something else at the same time.

As much as we value technological advances in terms of increased productivity and efficiency, not to mention enjoyment, there are consequences that affect every other aspect of our lives, relationships most of all. Such a barrage of stimuli allows for negligible downtime, making it even more difficult to recover from all the varied interactions.

The Impaired Therapist

The terms *burnout* and *impairment* are often used interchangeably in the literature, although there is a significant difference in that burnout may not necessarily lead to impairment sufficient to harm clients even if it most definitely shortchanges them in some ways. An impaired therapist, however, is dysfunctional to the point of actually hurting others, as well as himself. Moreover, burnout can be limited to the work setting alone, whereas impairment usually affects *every* domain in a professional's life.

Burnout, or rustout, may certainly be a common condition experienced by almost everyone at some time during his or her career. Serious impairment is probably limited to 10% of the profession at any one time if we count clinical depression, substance abuse, chronic illness, intense loneliness, boundary violations, and so on (Schoener, 2005; Reamer, 2015; Thoreson, Miller, & Krauskopf, 1989). Among those therapists who work with people who have experienced severe trauma, as many as 25% may struggle with corresponding secondary trauma or compassion fatigue—a condition with much quicker onset than the more insidious forms of burnout, countertransference, or impairment (Figley, 2002). Then there is also the so-called "wounded healer," who may be hobbling a bit but not to the point that it is significantly interfering with professional effectiveness (Zerubavel & Wright, 2012). I suppose *all* of us are wounded in some way shape or form.

Then there are those who suffer from the usual, pedestrian varieties of personality disorder, anxiety, and obsessive-compulsive disorders that led them to seek a profession in which they could "hide." We all know someone in the field who is seriously disturbed and consequently preys on clients through sexual exploitation, inappropriate value indoctrination, or other forms of pathological manipulation and control.

Dr. Narcissus is one such individual. Like more than a few charming manipulators, he has found the practice of therapy to be a haven in which to seduce people to do his bidding. Once upon a time, he entertained fantasies of being a true savior of humankind. Because he was brighter and better looking than most, and was endowed with special talents, he felt that he was entitled to accolades from clients and colleagues alike.

In the early days, his clients did not show him sufficient respect, nor did they feel sufficiently grateful for his efforts to help them. Some were even angry and put off by his arrogance. He began to find therapeutic work tedious and unsatisfying. With no other options available to him (like any seriously distressed person, he suffered perceptual distortions that clouded his judgment), he began to experiment with ways to make his work more satisfying.

It started innocently enough with requests that his clients show a little more appreciation. Things eventually escalated to the point where he seduced them emotionally, and a few times sexually, feeling that extraordinary individuals are exempt from the normal laws of mortals. After all, he felt that he was doing nothing wrong because he was providing a service to his clients.

After a close call in which a client threatened to file a complaint, and observing an increasingly litigious atmosphere regarding sexual exploitation, he limited himself thereafter to emotional seductions. He manipulated and cajoled as many of his clients as he could to become totally dependent on him. It reached the point where when he went on vacation, several of his clients booked rooms in the same resort at the same time so that he could continue to see them.

We are all familiar with colleagues who continue to operate even though they are doing great harm. If we were to confront them directly with suspicions about what we have heard, they would seem shocked and indignant. As mentioned, being distressed or wounded, however, does not necessarily mean that a professional is impaired. Presumably, it is possible to experience some degree of crisis or trauma in one's life and still conduct one's work, if not superlatively, then at least adequately.

It is unfortunate that when burnout does lead to significant impairment, it is the nature of the therapist's dysfunction to deny that there is anything wrong. There is a hole in the professional's conscience, evidence of sociopathy, or, more often, a kind of blinding attempt to save himself at the expense of others. It is when he can no longer deal with stress or keep symptoms of burnout under control that a therapist is most likely to engage in unethical conduct or to make self-serving decisions that harm others.

Whereas it is unlikely that anyone reading these words is seriously impaired (I suspect that such an individual would not be open to confronting the personal nuances of his or her work), there are many among us who can feel themselves slipping, inexorably, toward continued rustout and eventual distress.

The psychologically impaired therapist has probably ignored his problems for months if not years. His energy has been depleted, and a sense of cynical hopelessness has set in. He will infect many colleagues as well as his clients before the disease runs its course to retirement, disablement, or death.

To make it easier for therapists to ask for help, a number of state professional societies have organized hotlines for impaired therapists. In an effort both to reduce the proliferation of therapists who act out in their sessions and to control excessive drug and alcohol abuse among their colleagues, professional therapists stand ready to provide assistance where and when it is needed. We all have a duty and responsibility to promote not only the well-being of our clients and our own mental health but also the functioning of our colleagues as well. That boredom and burnout often lead to more severe personal consequences, such as depression, drug addiction, suicide, divorce, and the breakdown of professional effectiveness, is inevitable. We all entered the helping profession to make a difference in the world. The place to start is with ourselves—and then with our peers.

10

That Which Is Not Said

LIKE EVERY PROFESSION, the practice of therapy has its secrets that lurk in the background behind much of what we do. These are issues that are rarely spoken about even among ourselves, much less in public forums. I have alluded to several of these points previously, but I'd like to summarize them as the basis for what follows in this chapter about the taboo and forbidden in the life of a therapist.

Essential Secrets

I've always thought that one of the gifts—and burdens—of being a therapist is our commitment to some semblance of truth-seeking, plain-talking, and courageous challenges of life's paradoxes and incongruities. We have learned that secrecy and denial within families or groups can lead to all kinds of self-delusions and compromised functioning. And that's one reason why we supposedly believe in complete transparency and total honesty as the basis for our work and lives. Yet there are a few areas in which we often present ourselves as less than genuine and frank. Fair warning: this discussion is both uncomfortable and bewildering.

You may not agree with all of the issues selected. You may also justifiably believe I am exaggerating at times to make a point. But you will have to acknowledge that there is a shade of truth to the notion that the very foundation of what we do is laid on shaky ground.

Much of the Time We Don't Know What We're Doing

I don't mean to imply that therapists are not competent, skilled, highly trained experts who have a clear treatment plan and defensible rationale for what we do and why we do it, grounded in empirical research and evidence-based clinical experience. What I do mean is that a lot of the time we are operating in the dark, pretending that we know far more than we really do, and often clueless about what is really going on with a client at any given time. There. It feels good to say that.

Feeling clueless isn't all that rare for most therapists, who admit to having questions about their effectiveness about 25% of the time, often throughout most of their careers (Theriault & Gazzola, 2006). I don't mean to say that there is anything necessarily wrong with occasional fugue states in which we are wandering around as lost as our clients. We are required to pretend to possess far more confidence than we often feel and to provide answers to questions that we barely understand. We hold cherished theories that are sometimes not all that useful in making sense of what we are observing or experiencing in any moment of time. If you were pressed to be really honest and to rate on a scale of 1 to 10 how confident you are that your diagnosis of a given client is accurate, your understanding of this person complete and comprehensive, and your chosen treatment strategy the correct and best alternative available among all possible options, I'd be surprised (and skeptical) if you could score higher than a 5 or 6.

I had been working for several months with Kyle, who had been presenting symptoms of panic disorder. It was an easy diagnosis to make because of the clear narrative he presented, including sudden onset of heart palpitations, difficulty breathing, loss of control, unremitting anxiety, and feelings of impending doom. Further, there was never any precipitating event or any identified organic cause.

Kyle was a wonderfully responsive and cooperative client. He did everything I asked of him. He worked hard in sessions, practiced new skills outside of sessions, and had an amazing capacity for insight into his problems and their probable source. The only problem was that after all this time, the symptoms never reduced in frequency or intensity; they sometimes became even worse.

By mutual consent, we agreed that it might be a good idea to take some time off from therapy and perhaps consult with a psychiatrist for medication to manage the symptoms. This is not, however, the end of the story.

Several months later, Kyle scheduled an appointment that I assumed was to resume therapy. After he settled himself in his accustomed chair, he told me that he had recently sold his home, which required a thorough inspection.

I encouraged him to continue, all the while wondering why he was telling me this. I noticed that Kyle looked more relaxed than I'd ever seen him before. I assumed that all the things I had taught him had finally kicked into gear and that he had recovered from the panic disorder quite beautifully.

Kyle then proceeded to explain that during this home inspection, it was discovered that there had been a furnace leak in the house, producing toxic levels of gas that were actually the cause of his symptoms. Once the furnace was repaired, his so-called panic disorder disappeared. All along he never needed a therapist but a furnace repair specialist!

I think about Kyle a lot during those times when I feel so certain I know what is going on with a client and so clear about the symptoms, etiology, and best treatment. When I hear colleagues speak with such authority at conferences, supervision meetings, and in books about what they believe is truth in our field or in client experiences, I can't help but remember Kyle as a reminder that so much of what we pretend to know is merely illusion, conjecture, supposition, and myth.

Even When We Do Think We Know What Is Going On, Others Would Disagree

If you strenuously disagree with the first point and feel you that do have strong evidence to support your favored ideas about what is going on with your clients almost all the time, consider how many other highly knowledgeable and experienced experts would disagree with you. As convinced as you might be about any particular case conceptualization and treatment plan, as certain as you are about the best way to proceed, it is more than a little disturbing to admit that there are notable experts in the field who would strongly object to the path you are taking and maybe even recommend the exact opposite approach.

How often have you sought supervision with a number of different colleagues and been given *very* conflicting advice about what to do? How often have you heard passionate debates between respected therapists, each of whom advocates a radically different course of action? How can we possibly reconcile that a client comes in for treatment, presenting symptoms of depression, and might be told by a variety of mental health professionals that the best treatment is medication, or exercise and meditation, or brief cognitive therapy, or long-term psychodynamic therapy, or systemic family therapy, or . . . well, you get the point.

There are certainly points of consensus about which (almost) every practitioner would agree. For instance, most clinicians would subscribe to the notion that the relationship is a crucial factor in any kind of treatment, regardless of the interventions or strategies employed. There would also likely be agreement that good therapy requires some degree of increased insight *and* constructive action taken, especially the kind that leads to lasting change once sessions end. There is also pretty convincing evidence that such common factors are implicit in all good therapy. Nevertheless, in spite of a few points of agreement, many of the ideas you are certain about can be refuted by others who would passionately take a contrary position—with their own supporting evidence.

To add to our confusion, we can never really be certain that what our clients tell is us is going on represents even an approximation of truth. Clients lie all the time, not only about their symptoms and problems, but sometimes even about their identities. I once saw a client who made up a whole life for himself that was pure fantasy. I've interviewed other therapists who reported instances of their clients pretending to be terminally ill, neglecting to mention a fatal disease, faking suicidal intent, even lying about who they really are, or, in one case, even stealing the therapist's own identity—and wallet (Kottler, 2010; Kottler & Carlson, 2011). Therapy is an enterprise that is based on mutual trust, and sometimes that faith is compromised, leading to further doubt and questions.

But here's the good news: there is some evidence that therapists who have a certain amount of self-doubt, who continually question themselves and what they are doing, often do far better work (Nissen-Lie et al., 2015). They engage in constructive coping strategies such as trying to view the difficulties from multiple perspectives, soliciting lots of feedback from colleagues (and clients), and mostly giving themselves permission to be stuck and lost. This is in marked contrast to those who are far less proactive and instead reveal their frustration and complaints, most of which are out of their control.

We Can Never Be Sure If and When We Ever Help Anyone

This is the secret that really drives me crazy. There are clients whom we think—no, we are *positive*—we helped, yet we discover at some time in the future that they were "fooling" us or that the changes didn't last beyond a few weeks. As mentioned above, clients don't necessarily provide accurate and reliable reports on their progress, shading things in one direction or the other. It's also difficult to rely totally on the opinions of family members who may have their own agenda.

Clients tell us that they are making fantastic gains, but we later learn it was all distortion, denial, and fabrication. Even when we are reasonably certain that significant progress was accomplished, we rarely discover whether the changes lasted over time or whether there was a relapse. Further, we have trouble even deciding how best to measure positive outcomes, whether to trust client self-reports, family reports, or our own observations of behavior during sessions.

Think of cases in which you are certain, beyond any doubt, that you made a difference and that the helping effort was successful. How do you really know that the evidence upon which you are basing this assessment was truly complete, reliable, valid, and accurate?

Then there are supposed treatment failures that, you may later learn, were actually successes. A client drops out of therapy with no warning. There is no further contact and no response to any attempt to follow up. What does this mean? Did the person quit because of dissatisfaction with the results or because the goals were already reached? We live with the reality that most of the time we really don't know what happened to our clients after they stopped attending sessions.

Even When We Think We Helped Someone, We Can't Be Certain What Actually Made the Difference

You found a case that you are absolutely certain was a success. No doubt whatsoever. You have your evidence, and it is irrefutable.

Next question: What do you think made the difference and produced this result?

Whatever explanation you come up with, whatever thoughts you have about this cause-and-effect relationship, how can you ever be sure that this is what *really* made the greatest difference?

The obvious solution is to ask the client, during the last session or even as a follow-up some time later, what helped the most. This approach assumes that the client actually knows the answer, which raises other questions. If you've checked this out with your clients, haphazardly or systematically, you know that this is indeed a risky path. The response you get is often unpredictable and hardly what you wanted to hear. Clients will tell you all kinds of things you said or did that you don't even remember. They will ascribe the changes to accidental or serendipitous things that were completely unrelated to sessions. They will point to some incident that even now seems rather trivial and irrelevant. Or they will tell you they really don't know, shrug, and then make something up.

I am by no means suggesting that we stop asking clients to describe their views of what helped them most; rather, I am offering a reminder that such reports are incomplete and often flawed. One of the most important things we do in our work is to solicit meaningful feedback from consumers of our service about what we did that was most and least helpful. Nevertheless, there is uncertainty and confusion surrounding what we do and how and why it works.

What Don't We Talk About?

In addition to supervision and our own personal therapy, we do sometimes confide to friends, colleagues, and family about our own stuff. Yet there are still areas that remain mostly out of bounds; if we talk about them at all, they are in low whispers or in jest. One therapist confided, "The more I think about it, the more I realize how much of my work and my life that I keep to myself. After having seen over three thousand clients in my career, I could uncover a hornet's nest."

So, what is it exactly that therapists don't talk about much? There are a few authors who have examined this territory (e.g., Adams, 2014; Buechler, 212; Freudenberger & Robbins, 1979; Guy, 1987; Henry, Sims, & Spray, 1973; Kottler, 2015a; Kuchuck, 2014; Pope, Sonne, & Greene, 2006; Schwartz & Flowers, 2006; Sussman, 1995) and identified some of the central taboo topics. What are the secrets that we live with in various states of denial, or that we at least distance ourselves from?

We're Not Really Listening as Much as We Pretend

In theory, and as a myth, therapists are absolutely, completely, and continuously focused in sessions with laser-like intensity. We supposedly hang on every word uttered, immerse ourselves totally in the client's world, and exhibit the kind of hovering attention necessary to scrutinize the subtle meanings of everything said or done. We are always analyzing, processing, interpreting, making connections, formulating hypotheses, monitoring progress, revising diagnostic impressions, reformulating treatment plans, preparing the next intervention and the next one and the one after that—just as if we were in a chess match and thinking a half dozen moves in advance.

I don't mean to imply that there aren't some sessions that *do* hold our full attention, flying by so fast that we can't believe they're over in what seemed like a few minutes. I mentioned earlier that one of our secrets is that much of the time (sometimes most of the time), we are hardly present at all. There is a continual dialogue in any conversation, not only with the person to whom we are speaking but also with ourselves; psychotherapy is no exception. Sometimes we find ourselves lost in thoughts that are sparked by something that came up in a session. We are constantly personalizing content, asking ourselves how it relates to our own lives. Words, phrases, topics that come up, and images send us on little trips within our head, launch us into elaborate fantasies, and lead us to think things we would never say aloud.

Let's listen in on one sample of a therapist's inner dialogue during a session:

> Huh? What does that mean, that look? Is she avoiding eye contact? Hiding? Or just bored? Maybe she was just looking at her watch. I can't quite see the face of her watch to catch the time. Can I sneak a peek at my watch without her noticing?
>
> Gotta remember to make a note after the session about the names of her sisters. Carrie, Kyla, Meghan. Or is it Maggie? Damn. Forgot again. No, I think it is Meghan.
>
> Speaking of forgetting, I have to remember to return that call from this morning. I didn't have time to eat anything, and now my stomach is grumbling again. Where should I go for lunch? I'd love a good salad.
>
> Uh-oh. She's looking at me now, expecting me to say something. I wasn't paying attention. Doesn't matter. She keeps repeating herself, talking about her ex-boyfriend over and over. Whining. Complaining. She just doesn't get it that the relationship is over. And she won't listen to me anyway.
>
> Why is it so hard for me to listen to her? Why do I keep escaping like this? Is it me or her? I wonder if it's safe to bring this up with her. No, it would probably scare her away. But I should remember to bring this up sometime because I notice it keeps happening. I bet others find it hard to listen to her too. I should check that out with her. I'll ask her.
>
> "So, what do you make of all that?"
>
> Whew. That'll keep her going for a while. Where was I? Oh yeah, trying to stay awake. I need coffee. Hey, that reminds me: it's time I bought an espresso machine. I bet I'd end up saving money in the long run. I'll look up some reviews online after she leaves in . . . only 22 minutes.
>
> Oh crap. We have that meeting today. I should bring up this case and why it's so hard to stay present with her. But they'll ask me a bunch of questions I won't know the answer to. But it is interesting why I can't stay with her, and now I think this is really about me.

It is this last thought during this brief stream of consciousness that forces the therapist to confront her internal voice and its particular meaning.

When We Are Listening, It Is Often with a Critical Ear

In theory, therapists are supposed to be demonstrating compassion, concern, respect, warmth, and openness in our client relationships. That is what we strive for and what we are paid to deliver. However, the reality of what goes on inside us during sessions with certain clients is far different than advertised. There is a critical voice inside our heads, one that we rarely admit to, much less speak aloud. It is that voice that whispers, or sometimes screams, things like

- "What the hell are you talking about?"
- "Will you stop whining and complaining already? I'm tired of listening to this crap."
- "Give me a break! I can't believe you actually said that."
- "Whoa! That's just about the strangest thing I've ever heard."
- "If you could only hear what you sound like right now, you'd stop this nonsense and get on with your life."
- "Are you deaf or something? Didn't you just hear what I said? How many times do I have to repeat myself?"
- "When is it going to occur to you that nothing is going to change until you stop blaming everyone else in your life?"
- "Do I like you, you are wondering? You've got to be kidding me. I can barely get through this hour."
- "That is just about the sickest thing I've ever heard of. I can't believe you do that."
- "I swear, if you tell that same story one more time, I'm going to strangle you."

Granted, such critical thoughts are pretty compelling evidence that the therapist's compassion and empathy are compromised. But remember, these are *secret* thoughts that we rarely admit or talk about. That doesn't mean, however, that we don't have an internal running commentary that can often be quite critical and judgmental. In fact, of all the subjects mentioned in this book, this is the one that most therapists I interviewed wanted to talk about the most because it seemed so forbidden.

One therapist mentioned a client she has been seeing for quite a long time, someone she enjoys working with although "she's a bit of a storyteller." What the therapist means by this is that the client rambles a lot and goes off on tangents until she is forcibly reminded to return to the subject at hand. "She'll just talk and talk and talk and talk, going on and on, sometimes never getting to any point that I can figure out."

The therapist reaches a level of frustration where it is especially hard to restrain herself. "There was this one particular day when she was just impossible. And I know that some of it was my own issues because I had expectations, and I was getting very impatient. So after a while, I had tried a number of different things to see if I could get her to focus, and absolutely nothing was working. I just completely lost my empathy. And all I could hear was my own voice inside of my head screaming, 'SHUT UP! Shut up shut up shut up!' For the next few minutes all I could hear was my own voice inside my head screaming for her to just shut up. I don't even know what she was saying the whole time."

The therapist really had to work hard to calm herself down and regain some composure, silencing the critical voice. "I concentrated on my breathing and, you know, trying to find that empathy again. But it was really difficult. I had to really pay attention to my body and how I was getting frustrated and how it felt in my body. It took a while, but eventually I grounded myself. I decided to let it go and accept where she was and what her agenda was. Once I was able to do that I could accept her again. But the whole experience was agonizing."

Another example of a different kind of internal critical voice is told by a therapist who discovered something about a client that she strongly objected to on moral grounds. The client was talking about a family member she held in the highest regard who believed in the most sexist, oppressive attitudes imaginable. "When I heard my client talk about this person with such admiration, I couldn't believe it! This was my favorite client, and it felt like a betrayal. I could feel myself putting distance between us. This was hardly the first time I disagreed with a client's value choices, but this time I felt really disappointed in her." This therapist was especially confused about this incident because she had felt so unprepared to deal with it. "We learn in our training about how clients put us on a pedestal, but here was a case in which I had put *her* on a pedestal from which she fell." She had idealized her client and then, after realizing that some of her own core values were challenged, found herself becoming quite critical to the point that it definitely got in the way.

A third example of how a therapist's critical inner voice makes itself known is related to an ongoing theme of envy toward others. All throughout the week this therapist encounters clients who are far more successful in terms of financial security than she will ever be. Yet they are wounded and dysfunctional, possessing nothing special that she doesn't have. "I feel like such a fraud and hypocrite, so petty even admitting this, but you asked about secrets, right? So when I listen to some of my clients talk about all their accomplishments and opportunities, I think to myself, 'Why not me? Why don't I get to do that?' "

The therapist admits that this envy and critical voice are problematic for her in two ways: "Not only does it feel bad to admit I am envious about my clients' successes, but I tend not to believe people when they say they are happy for my own accomplishments. I mistrust that. So I'm not only limited in the joy I feel for others, but also in the good wishes I am able to take in and appreciate."

Although most of the clients this therapist sees are from disadvantaged backgrounds, it is the few from relatively privileged situations who most activate her critical voice. "I really do want to fully embrace and celebrate with my clients for what they are fortunate enough to have and own, or the opportunities they have that I will never have access to. If there is something I don't have and can't afford, the way to deal with it is to convince myself I didn't want it in the first place. This, you can imagine, creates its own world of 'things not said.' "

Sometimes the things we hear from clients are so disturbing that even a saint would shrink in disgust. A therapist had been doing an intake with a new client, listening to him go on and on for more than an hour about how his drinking problem was the result of his wife nagging him all the time. "Maybe he was trying to shock me or something, but he told me this one story about how he just wanted some peace and quiet. So what does this guy do? He tells me that he pulled out a gun, put it up to his forehead, and pulled the trigger—twice! He pulled the trigger of a gun pressed to his forehead twice just to get his wife to shut up!"

All the while he heard this story, the therapist made the appropriate sympathetic response, nodded his head, and kept his face blank, but inside he was thinking to himself: "What the hell? This guy is such a jerk, such a total jerk. I can barely stand being in the room with him. I just wanted to get him out of there. I was doing my best trying to be accepting and empathic, but I just couldn't hold it together. For the rest of the interview, all I could think of is what a lucky bastard he was that the gun didn't go off both times. I really hate to admit this, but his wife sure would have been better off if it had."

In each of these examples, therapists are just admitting that they are human and have personal reactions to what they hear, sometimes letting their guard down. This is not really so surprising or unexpected. And it isn't so much a secret as it is a subject that we don't talk about often except when pressed by a supervisor or when we find that the critical attitude is getting in the way of being helpful.

Feeling Superior

We may act with appropriate modesty and restraint, but deep down inside there is sometimes a feeling of being very special. Such a belief is certainly understandable given that we do have special skills and extensive knowledge. We do understand things that most others could never grasp. We hear nuances in language to which others are oblivious and observe subtleties in behavior that are invisible to the untrained eye. We can even appear to read minds because of our heightened sensitivity and ability to discern hidden intentions and motives, uncover unconscious thoughts, and predict what people might do or say next.

A therapist talked at great length about how listening to people's problems all day made her feel much better about herself. "I've had more than my fair share of failed romantic relationships," she said. "So when I hear about celebrities who break up, or my clients who are having trouble in their relationships, I don't feel like such a failure myself. Of course I also like hearing about other people's troubles because it helps me to forget about my own."

In this case, the therapist elaborated how she enjoys being with her clients, in part, because they are in worse shape than she'll ever be. "I do feel superior, and with good reason. Some of the clients I see are barely functional. In some ways, I feel safe around them because they can't hurt me. They defer to me. I feel confident and strong and secure."

Indeed we do spend most of our time in the company of those who are wounded, crippled, or unenlightened. We are used to being treated with a certain amount of respect and deference; after all, we are the closest thing to gurus that still exist in our culture. And we may come to believe over time that we really *are* smarter and more capable than most others, often because it feels like that is true.

Dysfunctional Colleagues

One of the most poorly kept secrets in our profession is that we have colleagues who are crazier than some of the most disturbed clients we've ever seen. They may have gotten into this work in the first place for reasons that have nothing to do with helping people. They enjoy manipulating and controlling others because they feel so out of control themselves. They feel a sense of power from exploiting others. In many cases, they just can't seem to help themselves: they are victims of the same kinds of mental disorders—major depression, personality disorders, panic attacks, schizophrenia—that afflict the rest of the population.

We certainly have more than our fair share of brethren who are psychologically troubled. Some are struggling with addictions or act out in ways harmful to themselves and others. As previously discussed, people choose this field for a variety of reasons that may have little to do with helping people but rather helping themselves. They may seek to stabilize their own lifelong depression, anxiety, or dysfunctional personality through the work they do. They may enjoy positions of power and authority that allow them to control and manipulate others. They may be trying to work out their own stuff by trying to help others with parallel issues. They may exhibit rampant narcissism that comes from taking themselves way too seriously.

Besides whatever dysfunctional coping style that therapists bring to the table, there is also the stress related to the job, driving professionals over the edge, wearing down their systems from the continuous immersion in clients' toxic material. Vicarious trauma, compassion fatigue, projective identification, relationship conflicts, collegial disputes, lack of support, financial problems, family problems, and just the grind of the job can lead to various forms of destructive self-medication. Substance and alcohol abuse are common coping strategies.

The media absolutely loves to ridicule therapists as unethical, outrageous, insecure, self-indulgent, sadistic, personally flawed, or seriously wounded, even as serial killers who eat their clients. In one study of over fifteen hundred films in which there was a therapist as a character, 80% of them portrayed the professional in a negative light as unethical, manipulative, incompetent, or evil (Flowers & Frizler, 2004). Perhaps this isn't all that suprising considering that within the medical specialties, psychiatrists are the least respected physicians in terms of their integrity, honesty, and ethics. Whereas generally most doctors are rated quite high in these dimensions by 70% of those surveyed, the majority of psychiatrists (59%) are perceived as lacking in these traits (Gallup, 2015).

I don't think of myself as particularly naïve about the rather eccentric members of our profession. Although the vast majority of clinicians are not only highly ethical and professional but also personally masterful in their own lives, there are a few among us who engage in the sort of bizarre behavior that makes our clients seem tame by comparison. Some of these folks are relatively harmless, even endearingly eccentric, but others are downright dangerous.

Raise your hand if you know somebody within the profession who is more than a little strange, if not downright disturbed.

I was assigned to supervise a therapist who was so anxious and fragile that she insisted that we sit on opposite sides of the room with the door open. I once dropped a pen on the floor, and when I stooped over to pick it up, she went into a catatonic stupor, fearing that I was going to hurt her in some way. I assume she had been abused by someone in a position of power, but she would never agree to speak about that. In fact, she would hardly speak at all.

The really amazing thing to me is that her clients seemed to improve in spite of her personal problems. They must have felt safe in the presence of someone else who was so vulnerable. It sure blew to hell one of my cherished beliefs that the essence of our therapeutic work takes place because of the ways we model personal effectiveness.

I've known therapists who scream at their clients, browbeating them into submission. I have heard of others who do things that seem so bizarre and inappropriate that it is amazing that anyone would ever come back to see them again—yet they have full practices!

I saw a new referral a while ago, and when I asked her what she expected from me, she said she hoped I would pay attention to her.

"What do you mean?" I asked.

"You know," she said, "like look at me and talk to me." "What else would I do?" I said, more than a little confused.

It was then she told me about her previous therapist, who used to polish and paint her nails during sessions. Once a month she would vacuum and dust the room during the conversation.

"And you put up with this for how long?" I asked.

"Not that long, just a few years."

About this same time, a friend asked me a question about his therapy. I was reluctant, of course, to get involved, but he assured me that he just wanted to ask a question. He had been seeing the same therapist for over 15 years and she had been some help to him, but recently he had been having some doubts about her approach.

Warily, I asked what they were doing together. He reported that this therapist was seeing him, his wife, and two adult children (in their thirties) for individual sessions once each week, plus seeing all four of them in a family session. That didn't seem unreasonable until he confided that this had been going on for years and that she insisted that he pay for everyone's treatment because he was responsible for all their problems. He estimated that he had paid her hundreds of thousands dollars. Even more disturbing: he admitted that things were only getting worse.

I could go on and on, but any of us can name our own examples of weird or dysfunctional therapists who can barely get along in their own lives, much less help anyone else. This might be our profession's dirtiest, darkest secret: that there are those among us who are severely disabled, if not predators who exploit others' vulnerability.

Our profession attracts the psychologically maimed and wounded for the best of reasons. Some of us were abused, neglected, or damaged as children. Others among us suffer from depression, anxiety, addictions, and other emotional struggles that led us to seek help and, perhaps ultimately, led us to seek training in therapy as a way to make the most from our experiences. Such painful trials and tribulations have had meaning and value in our lives to the extent that the lessons learned provided authenticity and greater empathy toward our clients who suffer in similar ways. Rather than disqualifying us, having been wounded can provide us with special understanding and compassion for others—*if* we are aware of these issues and work on them in supervision and our own therapy.

Maybe it is our being so used to multiple views of what is normal or impaired that leads us to be hesitant about confronting colleagues who appear out of control. Although we are ethically mandated to confront (and report) colleagues who are dysfunctional, this rarely happens. In bringing up these uncomfortable and negative aspects of being a therapist, my intention is not to air our dirty laundry but rather to make it far easier for us to talk about these issues with one another in more honest and constructive ways. As the next chapter elaborates further, it is the lies we tell—to ourselves and others—that eat away at our integrity and congruence.

11

Lies We Tell Ourselves—and Others

SOME OF THE negative personal consequences of being a therapist derive less from the pressure of clients, supervisors, and work schedules than they do from some form of self-deceit. We thus continue the discussion of some rather taboo and uncomfortable topics that may sully our image of maintaining the highest standards of honesty and truth.

Most of these forms of self-deception are harmless little fictionalizations that we are slightly aware of but choose to ignore. Others are buried deeper, beyond our consciousness, embedded within our system of denial, rationalizations, and distortions. "We flatter ourselves, and each other," one therapist remarks rather strongly, "we exaggerate, bluff, falsify, conceal, disassemble, hoodwink, over-simplify, bury our heads and avert our gaze with such skill and speed that we hardly notice" (Marar, 2008, p. 3). Therapists may lie most often to protect others from getting hurt, but also to protect ourselves with inaccurate or skewed case notes, carefully edited case presentations, covering up our mistakes, and exaggerating our outcomes. Therapists, like everyone else, also lie to ourselves and others about our abilities considering that something like 90% of practitioners believe they are better than their peers, which is also similar to the number of drivers who think they are superior to others on the road.

There are itty-bitty lies and those that are much more insidious. There are lies that are so obviously untruthful that we do not really consider them designed to dupe anyone. There are lies all around us—in the charters and policies and procedure manuals of our facilities, in the minutes of the board meetings and public advisory meetings, in the purposes of an organization: not only to help people or make the world a better place but also to make money, to provide tax write-offs, to pay off political favors, to keep a few people's egos or bellies well fed, or to satisfy some bureaucratic imperative.

We live especially with the lies that our clients bring to us every day. The really honest clients do not even pretend to disguise their fabrications. And we humor them as well, lying when we pretend to believe that they had a happy childhood, that therapy is such fun, or that the check they owe us is in the mail.

Nearly every beginning therapy session begins with a lie, when the client says things like "I want some help," when he really means, "I want you to fix me." If the client were really honest, the opening statement would go something like this:

> Look, I don't really want to be here. If you want to know the truth, I don't really have a problem; everyone else does. They're the ones who should be here, not me. So since you are asking me what I want from these sessions, that's easy: what I want is for you to agree with me. If that is not completely possible, then the next best thing is for you to do whatever you do to fix me. But I don't want to have to do any of the work. And most of all—absolutely no pain, please! I don't mind a little polite conversation, but don't push me, don't argue with me, and don't ever tell me that I'm wrong.

After clients tell their lies, then we respond with our own. After all, who would ever come back to see us a second time if we told clients what we really think and what was really in store for them?

> Look, I have no intention of doing what you want me to do. First of all, I can't fix anything; only you can do that. Second, you are the problem. I've only met you for 5 minutes, and already I have trouble liking you because you blame everyone and everything for what's gone wrong in your life but refuse to accept one shred of responsibility. Third, I don't have a clue what is going on with you, nor do I know if I can really help you at all.

Because this opening would not go over very well, instead we tell clients much of what they want to hear (in the first session, anyway); otherwise, they likely wouldn't return. We tell them that we're glad they came to us (a little lie, because we aren't so sure yet), that they definitely can profit from our work (a bigger lie, because we have no idea yet what is going on), and that we think that they have a good understanding of their situation (a nice compliment but a gross exaggeration).

We live with such frequent dishonesty from our clients' disclosures and reports—some of them unconscious omissions, others deliberate falsifications—that we sometimes forget the rough fit between a childhood memory and its repetition years later after being squeezed through the mind's protective sieve. This distinction between narrative and historical truth totally debunks the myth of the client as unbiased reporter and the therapist as unbiased listener. To support this idea, Spense (1982) reviewed the process of therapy: the client relates an unfinished story in finished form, creating meaning, transitions, and completion of memories that are actually quite muddled; more of the historical truth is lost during the process of translating images into words; finally, the therapist distorts the truth of what actually occurred even more by supplying contextual assumptions to fill in gaps. The whole basis on which therapy is built rests on very distorted, deceptive, inaccurate, exaggerated, and subjective information that may bear very little resemblance to whatever occurred in the client's life. In addition, the whole historical foundation of the profession was built on a lie—that repressed memories are real and that we all want to have sex with our parents.

One of the most influential training films of all time, the *Gloria* demonstration with Fritz Perls, Albert Ellis, and Carl Rogers, turned out to be a huge lie. In one investigation of the film's recording, Rosenthal (2011) interviewed the producer and participants, reviewed the transcripts, and researched Gloria's own story of the experience. And what he discovered was that Gloria was coerced and pressured by the producer, who was actually her therapist, to say that Perls was the best therapist to help her when that was not at all the case. In fact, she was fairly traumatized by her interactions with the blunt-speaking Perls, who called her a "phony" over and over as a way to provoke her.

Because it is difficult, if not impossible, ever to find out what really happened in a client's life—given the lapses of memory, the limits of language, the subjectivity of perceptions, and the influences of culture—we become comfortable with a certain level of deception, distortion, and half-truth. We settle for an approximation of truth, in our clients and in ourselves. The result of this situation, coupled with a mind trained to detect the intricacies of rationalization and intellectualization, is a therapist who lives under the illusion of Truth and Justice. But scratch us and we bleed. We are not all that we appear to be.

Games Therapists Play

We deliberately cultivate our aura of mystery and omnipotence, not to deceive, but to increase our influencing power. No self-respecting wizard or magician, or any professional for that matter, could expect to be effective if he gave away the tricks of his trade. And we have a set of special skills that we use to convince the Dorothys and Scarecrows in the Land of Oz that we are indeed powerful wizards.

For example, clients are constantly amazed at how we seem to know exactly when the hour is over, as if we had a special internal mechanism to sense the subtle changes of time. After years of practice, we are rarely caught glancing at the clock on the wall behind the client's chair when they are temporarily distracted.

We disguise our imperfections and lapses as well, believing quite rightly that they would interfere with our image as powerful healers. For example, we have developed an impressive array of options to disguise yawns. As we do not wish the client to know that we may feel bored or fatigued, we place the hand in front of the mouth in a pensive pose. Strategically sipping coffee also works quite well.

To counteract the temptation to yawn, another subtle therapist skill is the ability to look attentive during lapses into personal fantasy. We can keep head nods, furrowed brows, and uh-huhs going at the same moment that we are fighting our own dragons. Of course, sometimes we get caught, and the client may explicitly test our powers of concentration with, "Do you know what I mean?" That is the true test of the experienced clinician, which brings us to a whole new category of maneuver: what to do when you did not hear what the client just said. Even the most directive therapist will lapse back into her best Rogerian response: "My opinion is really important to you." Another excellent alternative goes something like this: "You've spoken at some length about this issue. I wonder if you might summarize the essence of what you think is most important?"

A knowing, mystical follow-up posture will often help us stall for time until we can come up with a more acceptable response. To err may be human, but it is not all that noble for therapists whose power may be undermined by lapses. A series of defensive ploys is often required for slips when, for example, our interpretations miss the mark. We can always backpedal and redefine the misjudgment as "only a working hypothesis" or "a possible theory," but certainly the client will lose confidence. One clever option is to reluctantly explain that the interpretation was actually a paradoxical maneuver specifically designed to elicit the reaction it did.

Two variations on this theme offer similar responses. Either when the client does not understand something that we just said or when we do not understand what the client said, we can act as though it's the client's fault.

A stony, quizzical face is quite effective in driving home the point that in close calls the therapist gets the benefit of the doubt. This implicit rule of thumb also allows us to sit silently when we do not know what to do next. The client may feel the responsibility to keep the ball rolling and say something emotional or intelligent.

Perhaps these strategies are necessary to increase the stature, omnipotence, and influencing capabilities of the therapist—but it is always at the expense of the genuineness, humanness, and presence that are so crucial in being with a client. People respond to us not only because of our professional competence but also because of our uniquely personal aura. The way we smile, laugh, love, and give, the way our eyes twinkle, teach clients as much about themselves as the most sophisticated interventions. Similarly, revealing our humanness, confusion, and ignorance can often be interpreted by clients as permission for them to do the same in a more open, honest relationship.

Counterfeit Intelligence

Another self-deception is the most universal among therapist frauds. There we sit among our diplomas and memorabilia acting as if we know exactly what we are doing. The collection of books and the wafting air of professionalism attest to our expertise. The client comes in insecure and off balance, so what does he know? It takes the average client a few sessions just to get his bearings, much less to decide whether this professional who comes so highly recommended is really a lightweight.

I can quote chapter and verse of any masters I have studied. I know exactly how to act like a therapist—that is, I have my penetrating stares, monosyllabic grunts, charming smile, and wise demeanor down pat. I know how to ask intelligent questions to keep the conversation flowing, and every once in a while to say something fairly intelligent. If pressed, I can even tell a persistent client what I think her problem is and what she needs to do to make things better. Most of the time, if she follows my direction, she will feel better (and—it is hoped—behave more effectively). But the truth of the matter is that throughout much of the encounter, I am actually quite confused, uncertain, indecisive, and awkward. On the stage or in the therapist's chamber, the audience rarely discovers such lapses in performance.

A very prominent and successful psychoanalyst with 20 years of experience admits, "I tell myself that because I've had so many years of experience, I can handle whatever walks in the door. But I don't know if I will or I won't. I lie to myself and to my patients to feel the confidence I need to manage a professional practice. In truth, I am extremely anxious every time I see a new patient. Will I understand him? Will I make an asshole of myself? Will I make a serious error in judgment? Will I know what to do? No. No. No. But I say to myself and to the client, 'Of course I can help you,' even when I think I can't."

Telling clients that we can definitely help them is certainly helpful even if it is not strictly true. Favorable expectations and placebo responses are set up principally by the therapist's belief in herself and the process. By communicating confidence, however false it might feel, we try to instill hope and motivation in the client. We would lose clients very quickly if after every bungled interpretation or misjudgment, we muttered under our breath, but within earshot, "Yikes. I blew that one." We would never get clients to come back if we were completely honest with them in the first sessions.

In other words, to get better, the client may need to believe in this lie and the others we'll be looking at. No physician in his right mind would ever let his uncertainties slip out, not just because he needs to protect himself from malpractice suits but because people must have faith in their healers. Just imagine if you overheard a physician say, in the middle of a procedure on you, "Oops."

Without faith, there can be no magic. And that faith is just important in our own belief system considering that holding high expectations for outcomes significantly increases the likelihood of better results (Connor & Callahan, 2015). That's the old placebo effect at work, not only affecting the client's positive expectations but also our own.

Certain lies—to ourselves as well as to our clients—may therefore be necessary, if not therapeutic. If lying to a client, deliberately or unintentionally, is unethical because it promotes deceit and deception, perhaps it is just as unethical to be completely truthful (whether it is in the client's best interest or not) just so the therapist can feel pure. Tactical deception, then, has its place in protecting clients from a reality that they are not yet prepared to face or in the paradoxical interventions that break stubborn destructive patterns that are resistant to more conventional attacks. Although lies can be very effective strategies, and quite useful in moving progress along, they are not usually a first choice. No matter how we rationalize the necessity of the lie, whether exaggerating our powers or our confidence, a certain amount of caution, modesty, and uncertainty is very helpful in keeping us from becoming too big for our britches. Just because we must tell the client that we know we can help him does not mean we have to believe it, too. But it sure helps.

The Pretense of Perfectionism

Closely related to projecting a false sense of confidence is the exhibition of counterfeit expertise. This occurs when we pretend to know or understand something that is actually quite muddled. There are times we nod our head in apparent agreement with what a client says and we actually have no idea what was intended. We hide behind pregnant pauses, stalling, giving us time to make up some response or answer to a question that is actually beyond us. We might even turn the question back to the client in order to hide our ignorance: "That's an excellent question! What do *you* think?" We are sometimes asked by a referral source or supervisor whether we can handle a particular case and immediately respond, "Sure, no problem," and then run to the nearest sources to bone up on this issue. And how often have you heard a client say after a week of reflection, "I finally understood what you were doing last session and what it meant," and had no idea what profound insight you were supposedly developing?

The pretense of perfectionism may be for the client's benefit, but it affects the therapist as well. If we believed that we really were as thoroughly competent and composed as the image we present to clients, we would be insufferable. Yet if we were continuously honest with ourselves regarding what we know, what we understand, and what we can do, we would be so riddled with self-doubt that we could barely function at all. The compromise position is to accept that we exaggerate our capabilities at times and that such distortion is sometimes necessary for the client's good, but that we should not for a minute forget that we are just pretending. Milton Erickson was fond of saying that if you can pretend very convincingly, then clients will pretend to make changes in their lives. And when things go well, after a period of time, they will forget they are pretending.

Feeling Indispensable

Any time we act for reasons other than to promote the client's growth, we dilute our honesty. This occurs occasionally, especially when we become more familiar with a client we have known for a while. At the same time we are taking care of clients, we take care of ourselves as well. This happens sometimes at the invitation of the client and sometimes by our own initiative.

Saying goodbye to a client is so bittersweet that many therapists encounter difficulty in letting go. There is sometimes an actual mourning process and sense of loss when a relationship ends. The client has learned her lessons well, accomplished her goals, obliterated her suffering, and (it is hoped) weaned herself of dependency on the therapist in the process. She feels strong, confident, insightful, and motivated to get on with the rest of her life. She also feels quite grateful to her helper, sad, nervous, and ambivalent about ending this relationship. The therapist shares many of the client's emotions: he feels excited, relieved, and probably confused as well.

Launching a client into the world leaves a vacancy in his schedule and his life. It means a loss of revenue and a disruption in a weekly routine that may have spanned months if not years. It also means saying goodbye to a dear and trusted friend.

Even when it is in the best interest of the client to leave therapy, when the clinician claims to be doing everything in his power to help promote autonomy, his behavior may reveal quite different intentions. After all, keeping a client locked into treatment, with no hope or wish for escape, can ensure a therapist a lifetime income. It is inconvenient to replace a "good" client who knows the rules and does not demand very much for her time or money.

We all know practitioners who keep their clients addicted to them for years. They teach people to need them, to require a weekly or daily fix just to function. Of course, some very disturbed people will need therapy throughout their lifetimes just to keep themselves out of the hospital. But here I am referring to those therapists who keep clients long beyond the point where they are doing them any good. One such psychiatrist has been seeing the same 20 clients two to four times per week for decades. His clients are so well heeled (and he is so reluctant to lose income) that when he schedules his annual vacation to the Caribbean, he reserves the wing of a motel so that his clients may join him and continue their treatment. It is his opinion, and his clients readily agree, that they just cannot function for 2 weeks without their doctor.

To a lesser extent, any clinician in private practice struggles with the issue of when to let clients go. It is easy to say that as long as they keep coming to sessions, they must be getting something from the experience. When I worked for a public agency, the longest I ever saw a client was for 10 to 15 sessions. At the time, I thought I was doing marvelous work. It can hardly have been a coincidence that when I moved into full-time private practice, where my livelihood depended on my ability to keep my schedule full, the average number of sessions I saw a client jumped from about 10 to 30. I had, naturally, convinced myself that this longer-term approach was much better for the client; it is more intense, more comprehensive, more elegant, more satisfying, more effective, and, yes, more costly.

Even during these times of managed care, when brief therapy is the order of the day, practitioners make different treatment decisions depending on their setting. If you are working for a public agency or school with hundreds in your caseload, your clinical decisions are likely to be different than those made by your brethren who earn a living from private income and have open spaces in their schedules.

One psychologist in private practice who is driven toward a goal of financial independence and yet is also very dedicated to helping people admits with great discomfort, "I lie when I tell myself I can see 13 clients in a day and not lose my effectiveness. I hypnotize myself into believing that so I can continue with this ferocious schedule I call my life. Especially, I lie whenever I say that I am not doing this kind of work to make a lot of money. Because I am." This is certainly part of what motivates many therapists in private practice—not only to enjoy freedom but to strike it rich. And this attitude affects the pace and style of what we do.

Many things can be said about therapists—that we are knowledgeable, dedicated, compassionate—but we have not been described as swift in our methods, at least historically. Even with the popularity of brief therapies and manualized treatments, we take our sweet time in getting to the heart of the matter, embellish our insights with poetry and stories, follow a tortuous route to a client's underlying fears. The lie to clients and ourselves is that we will rid them of their symptoms just as fast as we can. Even a first-year intern knows that if you take away the client's presenting complaints too quickly, he will not stick around for the best part of the show.

Absolutes

A psychology professor reveals, "It's difficult to admit I lie. I can't really think of any . . . well, maybe there's one. I tell my students to have faith in the human capacity for healing. I talk about it as an absolute, but it isn't really. There are a lot of people I don't trust or who can't take care of themselves. Their instincts are all wrong."

There is a tremendous difference between our theories and our actual behavior. To the public, to clients, to colleagues, we disclose our neat, coherent little model of why things work the way they do. Most practitioners, with little prodding, can articulate fairly detailed theories about human development, psychopathology, personality development, and psychotherapy. Together with these models of understanding, we also ascribe to specific systems of logic, morality, and epistemology. Finally, we bestow ourselves with titles to summarize the conceptual frameworks to which we owe allegiance. And therein hides the lie.

If the truth were told, clinicians do not always apply their orthodox theories in their sessions—and for good reasons. Once a person, any person, applies a method invented by someone else, it becomes a different method. Each therapist is simply too unique—with her distinct values, personality, demeanor, and voice—ever to practice therapy the same way another does. Moreover, the interactions with clients force us to think on our feet, instantaneously, instinctually, no matter what training we received. If we were to stop and think, to reflect on our theories, we would interfere with the smooth flow of action as well as paralyze ourselves with complexity. In other words, we do not really function exactly as we say we do, or even as we think we do.

In spite of our labels as social worker, psychologist, counselor, family therapist, or psychiatrist, in spite of our identification with particular theories, we act in accordance with client needs and our own intuition at the time. Most of the absolutes and rules that we say we follow are used only when appropriate or convenient. The most nondirective of practitioners occasionally gives advice. The most orthodox analyst reveals a distinctly human character. The most rigid cognitive therapist will also deal with feelings. The most passionate narrative therapist may still look at factors other than the dominant story and unique outcomes. And then there are the absolute imperatives of the profession that we all ignore at some time or another:

- *Don't give advice.* We do it all the time when a client is about to do something we feel would be incredibly stupid or self-destructive.
- *Don't answer direct questions.* But we do answer them when we get tired of playing games or when we know the answer and are dying to tell someone.
- *Don't talk about yourself.* Although this injunction may be desirable, it is idealistic and ultimately impossible.
- *Trust the clients' capacity for healing.* If they had sound judgment concerning what is best for them, they would hardly end up in therapy.
- *Don't get involved in your clients' lives.* This is possible only if you sleep through the sessions.
- *You have to like your clients in order to help them.* Some of them are genuinely unlikable.
- *Refer those clients who are beyond your specialties and expertise.* If we did this, we would grow very little and have very few clients.
- *Let the client lead the sessions.* If the client can't control his life, how is he going to be in charge of his cure?

For each of these absolutes, there are exceptions. For many of the rules of accepted standards of practice or ethical codes, there are times when we must make our own decisions in the best interest of our clients and their welfare.

Myth of Neutrality

One of the foundations of our work is that we are professionals and experts who, like judges or arbitrators, purport to be objective, detached, free of biases and prejudices, and morally neutral. Generations of therapists and clients have been deluded into believing the myth of neutrality in helping—that it is not only desirable but also possible to attain. We are cautioned to guard against exposing our true feelings, prejudices, convictions, and values, so that we do not impose our morality on others. Whereas those in pastoral counseling make no pretense of disguising their moral agenda, secular practitioners also have strong values of their own. It may be to adopt a particular lifestyle, a way of thinking or feeling, a political orientation, or a preference toward particular ideas. But essentially, we want to sell our values of health, risk, honesty, emotional fitness, autonomy, independence, and social justice. These are considered "good" values, so they are exempted from the neutrality gag order. But "bad" values, such as dependence, should not be communicated, even if we may sometimes wonder if there is anything so terribly wrong with two people contentedly stuck in a fused, parasitic marriage. There is room for much philosophical debate here—and that is exactly the point. As therapists feel differently about love, marriage, commitment, sexuality, and relationships, so they will work differently in their sessions. Some clients really understand this, so they ignore our lies.

The phone rings.
"Do you do marriage counseling?"
"Yes, I do."
"Are you for or against marriage?"
"That depends on the marriage."
"Let me put it differently. Do most of your couples stay together or get a divorce?"

Some perceptive clients are right on target with their queries. There are indeed therapists who stress commitment over divorce, abstinence over sexual exploration, sexual affairs over boredom, religion over education, travel over gardening, exercise over television, tea over coffee. We are hardly neutral, even if we try to keep our opinions to ourselves. We have opinions about everything a client says or does. And in the midst of our posture of supposed acceptance, unconditional positive regard, and neutrality, we are sometimes thinking to ourselves, *I wish you wouldn't.*

In spite of the myth, therapists are hardly value free, objective or neutral, and are, in fact, moral agents for their own beliefs. As human beings and members of society, therapists hold strong opinions about the nature of freedom, independence, responsibility, and productivity. Furthermore, there are many practitioners who believe that part of our role is to advocate on behalf of certain beliefs that are deemed desirable for the greater good.

A case could even be made that we ought to be more forceful with our values and less morally neutral, or at least do away with much of the pretense. If a suicidal client enters our office, we will do our best to convince him to develop our respect for life. Should a client who lives by her wits, a gambler, a risk taker, a reckless sensation seeker, wish our counsel, she will probably get a lecture on living more responsibly. We recommend the books that are most consistent with our life philosophy. In our hearts, we believe that what is good for us is good for everyone. Therapists who enjoy traveling urge their clients to travel more. Those who find peace running on a country road or worshipping in a church would probably prefer to have their clients do the same. If we choose not to impart any particular values, then we will push the big ones: that values are a good thing or that therapy is a marvelous experience.

If we do project our values during our work, what are the personal consequences for client and therapist? We must shoulder the burden not only of relying on our clinical judgment and professional skills but of knowing that clients will adopt many of our most personal beliefs. Are we really certain that the way we are living our lives would be all that great for the rest of the world? We can justifiably worry whether it is in anyone's best interest to adopt the values of a typical therapist. Some of our clients come in as just plain folks, naïve and sheltered. They may leave enlightened, but at the expense of their innocence.

A Therapist's Personal Skills

The preceding sampling of absolutes that are not strictly followed illustrates the discrepancy between what we say and what we do. These deceptions may contribute further to the stress and confusion that therapists experience.

Maybe this is our ultimate hypocrisy: while we push clients to expand their potential, strive for greater honesty, and improve their personal effectiveness, we sometimes continue a life of mediocrity. In our offices, we are stars—energetic, capable, creative, and powerful. Then we pack up our briefcases and head out into the world, fraudulent heroes.

There is often a major gap between the self that our clients come to know and love and the self that we expose to the rest of the world. We are taught to keep our distance from clients during accidental social encounters—supposedly to protect them from embarrassment because we have such an intimate knowledge of their lives. But another reason for this distance is to shelter them from the disappointment of finding out that we are really quite human. We feel shy and inept. We are not as witty and wise outside our realm. We are threatened by strange situations just like everyone else.

We are nevertheless aware of the myth of personal competence that we perpetuate. When a client complains of some self-defeating behavior or another, we smile knowingly and think to ourselves if not say out loud, "So how can you live with yourself, impaired as you are?" But how many times do we ask a client to master a skill that we have not yet mastered or confront a problem that is still unresolved for us? One charismatic therapist reveals his most painful lie involves the dissonance between what he asks his clients to do and what he is able to do in his own life. "In relationships, for example, I encourage people to be less defensive in their communication and more empathetic with their spouse, while I'm aware in my own life I don't deliver on that stuff at all." He notes a gigantic schism between his personal and professional selves, much preferring the latter over the former. "I struggle to integrate the two parts of me. If I weren't a therapist, I would do just fine because I would be less in touch with the ideal self I want to be. But I *am* a therapist and I'm trying very hard to do be more like the way I am when I'm in my office."

A therapist should be, beyond all else, a fully functioning model for others to emulate, a personally and professionally masterful human being. What are those idealized parts of ourselves that we access during work hours but are reluctant or unable to use otherwise? What are the skills and insights that we wield so masterfully with clients but somehow forget during personal encounters? Many, many professional skills do carry over to the personal realm. Most therapists, for example, are quite astute at picking up on the vulnerabilities of various people, filing them away, and using them to their advantage at a later time. Therapists are also adept at using their nondefensive confrontation skills or summarizing abilities during normal interactions. But then there are all those things that we know how to do, things we do every day, that we don't use as much as we could to enrich the quality of our lives and the lives of those around us.

A therapist talks about the hypocrisy of teaching to others what she hasn't been able to do very well in her own life. She recalled first going into practice in her early twenties, newly divorced with a 3-year-old child. "I wanted to launch my career by specializing in parent–child issues, an area which seemed to elicit a lot of questions with few professionals to answer them. I developed my own radio talk show on positive parenting and managed to convince a local newspaper that it needed a parent advice columnist, namely me. Oh hell! What did I know about parenting?"

Her career exploded on the national scene, which resulted in a reputation as one of the country's experts on parenting. Then she was remarried, to a man with two school-age children, and again she was confronted with the paradox of being a expert in an area in which she couldn't apply the knowledge to her own life. "Suddenly I had a family of three children. We were definitely not the Brady Bunch. My new family was an example of what *not* to do when blending two families. My greatest success was keeping my family from the public eye. I even hid my feelings of failure from my best friends. I continued to practice my lucrative and expanding profession even though I felt like a fraud and a hypocrite. I saw numerous therapists over those child-raising years and concluded, ultimately, that I was the kind of client to whom therapists refer as a failure."

She hoped that eventually her own clients would provide the answers she had been seeking by revealing their own successes, but it was not to be. To this day, the therapist is filled with shame about how inept she feels as a parent, even though she teaches parenting skills to others.

Focused Attention

When you are receiving monetary compensation for your time, you are more than willing to single-mindedly focus on another person. Through your body posture, eye contact, and other attending behaviors, you communicate your total interest in whatever the client is saying. You hang on every word, note the most subtle nuances of her nonverbal cues, sometimes even take notes on the most inane details of her life. You ask pertinent questions and further demonstrate your intense interest by frequently reflecting back to the client what you have heard. All of this is quite wonderful: the client feels appreciated and understood in a way that does not take place anywhere else.

A few hours later, you sit at home talking to your best friend on the phone while doing a crossword puzzle. Your mother calls and you half-listen to her while you open the mail. Your children or partner vie for your attention while you sit in front of the television or computer screen. You absentmindedly listen to your loved ones, all the while texting or emailing someone else. The focused interest that you are willing to sell to your clients you will not give away to the people who matter most.

Compassion—Toward Self and Others

No matter how bizarre or abusive a client becomes, we usually turn the other cheek. With total concern and complete empathy, we crawl inside someone else's sandals, boots, clogs, heels, wingtips, boots, or oxfords and feel what he is feeling. Because we fully understand the pain he is experiencing, we can be accepting and nondefensive in responding to his anguish. We can duck his anger and stifle our own frustration in not striking back.

A student comes to me upset about the grade he received on his paper. He is absolutely livid—something was activated in him by the grade or by some comment I wrote to him. He yells at me so loudly that I visibly cringe. He calls me names and tells me I am worthless, incompetent, and prejudiced against him. And I take it all. I just listen as calmly as I can. I don't defend myself. I don't respond except to nod my head, letting him know that I am listening. Suddenly, he literally collapses into a chair and begins to sob.

Throughout this interchange, I resisted the urge to fight back, to enforce respect and stop the verbal abuse. I did this because I understood immediately what was going on (which is certainly not always the case). I recognized that his outburst was not really about this paper, or even about me. And because I am a therapist, I was able to let things run their course before I attempted to work through the issue constructively.

We all feel self-satisfied after such a charitable gesture with a client or student. We reveal love instead of hate. We demonstrate serenity, clarity, and self-discipline. We resist the urge to become punitive, or even to defend ourselves. Then we get in the car to drive home. Someone cuts us off on the freeway, someone with an ax to grind for who knows what reason. We scream obscenities, make rude gestures, and tailgate the offender in retribution.

The other part of compassion that we feel toward others is less often directed toward ourselves. Neff (2015) points out that certain myths may make it difficult for us to give ourselves the benefit of the doubt the way we would for clients. There is a common belief that practicing such self-compassion is somehow selfish or narcissistic or implies complacency, self-pity, or weakness. On the contrary, she says, "When we care tenderly for ourselves in response to suffering, our heart opens. Compassion engages our capacity for love, wisdom, courage, and generosity" (2015, p. 47). It is about being kind to ourselves just as we are to so many others.

Patience

For someone who can sit still in a chair hour after hour, a therapist certainly has a hard time waiting in lines. Or perhaps I should own this one. I can sit in a therapy group that I am leading and wait as long as it takes for the other members to catch on to something that I picked up a long time earlier. I can wait months, even years, for a client to find the motivation it takes to make needed changes. I can sit in my chair for hours, sometimes five sessions in a row without a break, and maintain much of my focus and patience. Yet once I'm outside my office, I am a lunatic when it comes to waiting in line. I become impatient in slow traffic. I refuse to wait for a table at a restaurant for more than 10 minutes. I will not wait in line at a movie. So what's up with that?

Because we must wait so patiently during work, we may be reluctant to do so on our own time. Of all the qualities we must develop, patience is the most difficult: waiting for people to move at their own pace, waiting years sometimes before we can see a noticeable difference in a client's behavior. Yet put this expert "waiter" in a room full of people, and she will elbow her way to the front, if not to the center of attention, then to the head of the buffet line.

One therapist struggles with the disconnection between the way he is in his office versus the rest of his life. "I used to practice outwaiting a client during silences just to stay in shape. Now I think my greatest strength as a therapist is to allow my patients to take the time they need. My interpretations are usually subtle and understated. I wait for clients to hear them when they are ready. . . . If not [shrugs], we've got nothing but time."

The strange part of this to him is that people constantly tell him that he makes them nervous because he is always in such a hurry, the prototype Type A personality. "I have only one speed outside of my office—blazing fast. On the phone I refuse to be on hold for more than 30 seconds. That's my rule. I'd rather hang up and do something else. I got in a bad habit of checking my watch during sessions. I time myself going everywhere. People think I am the most impatient person alive. Only my patients know what I'm really like."

Well, it's unclear what any of us are "really" like when we are able to split ourselves into two very different individuals, depending on whether the meter is running or not.

Taking Charge of Our Own Lives

This may have been the chapter that was as uncomfortable for me to write as it was for you to read. Essentially, the point I have been hitting as hard as I can is that we have this wonderful opportunity to apply what we do with others to our own lives—and to do this more systematically and consistently. The lies that we tell ourselves are not terrible self-deceptions but rather strategies that allow us to work in a field that holds so many paradoxes and complexities.

The self-control of which therapists are capable is obvious. We ignore grumbling stomachs, the urge to yawn, and little voices whining, "Me, take care of *me*." We restrain our impulses to hug, shake, kiss, or strike a client. We sit immobile for hours on end.

How then do we excuse our frequent lack of self-control at home? Gone is the willpower to refrain from overeating. Gone is our ability to hold our temper. Gone is the resolve to stick with an exercise regimen. Where is the self-control that was so much in evidence just hours earlier? We plead exhaustion or a desire to escape from control. Time to relax in front of the television with a bowl of ice cream: "Will you kids shut up and give me some peace!"

There are many other things that we do regularly while working that we do not do on our own time. It probably could not be any other way. The lie is not in our inconsistency, not in our laziness and indulgences, but in our perpetuating the myth of our invulnerability. In many ways, it is helpful for clients to hold on to this myth. It empowers our role as models. It keeps their attention and stimulates hope. But it also is very confusing for the therapist who must lead a double life, disguising a secret identity.

During a lengthy interview for this book, one therapist was startled by being asked about his lies and self-deceptions. After several minutes of thought, he shrugged and said that he really could not think of any self-deceptions that he was aware of. He is a very honest person, and after years in treatment and supervision, he feels very clear and self-aware. I turned off the recorder and began to pack up when I heard him clear his throat and whisper: "Everything I've said to you is a lie. It is so important to me to sound and look good that on some level I'm always suspect. I try my hardest, and I still can't overcome my need to say and do things other people will approve of. I'm especially an impostor whenever I act like I know what I'm talking about. Even this is a lie."

This confession is familiar to me. And I realize that I've been unduly hard on members of my profession by implying that our transparency and integrity are somehow suspect because we are not always completely honest with ourselves and others. Of course we are something less than infallible, imperfect beings who sometimes shade the truth a bit in order to do our jobs and live with ourselves. Yet most of us are also intensely driven and committed to our own growth, just as we are for our own clients.

12

Alternative Therapies for Therapists

SOME OF THE problem areas that therapists confront are the predictable result of prolonged practice; some are the result of self-deception and self-destructiveness; still others are the inevitable side effects of being a therapist. These are, of course, in addition to the normal crises that every human encounters: the usual variety of personal conflicts, insecurities, mood swings, restlessness, financial pressures, family problems, indecision, and stagnation, and the fears of love, of death, of life. But unlike the public at large, therapists can sometimes be well versed in the techniques of avoiding therapeutic experiences—whether these involve counseling ourselves or getting help elsewhere.

Those therapists who do make personal growth a major life priority may, in fact, only go through the motions of addressing the issues. For example, one of the most popular alternatives for therapists who seek greater self-awareness and clarity used to be undergoing a form of psychoanalysis that is part of their training. Unfortunately, by and large, therapists often make miserable clients. When it comes to changing our own behavior, we can be highly skilled at pretense and acting.

A senior psychoanalyst admits this: "My biggest lie to myself is when I say I've been psychoanalyzed. Even though I was in analysis for seven-and-a-half years, I was a terrible patient. By no stretch of the imagination could one say it was successful, because I refused to allow several important areas of my life to be analyzed. Although I tell people all the time—clients, colleagues—that I've been analyzed, it's just not true. I've got a lot of work left to do."

Taking care of ourselves is not an option, but rather a mandate by our ethical codes. It is widely recognized that if we are not functioning at an optimal level, it is highly unlikely that we can be all that helpful to others.

Whether or not therapists seek enlightenment in the formal contexts of supervision, support groups, or psychotherapy, most are engaged, although not necessarily successfully, in counseling themselves. We just cannot talk to people all day long without hearing a little bit of what we say. We cannot teach people to talk to themselves differently without doing so ourselves.

The Therapist's Developmental Changes

As surely as we know that any client will move through a progression of developmental stages throughout her life or during the process of therapy, we know that we will experience a series of predictable, sequential, and logical changes during our professional careers. At other times, these changes can be sudden and the result of crises, critical incidents, or other life-transforming events.

Several critical incidents universally shape a therapist's development, the most obvious of which is the real reason the practitioner entered the field. As discussed elsewhere, usually little similarity exists between the publicly espoused motives (some variation of the theme "to save the world") and the private, perhaps unconscious, reasons (some variation of "to save myself"). We all have some hazy personal agenda that we have been following since graduate school that responds to an internal force that pushed us into helping others and keeps us there. That agenda may be to simulate the rescuer role that was familiar to us as children or to get therapy for ourselves without having to risk the inconvenience and cost of seeing a therapist. We have explored earlier how becoming a therapist is one way that some people seek to fulfill their need for power and control. Others are attracted to the opportunities for having successful relationships with minimal personal involvement. Still others who feel stupid can act wise, those who are selfish can pretend to be altruistic, and people who are timid can be assertive. One therapist relates, "If the truth be known, I couldn't care less about the money and status. I don't spend much anyway. I don't even like working indoors, so it is hardly the comfort factor that keeps me seeing clients. But I do like people being dependent on me. I really do. I get off on being needed. Nobody ever needed me as a kid. I guess because I never had anything that anyone else ever wanted. Now I do. And people will drive long distances, pay money, and jump through hoops for whatever it is I have. I like this feeling. No, I *love* this feeling."

There are both functional and dysfunctional motives for entering this profession. On the healthy side of the ledger are attitudes of idealism and altruism; a capacity for, and interest in, listening to others; intellectual curiosity; a desire for growth; a degree of warmth and compassion; and a tolerance for intimacy, ambiguity, and self-denial. These traits are sometimes balanced by hidden motives that are quite personally and neurotically driven: a desire for power, an interest in using others to work through one's own unresolved issues, unfulfilled loneliness and isolation, or even an intention to be exploitative for financial or personal gain. Here are just a few honest disclosures that some clinicians were willing to make:

Being voyeuristic: My life is kind of boring, if you want to know the truth. I don't really do that much other than hang out with friends and watch television. But I love listening to the crazy, wacky stories my clients tell. I love being able to ask them personal questions without them getting offended, things I could never ask people in any other setting. "So what's your sex life like?" "What possessed you to ever do something like that?" "What is your deepest, darkest secret that you've never told anyone before?" I just really enjoy being able to peer inside the windows of people's minds and hearts. Everything else in my life pales by comparison.

Needing to rescue: I grew up not feeling very important or very good about myself. I didn't feel useful to anyone, least of all myself. But now I get to save people. I know I'm not supposed to believe that or say that, but that's the way I feel. Every time someone comes in miserable and leaves better off, it's because I did something that helped—or that's what I'd prefer to think. I thrive on being able to save people like this, and it makes me feel important.

Being a know-it-all: People look up to me. I see my clients look at me with such reverence, such admiration and respect. Sometimes I say the most ordinary things, and they look at me like I'm some sort of god. I know stuff that others want to know. I make things look simple that others find so complicated. It makes me feel smart even though I know that I'm no better than anyone else.

Wanting control: I've never felt like I've had that much control in my life. I've been hurt in more than a few relationships. I get close to people, then something happens and it ends; I'm devastated. I haven't been in a good relationship for some time. Except for my clients, of course. And that's the point: they can't hurt myself. I'm the one in total control of those relationships. We meet on my turf. I'm the one who leads. I don't have to share much about me, but I can ask anything I want and expect an answer. It's the best kind of intimacy in that I feel loved and appreciated, but I won't be hurt no matter what.

Demanding respect: I don't make nearly as much money as my sisters do. I don't have the fancy office or the sports car. But people do look up to me. When they find out I'm a therapist, they treat me like I'm important, like what I do matters to people. I get respect, and I like that a lot. It's worth all the money in the world. And you know what? I respect myself. My sisters and friends might be successful in business, raking in the bucks, but I know that what I do really matters. And at night, I sleep like a baby because I know I'm doing my part to make the world a better place.

Wanting self-therapy: There was a time in my life when I was really suffering and I needed to see a therapist, but I was too embarrassed. I thought that was for the weak and spineless, those who were too stupid to figure things out on their own. So I did the next best thing: I trained to become a therapist. It was a sneaky way, I know, to deal with some stuff that terrified me. Well now I know better, but I still find that I get so much self-therapy every day when I'm working with my clients. I just learn so much every day.

What are the real reasons *you* became a therapist, beyond helping others? Why do you stay in the field when it might be easier to try something else? What are you searching for in books such as this? Your answers to these questions will give you the first clues to the critical incidents that shaped and continue to mold your development. These are precisely the areas that may have led us not only into the field but to our own therapy experiences as a client. These will continue to be the same issues we will always counsel ourselves about.

Many of us received much of our early therapy training growing up in our own families, where we acted as go-betweens, conflict mediators, and helpers. "We kept the peace when our parents argued; we took care of family members who were sick; we helped other family members avoid confronting their pain" (Anderson, 1987, p. 19). Although this configuration does not apply to every member of our profession, the scenario of being elected to the role of rescuer is a common one.

Previous experiences with therapy are often initial motivators to make the switch from client to helper. Many clinicians can trace their initial interest in the field, as well as their current style of practice, to their identification with a therapist who was instrumental in resolving some painful issues. There is a feeling of admiration for this powerful person who understands so much. There are feelings of gratitude and a wish to compensate for this guidance by passing it on to other generations.

Because they have never fully worked through their termination issues, some clients become therapists in order to keep their own therapy going. A beginning therapist talks about how her parents were so negligent while she was growing up that she was practically raised by therapists since the age of 14. "One after another, they all tried to help me, to teach me. Some of them were pretty lousy—they would yell at me and tell me to grow up. Others were fantastic and immensely important. Here I am a grown woman who has been in therapy, on and off, for 25 years. I started training as a therapist because I couldn't find anyone left to help me. I figured it was about time I started helping myself—and maybe I could help some others in the process."

The problems that will require the most self-counseling during a therapist's life are those that first appear during the training years. Just as your motives for entering the field and your previous experience as a client set the parameters for what you eventually will become, your education and supervision determine, to a large extent, the more specific forms of your professional style.

During his apprenticeship, an intern undergoes a radical transformation, only a small part of which involves the mastery of theories and skills; most of the changes involve a radical shift in his thinking and self-concept. Until he experienced what it was like to truly make a difference in people's lives he had rarely felt useful. As often as he felt confused and challenged by his work with clients, he was learning to trust his judgment and skills with greater confidence, an effect that affected other aspects of his life.

During therapist training, the fledgling therapist is exposed to both positive and negative models. If she is unlucky, she may even find herself caught in a political tug of war between teams of influence. For self-preservation, she will identify with one group or the other. She will find sanctuary under the wing of a mentor and find solace in the books that speak to her. She will work hard to win the approval of her peers and instructors and in so doing will create a problem of external control that she must counsel herself out of. For the rest of her life, she may fight against the bondage created by years of working for grades and affirmation. No matter how accomplished she becomes, she may yearn for the external approval that she grew addicted to in her youth. She may look to her clients to find out how well she is doing or measure her success by her income or scheduled bookings. But forever she may wrestle with the need for validation. This is the gift from her instructors, who taught her to depend on their grades, their evaluations, their commentary, and their approval to know how well she was doing.

Coupled with the need for external validation are the many internal changes a therapist undergoes. There is nothing like having your hair turn gray, your stomach turn finicky, your sleep habits change, or your memory become unreliable to facilitate a change in life philosophy, values, and therapeutic style. Spending day after day helping others deal with their failing health, decreased vitality, and developmental crises ought to make therapists better prepared to deal with their own. Yet in some ways it is worse because the clinician must live through someone else's midlife crisis a thousand times. We repeatedly experience, albeit vicariously, menopause and prostate problems. We live through the empty-nest syndrome, the launching of adolescents, and the meddling of in-laws more times than we can count. By the time we must face these same problems, we are already weary. We know what to expect and still cannot find ways to prevent those common conflicts between parents and children.

We must counsel ourselves through those endless existential confrontations that "civilians" can easily hide from but that therapists must face on a daily basis. Self-supervision is an integral part of what we do and how we operate. This is certainly no substitute for the necessary monitoring and supervision from other experts who are far more knowledgeable and experienced than we are, but one of the distinct advantages of our training is that it allows us to apply what we do with clients to our own lives; it is a key means by which we demonstrate self-care.

Self-supervision and self-monitoring take place in so many different ways. Each and every day that we talk to clients about their self-defeating behaviors, we cannot help but examine our own. Each session that we conduct leaves our heads spinning with all the things we might have done differently, all the things we resolve to change in the future. Each time we write case notes, we can't help but reflect on our clinical decisions and intervention choices, making adjustments in strategy or direction. And far more than that, we must continually monitor our personal biases and prejudices, our unresolved personal issues that get in the way, and our clinical skills that we are working to improve. Is supervision with a wise mentor critical in this endeavor? Absolutely. Is personal therapy desirable to help us look at our own stuff that might be getting in the way? Most certainly. But the act of internalizing the guidance of all our previous mentors and supervisors is what allows us to apply what we have learned to the daily, minute-by-minute process that we experience—both in our work and in our lives.

We confront the big issues: death, the fear of going crazy, death, and death again. And always around the corner lies angst—nagging, tugging, tenaciously holding on. Angst is the dread that accompanies a life devoted to enlightenment. Without some form of therapy, it can infect the heart, mind, and spirit, leaving the victim in a state of permanent disillusionment. Yet it is precisely this opportunity to look death squarely in the face, over and over again, that ultimately encourages us to face our own mortality, as well as to live our lives more intensely and passionately.

How Therapists Take Care of Themselves

Just as our clients prefer to exhaust all other means before spending time, money, and a certain suffering to get into therapy, many practitioners choose other options as a first line of defense. In many ways, we are ideally equipped for such self-care, given our training that has been designed to promote growth in others. Here is just a sampling of what some therapists do on a regular basis:

> My therapy is to do therapy. Being myself with my clients. I need a certain amount of contact with other people or I would stay alone. My clients affirm me; they challenge me; they push me to keep up with them.
>
> I get together with a colleague on a regularly scheduled basis, and we take turns being in the role of client and therapist with one another. As long as I can schedule my crises for the week when it is my turn to be the client, everything works out fine.
>
> My therapy is talking with my wife. Sharing with her my fears. Opening myself up to her feedback. I think self-disclosing wherever and whenever I can is therapeutic for me. Telling people when I'm afraid. Forcing myself to be honest about what I'm feeling.
>
> I travel a lot as a way to energize myself. When I'm away on a trip, I don't even think about my children, much less my clients. I don't know how I do it, but I do. Once I'm on the way to the airport, I let go of everything. The geographic distance creates a psychological distance. I shed my skin as a therapist and become a person in movement.
>
> I'm so damn driven and ambitious I had to find a way to slow myself down. I needed to do something just for myself—not for an audience, not for my résumé, not even for a sense of accomplishment. That's why I've been playing the guitar for 2 years and nobody has ever heard me. When I concentrate on the music, I can't possibly think about anything else. For a few minutes, nothing exists except my breathing, my fingers, the sounds I hear and feel.

> It started out that running was to be my therapy. It helped me sleep at night, forget my troubles, and do something nice for myself. Then I became obsessed and the cure became the problem. I developed knee and hip problems while training for marathons. After a while, I approached running like I do everything else: I became competitive and regimented. It was no longer an escape but another obligation. Now I'm down to just a few miles a day, and it helps a lot to keep myself centered.
>
> My therapy is gardening and digging in the dirt and watching things grow. My therapy is playing golf. My therapy is doing crossword puzzles. My therapy is being with friends, entertaining, going out. And sometimes my therapy is just doing nothing, just nothing at all.
>
> My husband is a wonderful help to me. He is very sensitive to me. He can sense what I need even before I do. He knows when I want to be hugged or when I want to be taken care of. I've been taking care of people all day long, so when I get home I need time to let go.
>
> When I'm surfing, waiting for the next wave, I don't have a care in the world. I sit in amazement as dolphins play around me. I watch pelicans fishing. I feel the pulse of the ocean, its incredible power that will give me the ride of my life or crush me like a bug. It takes such complete concentration when I'm out there that I can't think about anything else. By the time I stumble onto shore, my arms feel like noodles and my legs are shaking. All day long, as water continues to drip out of my sinuses, I'm reminded of that peace I feel on the surf.
>
> I live by certain rules. I never see more than eight clients in a day. I try not to see two appointments back-to-back. I spread them out over the week and leave deliberate holes during the middle of the day to feed myself, replenish myself. I read, go for walks, talk to friends during breaks. My therapy is in just the way I schedule myself so I don't feel overburdened.

These samples of therapeutic alternatives set the tone for what is possible in self-nourishment for professional helpers. Whether in the form of consultations, peer support, physical exercise, diversified hobbies, or self-supervision, alternative therapies are not just desirable but necessary in order for us to remain clear. The process of therapy itself takes place in a kind of meditative trance state with focused concentration on the present moment.

Incorporating meditation and other forms of self-relaxation into our lives is just one of the many ways that we practice with ourselves that which we've learned to help others.

Self-Therapy

The following self-administered therapies are further examples of what clinicians often do to keep themselves emotionally fit and spiritually energized. Keep in mind that no single choice is likely to make a difference by itself; it takes multiple strategies, consistently administered, to maintain a degree of healthy functioning.

When Therapists Talk to Themselves

There are many ways that therapists work to counteract angst and manage the transformations that are part of the helping lifestyle. Talking to ourselves as we would to clients is the most direct and effective cure. This self-administered therapy is especially advantageous in those situations in which we may be needlessly worrying about clients or having difficulty separating ourselves from others. If we find, during odd moments of the day or while tossing in bed, that we are unable to let go of our work, we may initiate a self-dialogue such as the following: "How am I helping my clients by spending time worrying about their welfare? If I'm not helping them, then what is this behavior doing for me? Inflating my sense of importance? Using magical thinking to prevent tragedy by anticipating it? Distracting myself from something in me?"

Consistent with, but not restricted to, the tenets of cognitive or narrative-based approaches is the ways that therapists talk to themselves internally when they are upset, either as a form of self-soothing or to challenge assumptions, beliefs, or thinking that are less than optimal. On a broader scale, those confrontations, interpretations, and challenges that produce the most dramatic impact on a client's behavior will do the same for us. After all, we are experts at talking people out of their suffering. We give pep talks that motivate clients to overcome their fears. We convincingly challenge them to let go of beliefs that are not helpful. We teach clients to talk to themselves so that they can carry our voices with them wherever they may go. At times when they balk or stutter, our words of encouragement come back to them. We repeat our favorite strategies of self-talk so often that they have become our personal prayers. During moments of stress or difficulty, they return to haunt us. There is nothing as uncomfortable for a therapist as catching himself feeling self-pity and hearing his own words in his mind, echoing exactly what he would say to a client in a similar situation.

It's through the testing of a particular intervention on ourselves that we first discover its possible utility in a session. A therapist who is gnashing her teeth in frustration over a difficult client notices that she calms down considerably when she reminds herself, "This is what I'm paid to do." Not only does this reminder help her calm down, but later, with the same client, she is able to urge the use of this identical strategy: "You get so angry at the customers for complaining about their purchases, so instead you transfer your hostility to me. But what do you expect to hear while working in public relations? Customers are expected to yell at you. So every time you let their whining get to you, just remember, their job is to complain; yours is to listen without feeling defensive."

We are constantly telling people how to talk to themselves. An adolescent mourning the loss of his girlfriend is instructed to tell himself that his pain is necessary and a sign of how much love he is capable of feeling. A woman who is straddling the line just this side of panic is urged to tell herself that the impending attacks will subside if she will remind herself of where she is and what is really happening around her. An obese man is cautioned that every time he reaches for food he does not need, he should tell himself that he is hiding from his pain. By teaching others to counsel themselves at will, the therapist internalizes the same therapeutic messages.

We may find it necessary to counsel ourselves in the same situations in which we recommend that clients talk to themselves more constructively:

- When you feel uncomfortable in social situations (*What have I really got to lose by approaching these people?*)
- When the car will not start (*Getting mad right now is not going to start the car.*)
- When you are about to lose your temper (*This just isn't all that important.*)
- When you don't get what you want (*Oh, well.*)
- When you are about to do something that might get you in trouble (*Is it worth it, and if so, am I willing to suffer the consequences?*)

There are also a number of instances in which the use of self-talk strategies are particularly helpful in a therapist's professional life:

- When a client becomes worse after an intervention (*I guess this means I'm not perfect and the client isn't yet ready to change. Time to try Plan B.*)
- When your mind drifts elsewhere during a session (*Concentrate, concentrate.*)

- When a client will not talk during a session (*Just relax. Take a deep breath. He'll talk when he has something to say.*)
- When a client fails to show up for an appointment (*Don't take it personally. Getting mad isn't going to help the client, and it surely isn't going to help me. What can I do with my time instead?*)
- When a session is interrupted by someone knocking at the door (*No big deal. Let me just deal with this and then get back to work.*)
- When a client does not pay his bill (*What an annoyance. How can I take care of this so that I won't have to think about it anymore?*)
- When there isn't enough work to do (*I guess it's time to hustle up some work. Things are always slow this time of year.*)
- When there's too much work to do (*The world isn't going to end just because I don't finish all of this stuff today.*)
- When a client becomes abusive (*Oops. I'm letting him get to me.*)
- When we feel blocked with a client (*What is getting in the way of my being helpful?*)
- When in spite of our best efforts the client does not improve (*I can't reach everybody all of the time.*)

When we listen to our own interventions and apply them to ourselves during self-dialogues, we demonstrate the true effectiveness of what we teach. After having said these things to ourselves and noted the results, we have greater conviction in what we say to clients. Again we note the interaction between the personal and the professional in our life as a therapist. As we stumble across some way of expressing a motivational or insightful idea during a session, we rub our hands in glee, knowing that we can use it again and again with other clients and especially with ourselves. And when we encounter a particularly poetic expression during social conversations, while watching a movie, or while walking in the woods, we smile inwardly and store it away for later use.

When Therapists (Try to) Solve Their Own Problems

A second set of strategies for therapist self-counseling involves treating ourselves as we would our clients by using our capacity for healing, nourishment, insight, and motivation to enrich our lives. This can range from simply noting our defensiveness in a threatening situation to designing an elaborate problem-solving package including short- and long-term goals, contingencies, reinforcements, and action strategies. By applying our therapeutic wisdom and skills to ourselves, we increase our personal effectiveness as we field-test our best interventions on our most severe critic, ourselves.

Those practitioners who are behaviorally inclined have a wide range of techniques at their disposal to help in defining and solving problems. Even therapists who work primarily with insight and deplore systematic training in decision-making are nevertheless quite skilled at helping people get to the bottom of what is bothering them and then address the situation. Whether we teach problem-solving skills directly or by combining them with other interventions, we are experts at understanding how and why problems develop and what can be done to solve them, or at least to live with them.

One psychologist feels especially successful at being his own best client when it comes to using his problem-solving system himself: "I am constantly applying to myself the model that I use with my clients. I try to define the problem I'm experiencing in specific operational terms. I look at the precipitating and contributing factors, the intervening variables, and why the problem continues to exist. I create a plan based on what I want and what needs to be done."

No other professional in any field works so intimately with the process of constructive thinking. As applied philosophers, we not only understand the intricacies of logic, ethics, metaphysics, and epistemology but also are readily able to employ their methodologies in solving everyday problems. We teach people how to think more rationally, to feel more appropriately, to behave more constructively. We can sort out the complexities of that chaos we call emotional disturbance. We know how to simplify the salient issues, shelve the distractions, and focus on the core issues. We are experts at ranking priorities in terms of their pertinence to desired goals. We can juggle the different loose ends while we determinedly push forward with a plan of action, then return to any number of related themes that were left hanging.

We are not only masters of deductive and inductive reasoning, practical philosophers who can cut through the gristle to the real meat of an issue, but also scientists by training and inclination. We use empirical methodologies to objectively evaluate the effects of any variable or intervention. We test hypotheses in our sessions with precision. We systematically collect the data that are pertinent to a particular case, isolate the dependent strategies, and then, with flexibility and stubbornness, try out any number of treatment variables while scrutinizing their impact on the client, on ourselves, on the flow and movement of the sessions.

That we can integrate so many skills and diverse bodies of knowledge into a coherent system of problem solving is testimony to our potential for an ideally healthful existence. As stated earlier, the hard part is applying all that we can do to help clients solve their problems to the resolution of our own issues.

Even with our defenses and subjectivity, with the limitations involved in using oneself as an object of self-study, we can certainly accomplish more than most of us presently do.

A social worker felt stuck in his job and couldn't see a way out. He had tried talking to a friend about his concerns, then tried therapy for awhile, but nothing much changed except that he'd been able to develop even better excuses and rationalizations for avoiding changes that felt frightening. "Sometimes I hate being a therapist for just that reason," he admits. "Why can't I be more innocent and trusting—just let things happen instead of analyzing everything?"

At one point the social worker just gave up, lost hope, and accepted that he was a failure as his own client—or anyone else's for that matter. But then a breakthrough came when he decided to just surrender to his feelings. "I'd done that lots of times before with clients. When they fight back or become defensive, I just let go. I tell them to keep their misery if they like it so much; they're just not ready yet to change. When I told a client that again for the fortieth time last month, it occurred to me I could do that with myself, too. I did. And that's how I ended up in my new job."

Just as this social worker applied what she does with her clients to her own life, we always have that same option, one not ordinarily available to those outside our profession. As we've covered before, we know things that most people don't know. We understand things that most people don't understand. We can do things that most people can't do. As just one small example, most therapists are highly skilled in using the techniques of reframing (from strategic therapy), accentuating the positive (solution-focused therapy), and identifying unique outcomes (narrative therapy). All these strategies share in common an emphasis on moving away from the negative, discouraging aspects of a problem to focus instead on what is working well. We are also fully aware that as therapists we must work within a paradox: we are forced to continually examine what is wrong with people even though we know that happiness and life satisfaction are associated with attention to the most positive aspects of life. This presents us with a challenge to remain upbeat and optimistic in the face of the barrage of despair that we encounter every day. It is a very good thing, then, that we know how to help ourselves when we are discouraged and frustrated by our work (or the depressing stories we hear), that we can change gears at will to focus on the most positive and fulfilling aspects of what we do.

It would be less than completely frank in this discussion to neglect that we all have a certain blindness to our own biases and mistakes. We blithely push forward with an agenda that we are certain is indicated yet the client wants no part of what we are selling. Or we are simply oblivious to aspects of ourselves that are off-putting to others, both in session and in our personal lives. That is why it is so crucial for us to solicit honest, meaningful, and regular feedback from those who know us and our work best, including our colleagues and supervisors, but also the most valuable input from our clients (Lambert & Shimokawa, 2011; Macdonald & Mellor-Clark, 2015; Miller, Hubble, & Duncan, 2007).

Journal Keeping

A number of painfully introspective writers, including Anaïs Nin, John Steinbeck, Thomas Wolfe, Virginia Woolf, André Gide, and Albert Camus, kept journals throughout their lives as a way to maintain their sanity and clarity after pouring out so much of themselves in their work. Carl Jung was the first to recognize the merits of the diary for a practicing therapist. It was in his *Black Book* that he first developed his theories, analyzed his dream and fantasies, recorded the events of his life, and conducted imaginary dialogues with his unconscious. Rainer (1978) found Jung's example inspirational, particularly when merged with the creative self-therapy approach of Anaïs Nin, who devoted her life to exploring psychological themes as a woman, a therapist, and a writer. Other well-known therapists, such as Carl Rogers, kept journals throughout their lives, providing us with a window to peer into their most private struggles.

Writing letters or emails to colleagues and friends can also be a form of self-therapy and catharsis for the therapist who is struggling with new ideas and insights or with her personal pain. Freud began his 5-year correspondence with his best friend, Wilhelm Fleiss, to explore his burgeoning theories and to promote his self-analysis. He did the same with trusted colleagues such as Jung, until conflict between them became untenable. These early pioneers quickly discovered that in the role of confidant to others, they must create a structure for the therapist to become a confidant to himself. Systematic journal writing serves just that function for therapists in several different ways:

It is a way to supervise yourself through difficulties with particular cases. It could be said that much of client resistance results, in part, from some blocking that occurs in the therapist. The journal provides a vehicle to explore the dynamics of being stuck with a client. We can examine our reactions as they are elicited by a session's content. We can keep track systematically of the interventions that we use with clients in given situations and note their specific effects. We can also outline in writing the facts and impressions of a case so as to structure alternative treatment plans, and do so in a way that is not necessarily a part of the official record.

The journal is useful for a therapist in following the patterns of professional behavior over time. When we encounter a client with concerns similar to those that we have worked with successfully—or unsuccessfully—in the past, we can review the interventions that we have tried before so as to avoid repeating mistakes. Naturally, journal writing is one of the most helpful structures for working through feelings of countertransference with clients. It is a process that often leads to surprises, new revelations and insights, fresh ideas, and honors the joy and curiosity of exploring the most important questions that we face. It is one means to rescue ourselves from shame and sorrow (Buechler, 2012).

It is a method of self-analysis. Freud's need to pour out his feelings accelerated during the period of his greatest introspection: "My own analysis is going on, and it remains my chief interest. Everything is still dark, including even the nature of the problems, but at the same time I have a reassuring feeling that one only has to put one's hand in one's own store-cupboard to be able to extract—in its own good time—what one needs" (Freud, 1897/1954, p. 227).

Extracting what one needs becomes a much simpler task if there is some repository where things are stored. The journal becomes a place to pour out your heart. It is the place for exploring hidden motives, unconscious desires, and unresolved struggles. It is the place for catharsis and free association, where dreams are expressed and analyzed, where the structure and patterns of life become more evident.

It is a vehicle for developing and recording ideas. Many novelists have used their journals to create intricate plots, sketch their characters, or record ideas they may someday use. All practitioners are also theoreticians. We harbor our own unique ideas about how the world works and how therapy ought to be conducted. No matter what school of thought we align ourselves with, we have our own individual notions about how best to work. The journal is the best place to articulate these ideas, to formulate our theories, and to grow as thinking beings.

It is a record of significant events. Therapists are more aware than most of the value in studying one's past in order to make sense of the present and future. By reviewing the history of a client's developmental growth and studying the critical incidents in a client's life, we come to discover what is creating the present complaint.

There are milestones worth recording in everyone's life: births, deaths, job changes, the loss of innocence, successes, and failures. Journal keeping helps us maintain our perspective on where we have been and where we are going. It is a way to remember things we have experienced. And best of all, it becomes a structure for committing ourselves to future goals. As we work toward these goals and counsel ourselves in the process, we become more personally and professionally effective.

Writing introspective journal entries or lengthy personal letters to confidants has quickly become a lost art, now replaced by brief posts on social media to inform others about what you are doing and how you feel about it. Likewise, emails have become the norm instead of letters, emphasizing brief communications that may lack depth and detail, not to mention deep meaning. It makes it hard to hold onto and remember the important events, thoughts, and experiences of our lives, especially as memory becomes more unreliable.

I've been keeping a journal since I was an adolescent, originally to make sense of the confusing things going on in my life at the time. Since I was a poor student, athletically challenged, and socially awkward (or so it felt at the time), I tried to find or create some semblance of comfort by talking to myself. After my father left and my mother became depressed and suicidal, I "consulted" with her psychiatrist at times as the eldest child. I think he might have been the one to suggest I try to write things down.

Since that time, for over half a century, I've kept a journal that eventually filled two drawers of a file cabinet. The journal contained my life's work, my thoughts and feelings about relationships, books I'd read as well as those I might some day write. I'd recorded all the important events of my life, my travels, outlines for research projects, my agonies and ecstasies. I wrote on scraps of paper, lined pads, menus, even a roll of toilet paper when that was the only option available. I'd even stuck into the folders letters from famous theorists I'd written over the years who'd been gracious enough to write back. My whole life was contained in these drawers, and I imagined that some day I'd have the courage to go back and review my life, either as an attempt to write my autobiography or perhaps just to conduct a life review. Thus far I hadn't felt ready yet to relive some of my many painful memories. But I'm getting closer.

There are, of course, other lessons for a therapist who spends his or her life helping others to let go of things that can't be fixed or controlled. We are usually so outcome driven, held accountable for discernable results, not just related to the practice of therapy but to all other aspects of life. "What have you *done* lately?" is a frequent query we are asked, or ask ourselves. But it turns out that the kind of critical self-reflection that takes place in a journal is exactly what we need most as an *experience* rather than as any product that results.

Physical Exercise

Therapists do their work in a chair, using their intellect and voice. While the mind remains active through its diagnostic and reasoning chores, the body remains inert, wasting away in some places and growing in others through neglect. Thus many of us find relief in physical exercise.

That therapists have jumped on the exercise bandwagon is not surprising. We who understand that total wellness requires the interaction of mind and body, who observe at close range how a sick brain can destroy a healthy body and how failing health can sap one's will, feel committed to the nourishment of our total being. Whether the activity is intended primarily for aerobic conditioning, aesthetics, entertainment, rehabilitation, or distraction, a regular exercise program serves a therapist's needs. The reasons for beginning such a program can be as varied as those for the population at large: to control weight, improve sleep, increase self-esteem, reduce stress, increase self-discipline, and prolong life. But we have other reasons to exercise: to engage in something nonverbal, to give ourselves silent time in an enlightened state—time for processing the day, for calming down, for beginning or ending a day of confronting other people's troubles.

"When I ride my bike," one therapist says, "the wind washes me clean. Everything I have soaked in during the previous days, all the complaints and pain and pressure, oozes out through my pores. I feel only the pain in my legs and lungs as I climb a hill, pumping furiously. Then I coast down as fast as I can, never knowing what is around the next turn."

It feels to him like, at least for a few hours, he is no longer "a receptacle for other people to dump their suffering in. Nobody catches me on my bike. There is no time to think, or I will miss a pothole in the road. And it takes too much concentration watching for traffic, pacing myself, switching gears, working on technique, saving my strength, and breathing slowly for me to consider anything outside my body. After a ride through the country, I feel ready again to face my clients, my past, and my uncertain future."

Just as we urge our clients to diversify their lives so they have multiple sources of renewal, therapists need a variety of means to recover from the demands of the job that don't rely on the same modes of experience and activate other internal processes related to the body rather than just the mind. Whether participating in spin or yoga classes, taking up running, walking, hiking, or cycling, the goal is so work off excess energy and better center ourselves.

Group Support

In addition to attempting some form of self-therapy to promote serenity and enlightenment, a therapist can initiate a number of changes to make life easier yet more stimulating. If group members impose certain rules to severely curtail endless complaints or criticism (such as occurs in many teachers' lounges), informal groups can provide a special source of energy. Many find group support to be a tremendous healing force for therapists in that there is a sense of sharing and of community; the embracing of relationships; and a universal, dynamic, and focused energy that everyone may draw inside his or her being. This is, of course, in addition to the usual transformational powers of a group in which the forces of cohesion and intimacy play such a significant role in creating a sense of community, belonging, and mutual identification. Most feel that certain key elements should be part of such a transformational group: several multi-dimensionally enlightened people; a setting that is conducive to an inspired process; commitment on the part of participants to release old patterns, to trust, and to be together; the infusion of love; and grace.

Such support groups, in some shape or form, spring up spontaneously in organizations. A room, a tree, or a bench may be designated as an informal gathering place where clinicians can meet during breaks or between sessions. This sanctuary is a place to get a back rub or to talk about cases. It is a safe place to unload and release the negative energy that has accumulated during previous sessions. Therapists who work in isolation often organize a weekly meeting of minds and hearts outside their offices.

All too often, rather than being a source of support and caring for one another, our colleagues become our greatest aggravation. We get on one another's nerves; undermine one another; compete for resources, promotions, and attention; challenge one another's competence and integrity; and fight political battles for control of policy. I am reluctant to admit how many jobs I have fled in my life because of the underlying tension, conflict, and overt verbal abuse that took place in the workplace. This job is hard enough by itself without making our lives, and those of our colleagues, more miserable through turf wars and petty squabbles over relatively meaningless issues.

Creating support among colleagues—preferably in our own workplace, or, if not, among others we have recruited in the community—is crucial to maintaining our sanity and centeredness. How are we going to help others if we don't find ways to nourish ourselves?

Friends and family supply a source of support for many therapists. We all need a place where we can go to cleanse ourselves, talk through our concerns, and tune up our mental and emotional functioning. I tell my students and supervisees all the time that they are not the only ones in training—so too are their families. And unless we are all prepared to keep our families informed about our struggles, to keep them part of our journey of being a therapist, they will be left behind.

Even with regular therapy and supervision, a clinician still needs daily support. This is often accomplished through debriefings at the end of the day with one's spouse, partner, with a special friend, or with colleagues. One therapist was already seeing a therapist each week, as well as a supervisor, yet still felt the need for something more to process all the stuff going on. "Talking to my wife every night and a psychiatrist friend occasionally took some pressure off, but that was still not enough. That's when I started roping some colleagues to join me for informal gatherings during the day. Whereas previously we had bitched together a lot—about the paperwork, insurance companies, or some departed associate—I began asking them for help. Pretty soon, we were all focused on the problems we were having and what we could do about them. It became not so much a therapy group as a bunch of people who were open to whatever happened."

In a support group for therapists, each participant presents a different nuance on the theme of professional depletion. Each of them attends the weekly meetings for different reasons, yet they all agree that the group is for mutual sustanance.

Tanya works experientially with her clients and thus opens herself up to a deeper understanding of her clients' worlds by accessing her own inner feelings. This highly personal and intuitive style is quite effective for her work, but she pays a dear price in being unable to fully metabolize and dissipate the pain and suffering that she encounters. She comes to the meetings each week in order to lance the wounds that have been festering inside her—the client whom she committed involuntarily to the hospital who screamed accusations of betrayal as she was carried into the ambulance; another client, a young child, who was the victim of satanic rituals but who is unable, as yet, to deal with the extent of his trauma.

Kevin mediates a lot of custody disputes. No matter which party he decides in favor of or what recommendations he makes, somebody is usually disappointed with his choice. Whereas he must appear before judges, attorneys, and colleagues as a paragon of confidence in his reports, inside he is wracked with doubts. Did he do the right thing? Who lied to him? Should he change his mind? Could he have done a more thorough job?

Kevin needs to tell someone, preferably a group of peers, about his doubts. The support group helps him come to terms with the realization that no matter how much he studies, how hard he works, how experienced he becomes, he will still never meet his own expectations of perfection.

Fred comes to the group for input on cases, he says. Maybe the others can think of something he might have missed. They do. Every client he struggles with presents issues quite similar to those he had not fully resolved. His habit of giving clients advice and recommending books for them to read is based less on their needs than on his feelings of inadequacy, his belief that as a therapist he is not really doing anything.

Paula recently noticed that she is perceived as seductive with a few of her male clients. She was bewildered by the number of men who had "fallen in love" with her, until group members pointed out that it probably was not a coincidence that this rash of love-struck clients had occurred at about the same time that her own divorce proceedings began.

Thuy has no specific personal issue that she is working on; she comes to the group for a "tune-up"—a sort of preventive maintenance to help keep her balanced. Alfredo also feels that things are going quite well in his life, both personally and professionally, but he knows, based on his past experience, that he cannot do this type of intense work, get close to others' maelstroms of pain, without occasionally getting singed.

On a more informal basis, several therapists from different agencies committed themselves to meeting for lunch every Friday. During the first few months, they spoke only about cases that they were stuck with or complained about their respective administrative staffs. Then they made a rule that they would limit their lunch discussion to subjects that would revitalize one another, focusing on encouraging one another to be more creative and innovative.

Adventure and Escape

One form of renewal that many practitioners prefer involves vicarious or actual adventure. Camping out in front of the television for an evening, or losing oneself in a 2-hour movie, is a wonderful way to turn off one's brain, sit passively, and allow other people to provide the entertainment. Escape fiction is an even better option because books take longer to get through and the "treatment" can be self-administered as needed. I would expect that fiction writers have rescued more than a few therapists from boredom or despair.

A similar phenomenon exists for practitioners who favor films that illuminate our professional work. I don't mean just those TV shows or movies that have therapists as main characters but also those that resonate with the main themes of our work or those that transport us as far as possible from these same issues. There is, of course, a direct application to the kinds of movies we might prescribe to our clients for similar purposes, to look at issues that are most salient in their lives.

Many therapists enjoy more active forms of adventure and escape in travel. Away from our office, home, clients, and colleagues, we regain a perspective on what is important. Eventually, there comes a time when we grow tired of living out of a suitcase and feel ready, if not eager, to return to that which we call work. In the meantime, certain forms of transformative travel have elements similar to those of good therapy may have more lasting effects (Kottler, 1997; Kottler & Marriner, 2009; Schaler, 2009; Wilson & Harris, 2006):

- *Mind-set ripe for change*: It is during trips that we are more open to new experiences and more likely to reflect on things in new ways.
- *Insulation from usual influences*: Liberated from the usual routines and people in our lives, we are much freer to experiment with alternative ways of being.
- *Getting lost*: Challenges along the journey present us with opportunities to become resourceful and solve problems in new ways.
- *Emotional arousal*: Just as in therapy, certain travel adventures stir us up and stimulate us in ways that we cause us to become more raw and vulnerable and thus more amenable to change.
- *Altered states and heightened senses*: All our senses become more sensitive when we spend time in novel environments. We see, hear, feel, and sense things that we might ordinarily miss.
- *Movement through time, space, and place*: There is something about being on the road, being away from home, that stimulates us in ways that nothing else can.
- *Facing fears*: Transformative travels are not exactly comfortable and convenient; we are often forced to deal with things that we'd rather avoid.
- *Public commitment of intentions*: As is true of group therapy participants, we are more likely to follow through on commitments if we tell others what we intend to do.

- *Processing experiences systematically*: For the changes to last, we must find ways to reflect on what happened and make sense of the experiences.
- *Transfer of learning*: Finally, in the best of circumstances, we generalize what we have learned from the trip to other aspects of our lives.

I mentioned earlier how there have been times in my life when I struggled to drag myself into the office. I was tired of my clients, annoyed with their whining, impatient and frustrated with their poky progress. I was just as perturbed with some of my colleagues, whom I was tired of babysitting (I was the clinical director of the agency). I was seriously thinking about a career change, but instead decided to take a trip to try and turn things around. I spent 10 days snow-camping in the wilderness, skiing across the Rockies, sleeping in igloos, processing my experiences each night with companions, and writing in a journal. It would be very difficult to come back from such a trip and not be transformed. The hardest part, of course, was keeping the momentum going once I re-entered my previous life.

I counseled myself and consulted friends about what I had learned. Keeping my resolutions firmly in mind and committing out loud to loved ones what I intended to do, I made dramatic changes to the way that I worked thereafter. I realized that I didn't want to be responsible any longer for a rebellious herd of other therapists. I didn't want to do therapy any longer the way I had been doing it. I needed to change how I did therapy, where I did therapy, and whom I did therapy with. Once I followed through on what I had learned while in the wilderness, the rest fell into place.

Since that time, I have begun to rethink ways to revitalize the lives and careers of therapists and other helping professionals by assisting them in planning and implementing transformative travels. For a couple of decades I have been taking groups of therapists, students, and volunteers to remote villages in Nepal, where we provide scholarships for lower-caste at-risk girls, or to refugee camps in the Middle East. Whereas the stated goal is to advocate on behalf of marginalized children and families, it never ceases to amaze me how the lives of the team members are transformed by the experience in ways that are truly remarkable. Some therapists return prepared to make major shifts in their work, their lifestyles, their relationships, and the ways they think about themselves and the world. These journeys have had such a profound impact on me that I've reconceptualized the very foundation of what I do as a change agent, applying concepts from what we do in therapy to a different arena altogether.

It's interesting that one of the things that many of us have discovered about therapeutic travel experiences is that they tend to exert the most power and influence precisely when things go wrong or when you are required to deal with new challenges that had previously been beyond your capability. These are the times when growth and learning most often occur, especially if the experiences are structured in a way that is consistent with how we think about our work in more conventional settings. This means specifically encouraging ourselves (or our clients) to get way outside our comfort zones and visit places that will most likely test us in new ways. It means trying to "go native" as much as possible, meaning adapting to local customs and fully immerse yourself in this novel world, all the while suspending the usual critical judgments when things are different and unfamiliar.

One of the outcomes frequently reported by therapists who undertake transformative journeys is that they make new decisions about how they want to spend their time upon their return. It often takes getting away from our normal environment and influences for us to sort out what is most meaningful and important. One common realization is the importance of setting limits that we have not introduced or enforced previously.

Setting Limits

Thus far, many of the options presented involve a commitment to do something on an ongoing basis—another obligation of sorts—whether that involves exercising, investing in relationships, self-talk, taking breaks, or anything else. Yet for those who are overstimulated and overwhelmed, the key is to set clear boundaries about what you are willing and unwilling to do. This begins with knowing what your limits are in the first place and making sure to stick within them. There are some therapists who can comfortably see 15 clients a week and others who can see double or triple that number without ill effects.

For those in private practice it's always difficult to say no to any new referral because of the fear that new clients might stop coming. For those who work in the public sector, there is sometimes no choice regarding workload. Nevertheless, it is important to do what we can to create as much space as possible for recovery, reflection, and revitalization. This means declining new referrals, new opportunities, new requests that are not a priority. It means reducing the number of client contact hours and building in more breaks between sessions. It means restricting availability to clients and colleagues after hours. It could also mean cutting back expenditures and expenses so you have more freedom to work fewer hours. It also helps considerably to set limits with respect to your accessibility, turning off your mobile device at times, choosing not to answer a message or call right away, and giving yourself downtime with the usual distractions and disturbances.

The recurrent theme is modulating the amount of control you exercise in your personal and professional lives. For those who have overly permeable boundaries, this might mean shoring up the protective walls to allow time for more self-care; for others whose boundaries are far too rigid, developing flexibility might be the appropriate solution. Regardless of the desired path, we have learned all too well that entrenched patterns are difficult to change without a professional guide along the way.

When All Else Fails: Therapists Seeking Psychotherapy

The vast majority of therapists have been in the client's chair at some time in their lives, with estimates ranging from 50% for practitioners in general to 98% of psychoanalysts and 91% of humanistic therapists (Malikiosi-Loizos, 2013; Norcross & Guy, 2005). Obviously one's theoretical orientation would influence the choice given that some approaches would absolutely require sitting in the other chair to gain experience and work through personal issues, while others might even discourage it as completely unnecessary.

Therapists report being reluctant to seek such assistance because of fears of exposure, concerns about confidentiality, feelings of shame, avoidance of transferring power to an authority figure—in other words, all the usual excuses that anyone would use. In addition, however, therapists might also hold the belief that they can fix their own problems if just given enough time to do so. The overriding fear is that admitting personal problems may be interpreted as evidence of incompetence. When therapists do decide to seek outside help, it is usually related to dealing with stress, relationship issues, depression, anxiety, and conflict resolution and less frequently for career counseling or substance abuse (Norcross & Connor, 2005).

Even with these concerns, 90% of those who have entered therapy as a client report that it was incredibly helpful along a multitude of areas (Orlinsky, Norcross, Ronnestad, & Wiseman, 2005; Probst, 2015); first and foremost it allows them to learn so much more about the process from the other chair. They simultaneously hovered between roles of a client immersed in the sessions, and a critical observer, noting the impact of particular skills, interpretations, strategies, and methods (and yes, this *definitely* gets in the way). This helped them not only to learn new approaches to their own clinical work but also to realize what *not* to do in the future. They also reported afterwards that they felt increased respect and admiration for their own clients because of the courage it takes to do the work each week. One therapist, for example, listed all the ways that she was changed unexpectedly by sessions she attended, becoming far more patient with herself and others, improving her tolerance for ambiguity, uncertainty, and complexity, increasing her faith in the power of therapy as a transformative experience, and basically learning to love her own clients more than ever (Butler, 2014).

For any of us who specialize in treating other therapists, there are some obvious challenges related to maintaining boundaries and clarifying expectations for confusing roles. Such relationships tend to be more informal and so more subject to shifts in what might be expected. Therapist-clients would also be more inclined to be critical, analytic, and challenging, wanting to pull the curtain back to see what magic lies behind it. In some ways we are ideal clients because of our degree of sophistication and the fact that we speak the same language, whereas in other ways we can be quite resistant and hard to pin down.

One can only wonder about the number of practitioners who won't seek therapy for themselves, even when they are struggling with something they can't handle themselves. Several therapists interviewed for this book declined to comment on their method of working through their own problems. Just before abruptly terminating the interview, one respondent exemplified the hostility and defensiveness that this issue can arouse: "You ask me what I do when I encounter personal problems. One thing I would *never* do is see another therapist. I might try to work it through myself first and then talk to my wife, but I just wouldn't go to anyone else. I just don't trust other professionals. And even if I did, I've never had a reason to go."

Although this response is hardly typical of our profession, it occurred often enough to merit closer inspection. We may not all be as rigid, threatened, and mistrustful as this particular therapist, but many of us do seem to feel that therapy is for others rather than ourselves. No less than a dozen therapists responded to the questions about their personal problems with a simple, "I can't think of any."

At first, I wondered whether there might really be some among us who have attained a state of nirvana, perfect specimens of emotional and behavioral functioning who have transcended the problems of mortal beings. More than likely, questions that ask therapists to look at their vulnerabilities elicit the same kind of reactions as they would clients. We deny that we have problems. Those that we grudgingly admit to, we think we can handle ourselves. We become defensive and irritable; we prefer our illusions of grandeur.

Because therapists both see behind the wizard's curtain and inhabit that space, we can be particularly challenging clients in our own psychotherapy. We have little tolerance for the usual practices that might work with less sophisticated clients. There is a part of our brain that is always observing the treatment methods critically, naming the techniques, wondering about the choices made, acting as much as a spectator as a participant in the process. Furthermore, if we really want to play games, there is nobody more skilled at doing so.

There was a time several years ago when I was quite unhappy with the trajectory of my life and my career. I felt stuck and didn't know how to extricate myself. Like most people, I first tried to handle things on my own, offering the usual excuses that I didn't have time, couldn't afford therapy, or could never find a professional who would meet my exacting standards and see through my usual ploys.

Not content to consult with just one therapist, I was such a critical consumer that I scheduled appointments with three different practitioners in the same week. I was burned out with work and depressed about my life situation; I felt trapped and helpless to do anything about it. Like most prospective clients, I had already exhausted my personal resources and most of the coping strategies mentioned in this chapter. Nothing was working: I felt desperate and hopeless. After getting in two serious car accidents within a short time, neither of which seemed to be my fault, I was faced with the realization that I had to get help.

The first therapist I consulted was a mean son of a gun—direct, blunt, and, in my mind, heartless. He began the first session by asking me about my earliest memory, which I related was holding my brother in my lap on the way home from the hospital immediately after his birth.

"How did you feel holding your brother?" he asked me. Truthfully, I couldn't really remember, but the guy scared me, so I tried my best to come up with a suitable answer. "I was scared," I told him.

"Scared?"

"Yeah, I mean I was only 3 years old, and my parents were letting me hold this brand-new baby. I was afraid I might drop him or something."

"I see," he said to me. Then a long pause. "That's really your problem, isn't it?"

"What's my problem?" We'd been in session all of 20 minutes and already he had me diagnosed. That was impressive indeed. So far I had told him that

I was tired of being a therapist and was considering other career options, maybe teaching or practicing in another setting.

"You obviously have a problem with responsibility," he told me with what appeared to be a smug smile.

"I do?" This was surprising because I was one of the most responsible individuals I knew.

"Absolutely. You were afraid of holding your brother. And now you're afraid of the hard work of being a therapist. You want to run away from the responsibility just like you have done your whole life." Then he crossed his arms and looked at me as if he dared me to answer his accusation.

I sat sobbing in my car after that session, thinking that if this is what being a client in therapy was really like, I'd rather endure my suffering, even risk another accident. I felt some possibility of hope with the prospect of two more therapists to go.

If the first therapist was cruel and heartless, the second one, Glinda (as in the Good Witch from *The Wonderful Wizard of Oz*), was warm, caring, supportive, sensitive, and accepting. She reassured me that everything would be all right. She told me that I had a right to feel the way I did. She agreed with me that the first therapist had been out of line. It was clear to me she would agree with almost anything I said. So I fired her as well.

I warned you that this was a story about therapists being difficult clients, didn't I? I figured I knew way too much about how therapy worked, enough that perhaps I was immune to the magic. My standards were just too high. I had reasons to disqualify almost anyone I might see—too mean or too nice. I also realized that if I was ever going to get some help, I had better undergo an attitude adjustment and let go of my need for control. I say I trust the process; now it was time to prove it.

If the first therapist was too cold, and the second was too hot, then the third was just right. Maybe it wasn't him at all, but rather my willingness to do whatever it took to be a good client. I could hear echoing in my mind all the admonishments of hypocrisy that have been repeated throughout this book: What the heck was wrong with me that I believed so passionately in my clients asking for help, when I was so resistant to doing so myself? Or I would ask for help in a way that it could never be acceptable to me.

There will be times in our lives when each of us will face challenges that seem beyond us. We shake our heads in befuddlement when some clients express their extreme distaste and reluctance for what we do, having been stubborn and unwilling to ask for help when they so desperately needed it. Yet there is little doubt that our own reservoir of energy is slowly depleted with every session, until such time that we also need replenishment. Whether you find peace in a church, mosque, temple, or synagogue, a theater, garden, sports arena, or on the road is beside the point. The important thing is to do something for yourself so that you can take things less personally, adjust your expectations to realistic levels, break away as you need it, and talk to yourself as you do to your clients. Most of all, by doing something for yourself, you demonstrate that you take your own growth just as seriously as you do that of your clients.

13

Toward Creativity and Personal Growth

THERE IS A long and distinguished history within our profession of famous therapists doing some pretty unusual things to get through to their clients. Stories of Milton Erickson, Carl Whitaker, and Fritz Perls abound about some of their stunts—slapping a client in Perls's case, and breastfeeding a client or sleeping during a session in Whitaker's case; and there are so many books written about Erickson's creative interventions, they are impossible to catalogue. In more recent times, this tradition has continued through the work of brief and solution-focused practitioners who resort to all kinds of innovative ways to get through to resistant clients.

There are some writers who believe that therapy, as a profession, could quite legitimately be housed in an academy of dramatic arts instead of a school of education, health, social work, medicine, or liberal arts. "In this setting, therapists would speak of their craft as professional conversation, strategic rhetoric, or even a genre of interactional theater" (Keeney, 1991, p. 1). Indeed, when Jeff Zeig, Ericksonian therapist and founder of the Evolution of Psychotherapy Conferences, wanted to take his clinical skills to the next level, he did so not just by studying the recordings of all the most prominent clinicians but also by taking acting lessons to increase his capacity for improvisation, spontaneity, creativity, and innovation.

Treating the practice of therapy as a creative or dramatic art certainly has as much merit as viewing it as applied science. If science is therapy's brain, then creativity is its heart. It is the source of our intuition, the flexibility that leads to innovative models, and the energy that drives our most inspired inventions. Creativity is the essence of what makes each of us so uniquely powerful and influential.

Therapists must be creative because so much of what we do is spontaneous and improvisational; we react and respond in the moment to whatever is happening. We are creative in the ways we organize our knowledge and research base so that we can retrieve stuff on demand. We are creative in the ways we frame and understand client issues, in the ways we modify and refine our clinical style, and certainly in the methods by which we deal with the impasses that inevitably occur. Creativity also plays a role in the ways we maintain a freshness in our perspective, in the ways we stay energized and continue growing, learning, and improving our effectiveness. Finally, we are creative in the sometimes ingenious ways we help clients break loose from their rigid, self-defeating patterns, to think, feel, and act differently.

Everything comes together for us in the creative process. When we experience a major insight it neutralizes boredom, burnout, and other professional hazards. Through an innovative procedure, we share our passion for discovery with the client.

The creative journey toward a new understanding, for the client or the therapist, follows a progression from the familiar to the unknown. During this passage, there is a movement from stable ground to confusion, frustration, and self-doubt. It takes courage and a certain degree of risk to be creative, given that we are breaking new ground or experimenting with something that has not been tried before. Whether part of a gradual evolution or a period of stunning insight, creative breakthroughs are what keep us most engaged in the process of doing this work.

The Urge to Create

Therapists are, at least theoretically, self-actualizing people. Abraham Maslow eloquently connected this intrinsic growth motive with the urge to create. He described one of his subjects, a psychiatrist and pure clinician, as follows: "This man approached each patient as if he were the only one in the world, without jargon, expectations, or presuppositions, with innocence and naïveté and yet with great wisdom, in a Taoist fashion. Each patient was a unique human being and therefore a completely new problem to be understood and solved in a completely novel way" (Maslow, 1968, p. 136).

Personal growth and creativity are synonymous in the life of a therapist. The very process of therapy involves discovering and creating new patterns of meaning in people's experiences. Ideally, it is possible to use our creative thinking for the benefit of enlightenment. We do this in our office as well as at home. A child therapist works in solo practice but never feels lonely or isolated; instead she finds the solitude more conducive to trying things her own way. Like many of the therapists I've interviewed, she didn't think of herself as particularly creative but admitted that sometimes she does things she might agree are a little unusual. "The way I do therapy always changes. I use art or music or movement or anything that strikes me at the time in my sessions. I trust that aspect of myself." She also tries to be congruent between the creative spirit she tries to empower when working and how she practices that in her daily life. "I think the way that I live is creative. I have a great sense of humor. I do a lot of sometimes wacky things. There have been times I've awakened the kids at 2:00 a.m. to drive downtown for ice cream. Or sometimes I like to do crazy things like hide from my husband when he comes home from work and then jump out and scare him."

Why do we experience the urge to create? On the simplest level, the most basic of all human drives is to create another life in our own image, to perpetuate our gene pool. Our survival as a species has depended not only on the persistence of our progeny but on our abilities as versatile, cunning, and creative problem solvers.

Therapists have more than their share of creative energy. Our ideas live for generations through every client we help. People may forget their grocer or their fourth-grade teacher or their neighbor, but they never forget their therapist. What clients will remember about their therapists is likely to be a particularly novel idea that they introduced or a familiar concept that was presented in an instructive way. For this reason, a therapists will live as long as their ideas survive.

Resistance to Creativity

On first sight, creative acts are often viewed as a form of deviance. A brief glimpse into our field's history reveals a number of contributions that were initially scorned and ridiculed. Neither Freud, nor anyone who has come on the scene since, has had an easy time finding a sympathetic audience for his or her radical approaches to helping.

While teaching at the University of Chicago, Carl Rogers agreed to present a lecture at the University of Minnesota, home of E. G. Williamson, the founder of advice-giving counseling and the guidance movement. At the time, in addition to this directive style of treatment, the other dominant therapies were the behavioral controlling techniques of B. F. Skinner and Freud's psychoanalysis, which were, by then, firmly entrenched in the United States. Perhaps with some naïveté, Rogers ventured into this territory to talk about a focus on the present instead of the past and an emphasis on emotional expression rather than on behavior or thinking. "I was totally unprepared for the furor the talk aroused," Rogers wrote, "I was criticized. I was praised. I was attacked. I was looked on with complete puzzlement." Yet it was precisely this controversy that got his attention and inspired him to develop his ideas further: "It would seem quite absurd to suppose that one could name a day on which client-centered therapy was born. Yet I feel it is possible to name that day and it was December 11, 1940" (quoted in Kirschenbaum, 2009, p. 109).

People are threatened by new ideas that challenge what they think they already know. Resistance to creative thinking is much more the norm than the exception. Especially in the evolution of science, professional thinkers have much preferred aesthetics and symmetry in their ideas to the chaos of reality. Boorstein (1983, p. 86) comments on why it took so long for explorers, who long had the necessary technology, to find and plot the geographical world: "The great obstacle to discovering the shape of the earth, the continents, and the ocean was not ignorance but the illusion of knowledge. Imagination drew in bold strokes, instantly serving hopes and fears, while knowledge advanced by slow increments and contradictory witnesses. Villagers who themselves feared to ascend the mountaintops located their departed ones on the impenetrable heavenly heights."

One scientist who sought to climb the mountain and find out for himself why so many people depart life before their time was Ignaz Semmelweiss. Koestler (1964) mentions his case as an example of the inevitable and stubborn resistance that accompanies any creative act that revolutionizes our thinking. In 1847, Semmelweiss discovered that it was the filth, bacteria, and residual cadaveric material on a surgeon's hands, that had caused infections in patients who became worse after operations. He was the first to suggest that it might be a good idea for doctors to wash their hands in chlorinated lime water before touching a patient, an innovation that significantly reduced the mortality rate from infections in the hospital. Rather than being honored or rewarded by his colleagues, he was denounced for implying that doctors were "murderers" since they were allegedly killing their patients with so-called germs on their hands. Alas, Semmelweiss eventually died in a straightjacket, raving mad.

A similar but no less dramatic fate of ostracism befell many other creative geniuses—Copernicus, Galileo, Darwin, Mozart, and van Gogh, to name but a few representatives of their fields. In most cases, a creative idea is first viewed with suspicion and resentment. Perhaps this probationary period is constructive in that it filters out many worthless eccentricities; innovators who can stand the test of time and the criticism of their peers endure.

Creativity is often resisted in therapy because it usually involves breaking rules. Our culture may endorse the idea of creativity, but it certainly does not embrace new structures that render the old ones obsolete. Bloom (1975) mentions how creative acts within our field often stand in opposition to the structures that were built by those currently in power. Inevitably, there will be tension and conflict before the new ideas can be accepted. When we are breaking rules for the sake of finding successful, novel solutions to client problems, Bloom offers the reminders that, first of all, all rules will eventually be broken. Second, if you are going to stick your neck out and experiment with something new, be prepared that some people are not going to like that. Third, assume that every client deserves to be treated as a unique and individual challenge that deserves a creative solution. Finally, because creative efforts almost always involve some risk, it is advisable to be cautious and recognize that they could do more harm than good.

Risking and Creativity

The mentality of the beginner in this profession is to avoid creative or risky behavior for fear of harming somebody. The midcareer professional may also avoid creative or risky activities in favor of what is tried and true. In both instances, the clinician is locked into a safe, predictable style of working that may produce consistent if unremarkable results.

Risk and fear are inseparable. There cannot be the possibility of gain without the possibility of loss—no matter how carefully one anticipates and prepares. Taking risks means, to some, the possibility of making the wrong choice. In almost all cases, it means breaking away from the status quo. It also means dealing with unknown consequences.

The risk in trying something new in therapy is that it is possible, if not probable, that it won't work in the first few attempts. We risk losing our way. After attending a workshop, or reading a new book, there is often initial excitement about applying some new idea. The first few times we practice what we have learned, it feels awkward and contrived. After some period of time, we are able to incorporate the method into a style that is reasonably smooth. Finally, in the last stage, we are able to internalize the technique, to make it part of ourselves, in such a way that it no longer belongs to someone else.

The process of doing therapy awakens in us the sense of ourselves as explorers. We teach others to discover uncharted territory, to learn survival skills and apply them in conditions of maximum stress. We teach people about their limits and their capabilities. We help people take controlled risks, where much of the danger can be anticipated.

Risk—the possibility of failure or loss—cannot be avoided if the possibility of success is to have any meaning. There are risks of emotion that involve honestly and spontaneously expressing feelings, admitting fear, or professing love. There are risks of growth in giving up control, in being yourself, or in trying something that has never been attempted before. There are risks of intimacy in working through vulnerability, jealousy, and trust. There are risks of autonomy in cutting off dependencies and being more responsible. And there are risks of change that involve breaking old rules, patterns, and habits and moving into the world of the unknown.

There have been certain conventions within the profession that have been considered sacrosanct, for example, that sessions are 50 minutes long or that the interaction should only take place between participants sitting in chairs in an office even though there is no particularly compelling evidence that those factors must be honored; after all, they are more for the convenience of the therapist than they are for any reason related to better outcomes. Jacques Lacan stirred quite a controversy when he suggested that sessions should only take as long as a client actually needs on any given day. He would thus refuse to take appointments and just ask people to show up in his waiting room if they wanted to see him. He would then determine if they needed just 5 minutes or 2 hours, depending on the nature of the problem and their willingness to do deep work that day.

Changing the format, structure, or context of therapy is certainly risky when it is outside the usual expectations of what is considered standard treatment. Yet some therapists are pushing those bounds and still remaining carefully attentive to any possible ethical breaches or the consequences of boundary "crossings." One investigation looked at those therapists who take their clients on field trips or conduct their sessions outside the office, even if just going for a walk (Revell & McLeod, 2016). Would such an activity increase the risk of possible improprieties or misunderstandings within the relationship? Possibly. But the study also offered quite a number of advantages helping work through an impasse, improving the relationship, building deeper trust and intimacy, fostering greater openness, and creating an overall sense of well-being. Likewise (and perhaps not surprisingly), the therapists really enjoyed these kinds of sessions as a change of pace, creating more variety in their day, invigorating their energy, and reducing stress. In addition, if we may rely on their self-reports, they said fairly consistently that they were easily able to concentrate and focus on the conversations without feeling distracted and also did some of their best work during these "walk and talks."

Nevertheless, there are risks associated with doing anything creative or innovative that is not currently in widespread use or empirically tested. Yet we all find ourselves in situations where we use our best judgment and take a leap of faith, (hopefully) certain that we are doing this for the client's own best interests rather our own convenience and preference. Our intuition—or perhaps impulsiveness—leads us to try something we've never done before, not at all sure about what will happen.

I have a home office where I occasionally see clients, and I was having some work done on the house, so I notified a scheduled client (another therapist) that we could reschedule in the future or else just walk to a nearby coffee shop where they had a private room in the back. I felt a bit uneasy suggesting this option, but the client readily agreed, so off we went. During the walk itself, I could tell we both felt awkward with this novel arrangement, but things quickly loosened up, and we ended up talking about things we never had before. When the next week the construction was still not completed, I offered another alternative to sit on our back patio, since I still felt uneasy about going to a public place. Once again, the session was groundbreaking in a number of ways. But the thing that struck me most about these two very different conversations is that we both had almost perfect recall of everything that was said and frequently referred back to the "coffee shop session" or the "patio session" once we resumed our normal structure. It got me thinking that if the goal of what we do is to create novel interaction experiences, the kind that produce lasting changes, wouldn't we better off changing things up once in awhile to keep things fresh and exciting?

I don't mean to advocate specifically for conducting sessions outside the office, but just to stimulate thinking about ways we could be more innovative, creative, and experimental without jeopardizing client safety and welfare.

Creative Problem Solving

What we do, in part, is helping people to solve problems for a living—or if not to resolve them, at least to learn to better understand and live with them. Since by the time clients arrive in our offices they have already likely exhausted most of the obvious solutions and tried whatever they—or anyone else—could think of, our task is often to help them consider far more creative options.

Some of the best examples of creative problem solving come from the family therapy practitioners who seek to break rigid hierarchies of power and vicious circles designed to repel any outside intervention. This takes place through (1) helping clients find new ways of getting unstuck from their perceived hopeless situations, (2) not being confined by any single theory, (3) accessing unexpected and unknown resources, (4) embracing the complexity and paradoxes inherent in family issues, (5) being flexible about the ways conflicts can be resolved, (6) always questioning everything and why things are done that way, (7) thinking outside traditional parameters of what is supposedly appropriate, (8) being spontaneous and doing things that are improvisational, (9) embracing humor and playfulness in interactions, and (10) trusting intuition as well as logic. Innovation and experimentation are the hallmarks of these strategic helpers who rely on strange, novel, sometimes hilarious means to initiate change in difficult clients.

When intuition and creativity are combined with our natural heritage of empiricism, philosophical inquiry, and the rigorous application of scientific methodology, we have at our disposal a process that is both creative and cautious, radical and responsible. As mentioned, clients come to us only after they have already exhausted the more traditional and obvious problem-solving strategies. They have discovered that drugs do not always work for very long, nor does blaming others or wishing that problems would magically vanish. Hiding under the covers feels safe until you have to change the sheets. Faced with nowhere else to go, all other options eliminated, they walk into the therapist's office, defeated. Obviously, the cure will be found in something that the client has not yet tried or, in the case of very difficult clients, in what no other therapist has yet discovered.

While doing trauma work after an earthquake, one woman approached me with a paralyzed hand that she claimed no longer worked at all and had no sensation whatsoever. She had already been checked out by our surgeon, who found no organic cause for the problem. When I asked her what she had already tried to fix her hand, she repeated a long list of things that others in her village had suggested to her, none of which had any effect whatsoever.

Since she claimed that she had not actually been injured by any falling debris, I asked her how she came to end up with a "broken" hand. She told me that at the moment of the shock waves that brought buildings down all around her, she had grabbed ahold of her mother to steady themselves as the ground rocked back and forth. Ever since that terrible moment, her hand had stopped working.

"Hmmm," I muttered, having no idea what to tell this woman. This was like one of Freud's earliest cases of hysteria in which someone develops psychosomatic symptoms as a result of some trauma. Since I had always treated such cases as "fairy tales," I was now completely at a loss for how to proceed. Given the language difficulties we already had communicating, her extreme level of anxiety, and her insistence that the problem was likely the result of some act of the gods, it was pretty clear that nothing I had ever tried before would likely work in this case. So instead I threw everything into the wind to see what might blow back at me. Before I could even consider how bizarre this was going to be, I instructed the woman as follows, based on some hazy recollection of what a shaman might do to promote spiritual intervention: "For the next 3 days and nights, I want your mother to rub warm oil into your hand, slowly massaging each part. I also want you to take one of these pills each evening, which will also help considerably." I then ceremoniously handed her three aspirin.

Did this rather strange intervention have the desired effect of curing her broken hand? I have no idea because we had to move on to the next village where there were hundreds of additional people requiring medical and trauma care. It was out of desperation that I was forced to come up with an intervention that, rationally, made little sense but, in a strange way, made perfect sense to the client as a viable solution to her problem.

Creative Thinking

In spite of the common belief that creativity is some sort of innate trait that one either has or doesn't have, it can be more functionally thought of as a type of mental process that we engage in every day in all sorts of ways. In most cases, it doesn't represent some major innovation or breakthrough as much as it involves an adaptation of something that's been tried before; in the context of therapy it is almost always a collaborative partnership.

In an essay for researchers on breaking out of their conceptual ruts and away from the tendency to think as clones of one another, Wicker (1985) offered the advice that may be applied with equal usefulness to the fostering of creativity in therapists:

- Adopt a playful, whimsical attitude by exploring unusual metaphors.
- Constantly tinker with the assumptions of your operating principles, especially those you hold most sacred.
- Attempt to expose hidden assumptions by increasing your awareness of implicit processes in your work.

The therapist functions much of the time as a detective. First, she attempts to figure out the "crime" that a client feels he has committed that is bad enough to warrant symptomatic punishment. She interviews the suspect, reconstructs the scene, and carefully gathers evidence. She formulates a motive, a hypothesis regarding how and why the symptoms appeared. She deduces a modus operandi, a signature to the crime, a pattern in which the current symptoms fit the client's characteristic style. She gently interrogates the client, squeezing out a confession that will exhaust the need for continued self-punishment. In these activities, it is the therapist's willingness to enter the client's world, to sift through all the information available, and finally to connect events and intuitively interpret their meaning that will solve the problem. To accomplish these tasks, the therapist must be a creative detective, must be able to see beyond the obvious to the often disguised and subtle clues that lie embedded in a client's behavior.

Dimensions of Creative Practice

Having studied the work of several writers about the creative process in therapy (Beaulieu, 2006; Carson & Becker, 2003; Gladding, 2008, 2016; Keeney, 2009; Kottler, Carlson, & Keeney, 2004; Levy, 2014; Rosenthal, 2001) and interviewed prominent therapists about their most creative breakthroughs (Kottler & Carlson, 2009), the following themes appear to be most significant in leading to innovation in practice.

Admitting you're lost. Before you can invent something new, you first must be willing to recognize that you have already run out of available options. You have already exhausted what you know, repeated your favored methods, and now realize that you are going to have to find a way out of this maze by trying something that you (or maybe anyone) have never tried before. That feeling is both exhilarating and sometimes terrifying.

Questioning cherished assumptions and conventional wisdom. Like most people, you do what you do, and do it the way you prefer, because that is the way you've always done it (at least lately). We get into routines that effortlessly guide the ways we work and live our lives. We drive the same routes to get to familiar places. We order the same things off the menu and prepare our meals in the same way. When doing therapy, we sit in the same place and begin sessions the same way, doing what we can to maintain stability, predictability, and sameness. Rarely do we question why we do things this way and why we can't make adjustments, or even radical shifts, in our procedures. If the goal is often to shake things up for clients, to provide novel and memorable learning experiences, why can't the participants sit in different places each session? Or better yet, why not rearrange the furniture, or even the location of each session? There are infinite ways we can change what it is we do, not for change's sake, but rather to keep our clients alert and engaged.

Embracing mystery and confusion. Typically therapy is defined as an enterprise that helps clients make better sense of their lives. We are all about promoting understanding and insight, finding or creating meaning. Yet most healers of the world see their jobs as honoring the mystery of life, and, rather than making sense of things, they do things that are deliberately and strategically designed to be confusing. Their goal is to turn off the analytic brain and instead embrace direct experience with all its uncertainty, confusion, and power. Thus therapeutic tasks and ordeals are designed *not* to follow logically from the presenting problem but rather to emerge from intuition and a felt sense of what might be useful.

A self-respecting shaman would tell you that rather than reading these words about creativity, what you should do instead (and feel free to follow these instructions) is (1) tear this page out of the book; (2) write down in the margins of the page free-associated words and images that have come to mind as you read this far on the page; (3) carefully fold the page in half, then into quarters; (4) place the folded piece of paper between your pillowcase and your pillow; (5) go to sleep with the page under your pillow and allow yourself to dream whatever is stimulated by this procedure; and (6) don't attempt to make sense of the dreams you have—just follow them wherever they may lead you.

Okay, maybe I just lost you. But my point is that creativity often involves doing things that are designed to honor mystery and confusion rather than always trying to erase them by providing the illusion of understanding. This helps not only our clients but also ourselves to increase our tolerance for ambiguity, complexity, and confusion—which is much of what life is about.

Cognitive flexibility and fluency. Most studies of creativity define the process as the ability to generate multiple solutions to a problem, as many as possible. One of the things that clients soon realize is that the more options they have at hand to deal with a situation, the more empowered they tend to feel. It is similar with therapeutic practice: the more different ways we can look at an issue, the more flexibility we have in addressing it from multiple perspectives. This is the essence of reframing seemingly intractable problems in different ways, leading to more creative solutions. Also, the lesson learned from some kinds of solution-focused therapy is that if you try something and it doesn't work, try something else—anything other than what you are already doing.

This is something we try to teach to clients but don't practice as often as we could in our own behavior.

Thinking outside the box. This is a common description of creativity, but such thinking is sometimes difficult to imagine when we are *inside* the box. Among the interviews we conducted on creative breakthroughs (Kottler & Carlson, 2009), a few examples of this phenomenon stood out. Ericksonian Michael Yapko described how he demanded that his client give him $1 million in order to demonstrate how unrealistic it was to keep asking someone for something that he will never give, in this case a father's approval. Narrative therapist Steve Madigan talked about the way he worked with a hospitalized patient who was inconsolable in his grief over the death of his young daughter. Madigan gathered together all of the man's friends and relatives to initiate a letter-writing campaign of support. Feminist therapist Laura Brown heard a client talk about how she felt stuck in a box, and so structured several sessions in which the client actually sat inside a huge box, finally breaking through when she felt ready. Researcher Scott Miller mentioned a case in which he pretended to be Sylvester Stallone in order to challenge a client's insistence that he was actually Rambo. In these and so many other cases, the therapists tried things that previously had been unimaginable; they were encouraged to experiment with new strategies that they'd never considered before.

Uncertainty and ambiguity. Almost by definition, being creative means we are operating in the unknown, without familiar landmarks or guides. The more we learn to increase our tolerance for this uncertainty, the more likely we are to be willing and able to visit new places in our work with clients.

One counselor describes how she lives with the experience of "not-knowing" the true impact of her work, yet still forges onward to be as creative as she can. She considers herself fortunate (in some ways) that she actually lives with her clients, who are students in a boarding school, since she can chat with them in their natural environment and learn all kinds of things about their lives that would otherwise be unattainable. "It's like being surrounded by a hundred teachers. It's the perfect environment to work collaboratively, experientially, and creatively. I can work from canoes, on the beach, by the campfire. I meet the families and friends."

As much as she enjoys the diversity of options, she still admits that it's hard to tell when she's making a real difference in their lives. "Every time one of them stumbles, I worry that I haven't done enough for them so, sometimes, I return to traditional cognitive strategies. I stop trusting the process or get lazy or scared," which she admits almost always backfires. "Emotions escalate, heels dig in, trust is lost. And even when formal interventions do unfold gloriously, within a day or two, a new crisis develops. So I never have a sense of completion, efficacy, or acknowledgment. And I know that growth is in the hands of the client, so I may never attain a sense of competency or equilibrium. That off-balance feeling is always hovering."

It may very well be that it isn't what superlative therapists do *in* sessions that is as important as all the reflective time and energy they spend *between* sessions thinking creatively about their cases (Miller, Hubble, & Duncan, 2007). So if the goal is to be more creative, one way to do that is to work at it and make it a major priority in your life and work. This is true not only with respect to clinical practice but also when it comes to using our skills to make a difference in the wider world.

On Wisdom and Creativity

Whereas creativity is often a learned or developed trait or behavior, most philosophers have struggled to define the nature of wisdom, much less its particular attributes. One can be wise without demonstrating creative thinking; likewise, one can demonstrate creative actions without any semblance of wisdom in how they can be useful.

Being a therapist is as much a lifestyle choice as it is a job or profession. It means a life devoted to the pursuit of wisdom, especially the practical kind that can be passed on to others. Although wisdom is usually associated with being highly experienced or elderly, there are a number of other traits that have been identified as components of this characteristic (Korkki, 2014). Wise elders and therapists have a far more nuanced reflection on accumulated experience, able to recognize patterns and subtle differences with a certain clarity and vision. They are able to demonstrate both a high degree of emotional regulation, as well as tolerance for individual and cultural differences. They have a highly developed understanding of life's priorities, and yet can face existential despair with faith and humility.

This description of wisdom is actually the ways that older, more mature practitioners display their creativity. Originality has been normally associated with the energy and passion of youth, yet older therapists make their own innovative contributions by relying on their signature strengths instead of dwelling on their age-related losses that may make daily functioning more challenging in some ways (Kottler & Carlson, 2016). For older therapists, this means possible compromised memory functioning or reduced energy, but it also means having far more diverse life experiences and "messier" minds that can lead to extraordinarily creative behavior when several internal strategies are frequently employed (Gregoire, 2014), the first of which, ironically, is lots of daydreaming. It turns out that the creative mind needs downtime to roam in undisciplined, unstructured ways. This means giving oneself the time, space, and permission, to sit or walk around with no other agenda except to let our thoughts and feelings wander where they will.

Whereas behaviors that promote creative thinking and action involve a marked lack of structure, this must be tempered with some degree of careful, critical analysis of what we have noticed, observed, and sensed is going on. Therapists are ideally suited for such scrupulous observation and analysis because of the nature of our training: Who else is more qualified and experienced in figuring out the meaning and nuances of behavior or life's most challenging questions?

Creativity is most often triggered by seeking the "silver lining" in any situation or opportunity, looking for the learning experience or lesson that might prove useful. That is one reason why many master therapists prefer not to look at their so-called "failures" as anything other than valuable feedback regarding what needs to be altered or changed. With successful aging comes an acceptance of one's limitations and unrealistic expectations, helping to convert some novel idea into very practical and realistic application. But there are still certain risks associated with any new or experimental strategy that has uncertain outcomes.

Erik and Joan Erikson wrote eloquently about the wise and creative spirit associated with later maturity that is driven by the developmental stage of generativity. In most cultures around the world (except increasingly in the West), elders are afforded status and honored, not only for what they have accomplished in their lives, but for their role within the community as advisor and sage. Elders are expected to devote their latter years to serving others, using what they have learned to mentor and guide the next generation.

As therapists age and attain "senior status," many find a yearning to apply what they know and understand to settings outside the usual and customary domains of an office. With time running short, the aging clock ticking away, they may feel a commitment to make a difference on a larger—or at least different—scale. It is one thing to work with a single individual for an hour and quite another to devote time to promote systemic changes within a group, organization, or community. I've talked a lot about the ways that therapists remain vibrant, creative, and professionally engaged through a process of periodically reinventing themselves. This has been especially the case with clinicians reaching way beyond the restrictions of therapy sessions to "do good" in other contexts.

There's been a lot of talk (but a lot less action) about the therapist's role and responsibility to advocate on behalf of the marginalized and oppressed as well as promote an agenda of social justice. Most therapists are so busy and overwhelmed with their day jobs that it's hard for them to find the time, much less the opportunity, to intervene creatively on a more systemic level. Yet therapists are becoming increasingly involved in community and world affairs and finding this to be among the greatest satisfactions of their lives. Mary Pipher (2013) mentions how there have been times she has felt such despair at the hopelessness of addressing certain environmental or social issues that it just made her head and heart hurt. "So I decided to get to work," she says, "because action has always been what pulls me out of despair." This realization is what led her to use her therapeutic and leadership skills to organize efforts in her community.

Therapists are redefining their roles, embarking on spiritual quests as concerned citizens of their communities (Norcross & Guy, 2007; Rojano, 2007), catalysts for social change (Doherty, 2008), advocates of social justice (Aldarondo, 2007; Bemak & Chung, 2008; Kottler, Englar-Carlson, & Carlson, 2013), and agents of transformational change in global human rights (Kottler, 2008; Kottler & Marriner, 2009) and political institutions (Roy, 2007). More and more often, there isn't just discussion of issues related to the therapist's responsibility with regard to issues of poverty, deprivation, inequity, racism, oppression, violence, genocide, starvation, abuse, and catastrophe, but also increased action on these fronts.

Since I am certainly one of those aging, elder therapists, I've had plenty of time to reflect on ways that my knowledge and skills might be put to more creative use outside the traditional office. More and more often during recent times, I've tried to expand ways that I might apply what I do to help those who would never have the opportunity to seek the services of a therapist. I've taken students to work in orphanages in Cambodia, schools in India, a leprosy colony in Ghana, refugee camps in the Middle East, conducting home visits in Nepal, volunteering with homeless residents in our local community, all designed not only to make a difference in these settings but also to inspire new therapists to make this a part of their life and professional mission. It is from stretching ourselves in new and different ways and contexts that both our wisdom and creativity are helped to grow.

Doing Therapy as a Creative Enterprise

It often seems like there are two opposing points of view related to practicing therapy. One approach emphasizes reliability and consistency in interventions. Some believe that to minimize chance variables and maximize intentionality, it is crucial for therapists to be able to replicate what they do. When you find something that works—a particular anecdote or metaphor, a structure or intervention, an interpretation or technique—you should, according to this approach, use it again and again because of its demonstrated effects. Not to do so is to cheat the client of an empirically tested remedy that is known to be useful.

On a smaller scale, we may tend to rely on the same anecdotes, examples, and verbalizations that we have honed over time. One standard and reliable response to the client complaint, "I'm not getting any better," might be to to reply, "Then the therapy must be working, because it is helping you become uncomfortable and therefore more motivated to change." Relying on this well-tested response may be consistently effective, but in time the therapist using it may begin to feel like a computer that spits out a canned answer in response to any given button that is pushed.

Some dedicated and very successful therapists do not mind sacrificing their own fresh involvement in the spontaneous process of change for the sake of telling a client something they have told a hundred other clients previously. One clinician explained his rationale for consistency in his therapeutic formula: "Look, I've worked a long time to perfect my favorite metaphors. I have no right to exchange them for as yet unproven examples just for my own amusement. Of course I get tired of saying the same things to all my clients, but that's what I'm paid to do."

Another perspective conceives of each therapy session as an individual masterpiece. It may (and probably will) contain elements in common with many other works of art in the same style. The same themes repeat themselves. The process of change generally follows a predictable pattern, even if the client's individual history and the therapist's characteristic style vary. Such a clinician attempts to translate her energy authentically in every session, to create each therapeutic work of art with personalized appeal. In the words of one practitioner, "I have this rule never to repeat myself, or at least not in the precise way I expressed something before. Even if I don't alter the story, I will tell it in a different way or relate it more specifically to the life of a particular client."

This sounds like an a lot of additional work, but she can't get the fantasy out of her head that some day her clients might somehow meet one another and compare notes about what she said to them. "I can't stand the idea that they might discover I told them the same thing. It is much harder on me to stay on my toes and think of new ways to get points across, but it's worth it: I'm always learning and getting better. And I never get bored."

The practice of therapy can indeed be an exercise in creativity—especially in the ways we play with language. We are playwrights in that we spontaneously compose and direct dialogue, acting our various roles of a nurturer, an authority, or a character from a client's life. We are poets in that we create images and metaphors to illustrate ideas. Over the years, most practitioners have compiled in their heads a wonderful library of helping stories and therapeutic anecdotes that they have borrowed or invented. These represent the sum total of a practitioner's lifework. One of the things we do so well as we walk through life is collect things that may be useful in a session at a later time.

Considering that creativity is essentially the discovery of an analogy that connects along multiple planes, therapists are original thinkers of the first order. We use humor and parody to defuse tension with a client, to confront the client in a less threatening way, or to discuss taboo subjects that might be more difficult to approach from a more direct angle. Implicit in a humorous anecdote or pun could be the nucleus of a major insight, one that the client may first laugh at before considering the painful truth that the punch line contains.

Laughter, we know, has a cathartic value of its own. The therapist's occasional role as a court jester who seeks to coax a smile out of the frozen features of despair represents only one way that humor can be used in the therapeutic process. Koestler (1964, pp. 91–92) found humor to be the best single example of how the creative mind works: "To cause surprise the humorist must have a modicum of originality—the ability to break away from the stereotyped routines of thought. Caricaturist, satirist, the writer of nonsense-humor, and even the expert tickler, each operates on more than one plane. Whether his purpose is to convey a social message, or merely to entertain, he must provide mental jolts, caused by the collision of incompatible matrices."

The preceding theory of humor could also be a description of therapy itself: helping people break away from stereotyped routines, providing mental jolts, and especially encouraging thinking on multiple levels. In this routine, the therapist is a scholar and practitioner of originality par excellence. Each and every client presents us with her perception of a disturbing crisis or a serious problem that has no solution. Because we are capable of viewing any behavior on many levels, we do not experience the same feelings of being stuck as the client does. We can reframe the problem in a different light, change its shape in such a way that it may be solved more easily. Often this simple maneuver of looking at the same old problem from a different angle is sufficient in itself to provide immediate relief.

Originality is evidenced in the therapist's thinking and behavior in other ways as well. When we stop to consider the conditions that are likely to spawn creative acts—that is, permissiveness, absence of external criticism, openness to new experience, acceptance of novelty, an emphasis on internal control and individual autonomy, flexible problem solving, integration of cognitive-affective dimensions, and psychological safety and support—we realize that we are describing the experience of therapy. The client and the therapist interact within an environment that is designed to promote the maximum amount of creative thinking. Each gives the other permission to experiment with new ideas and novel approaches to problem solving. The client is encouraged to consider unusual ways of looking at her life, her goals, and the methods of getting where she wants to be. While a client is attempting to go beyond previously defined limits and choices, the therapist is busy processing all the information that has been presented: past history, current functioning, complaints and symptoms, and interaction style are collated in the brain until finally there is a startling moment of revelation. By combining all the data in a unique and organized way, the therapist invents a creative interpretation of the client's behavior. Further innovation is required to determine the best way to facilitate the client's insights and, later, to help her act on the knowledge in a constructive manner.

For those therapists who value creativity in their work, innovative strategies become second nature. More important, such therapists become less certain of what they already know. For centuries, helping professionals were absolutely certain that the mentally afflicted were possessed with demons that needed to be exorcised. It is arrogance of the intellect that led to the Dark Ages. In contemporary times, those of us who are possessed with the single-minded devotion to a way of doing things, without consideration for revision and evolution, will hardly advance the state of our profession. Creative therapists now employ all kinds of alternative modalities to promote *shared creativity* in the relationship, whether through movement and dance, visualization and imagery, dramatic enactments, play, writing, art, experiments, and the use of all kinds of technology as adjuncts. Yet these are all just "tools" like everything else we do since it is actually "our empathy and understanding, love and caring" that really make the greatest difference (Levy, 2014, p. 26).

Creative therapists listen to the voices inside them. They pay attention to what does not make sense, even though things may have always been done that way. They are constructive rule breakers. They take cases that make them feel uncomfortable. They treat each case as if it were unique. And most of all, they enjoy the company of other people who challenge their ideas. They find their creativity nurtured in their interactions with colleagues and especially with clients.

The mutual creative energy fostered in the client and therapist as they encounter each other is a final factor in the chain of consequences that are part of their reciprocal influence. For Bugental (1978), being a therapist was much more than making a buck or belonging to a prestigious profession. It is "an arena for my creativity and endless raw material to feed it. It has been the source of anguish, pain, and anxiety—sometimes in the work itself, but more frequently within myself and with those important in my life in confrontations stimulated directly or indirectly by the impact of the work and relationships with my clients" (pp. 149–150). According to Bugental (1976), being a creative therapist involves the process of becoming more aware. It is not necessary for us to do anything to ourselves, to change anything in our lives, to alter our style of helping. Rather, we can be more aware of ourselves just as we are. This process involves recovering our own vision that has become unduly influenced by our mentors and not influenced enough by our own experiences.

This is where the book begins, not ends. This is the part of our journey together where you decide what to hold on to, what to remember, what to make your own. And as you well know, the prognosis is pretty poor given how little we remember of any of the books we've read, workshops we've attended, or training experiences. What will you take with you from this exploration to access greater compassion? To embrace the unknown, the complex, the inexplicable? To seek out new and more diverse mentors among staff, as well as from the larger world? Most importantly, what aspects of our conversation (and it was a dialogue between us) will you share with trusted friends, family, and colleagues?

The creative process is such an integral part of *being* a therapist that it is difficult to avoid integrating what we learn in our work to our personal lives. Our clients do indeed change us almost as much as we change them. Even though we know, understand, and enforce the rules and guard against infection by clients, and even though they are amateurs at influence, befuddled and distracted as they are with their own concerns, we cannot remain completely unaffected. We are touched by their goodness and the joy and privilege we feel in being allowed to get so close to a human soul. And we are sometimes affected by their malicious and destructive energy. Whenever we enter a room with another life in great torment, we will find no escape from our own despair. And we will find no way to hold down the elation we feel as a witness to another person's transformation—just as we are the catalyst for our own.

14

On Being a Client: How to Get the Most from Therapy

"I'VE BEEN IN therapy for several months and I've been seriously wondering if my therapist really gets me. He seems like a nice guy and all, and he came highly recommended from a friend, but it feels like most of the time we are just having conversations about stuff but I don't feel any better. How do I know if it's worth continuing with him? Or, I guess a better question, is how do I tell him that our sessions aren't helping me?"

Although the main audience for this book has traditionally been therapists and counselors, it has been available to the general public for many decades, leading people who are currently in therapy, or contemplating such a decision, to search for advice about their current and future therapeutic experiences. Such clients, or prospective consumers, sometimes feel confused or dissatisfied in some way with their current course of treatment and want to know what they could—or should—do to change the way things are going. In many cases, they just want to know when it's time to quit altogether and find someone else who might be a better match, or else the best way to inform their therapist how unhappy they are with the way things have been proceeding.

These are always very delicate questions to address because, on the one hand, I want to be supportive, yet on the other hand, I realize I only know a very small part of the story and I also don't want to do or say anything that might somehow compromise the therapist's efforts. I am aware that sometimes I'm just a convenient means by which some people might "tattle" on their therapist, or use me as an excuse to get out of something that they find uncomfortable. I also realize that the client's perception and experience of what is happening—or what is *reported* to me in an incomplete message—is just one part of the whole relationship and its meaning.

Nevertheless, there is considerable research to support the idea that therapy doesn't work very well if both (or all) parties are not on the same page, are not (mostly) honest with one another, and don't regularly share their responses to what is going on and how they feel about it. So often, clients simply don't tell their therapists about things they like—and those they don't—because they don't want to disappoint an authority figure.

Like any other professional guild, therapists are a pretty diverse group (perhaps even a *lot* more varied that others). We not only have dozens of different approaches but also some rather unique and personalized styles in terms of the ways we like to work. It is no surprise that a client might consult several different professionals and become increasingly confused after hearing just as many diagnostic impressions regarding the problem and even more ideas about the best way to deal with the issues. In addition, it is certainly true that some professionals are more capable than others. How is someone who is currently involved in therapy, or considering becoming so, to determine if he or she is getting the most out of sessions? And if benefits and results are being compromised in some way, how can one take the initiative to get more from the experience?

There's a lot of training to become a therapist, but not much in the way of preparation for how to become a great client. Some sources review the basics for how to choose a therapist, what to talk about while you are there, and how to optimize the sessions to better meet desired goals (Bates, 2006; Edelstein & Waehler, 2011; Trosclair, 2015; Zimmerman & Strouse, 2002). The following discussion is designed to demystify some of the secrets.

Some Key Questions That Clients Might Have About Therapy

Let's acknowledge at the outset that psychotherapy is a pretty strange enterprise. You sit in a room with someone whose job is to listen to your story, ask questions, and then talk to you about what is most upsetting. This professional doesn't actually *do* anything besides talk—she doesn't do any procedures, surgical interventions, or, in most cases, even offer any drugs. It's just about talking with one another, with the anticipation that such conversation will cure, if not ameliorate, any disturbing symptoms of depression, anxiety, loneliness, or confusion. That's pretty remarkable in itself, but then consider that there is not necessarily universal, much less standard, agreement on the best way to proceed. As mentioned repeatedly in this book, we don't even fully understand how and why the process works—and if we think we do, there's likely a half dozen alternative explanations that may directly contradict what is offered. So, if you aren't confused, you aren't paying attention. You should have *lots* of questions. I've been doing this an awfully long time and I *still* have lots of questions.

1. First of all, how do I know if I need therapy?

Not many people actually *need* therapy, but it sure is useful and helpful to most people most of the time. Whereas it used to be the case that therapy was for those with severe emotional disturbances or mental illness, nowadays the field has expanded to serve a wide variety of concerns, problems, and issues. This can—and still does—include rather serious emotional or behavioral problems but also covers those who are experiencing some adjustment difficulties, problems of daily living, or just want someone to talk to about ideas and feelings.

Rarely does anyone seek therapy as a first, or even a second, choice. It is expensive. It is time-consuming. And it often hurts, or at least is uncomfortable at times. But if you are suffering in some way, or just plain confused or lost, or perhaps just have something on your mind you'd like to sort out, then therapy is indeed an excellent option. Most people are very satisfied with their experience, and, contrary to popular belief, it doesn't need to take a long time; some people get what they want in just a few sessions, while others enjoy the process for years, as long as they are making continued progress.

With that said, you probably could benefit from therapy if you are consistently not getting what you want in life or if you don't feel you are satisfied with the way things are going. Whereas mild or severe depression, loneliness, anxiety or severe stress, previous trauma or abuse, addictions or bad habits, ruminations, interpersonal conflicts, family problems, career dissatisfaction, poor school or work performance, and physical symptoms that appear to have some psychological component to them are all common reasons why clients seek help, some people also do so because they need a place to work things out without concern for being pressured by someone who might not have their best interests at heart.

You might also consider therapy if others in your life, especially friends or family members who know you well, believe that you have problems that you appear to be unwilling to address. While it may be true that this pressure is more related to *their* difficulties rather than your own, when you receive consistent feedback from more than one reliable person, it is time to consider that there might be something worth examining.

Could you talk with a friend or colleague instead? Of course. But the reasons why people seek a therapist, and even pay for that privilege, is because they want someone who is reasonably objective, who won't meet his or her own needs, who will likely respond in a caring yet honest way. It also helps that a professional has so much more training than a "friend," especially with regard to differential diagnosis, treatment strategies, listening and responding skills, and especially a deep understanding of the issues presented.

2. What do people talk about in therapy?

There is usually a balance between the therapist and client each talking to one another, and it is usually not a good idea if only one partner in the process carries all the conversation. Some clients complain that their therapist never says or offers much and appears rather passive; others don't like that their therapist talks constantly, almost all the time, rarely allowing them to get a word in. Probably either extreme is not ideal, since there should be an exchange of thoughts and feelings during the interaction, one in which each person has a chance to engage with one another in a spirited, meaningful way.

It is certainly the case that some approaches emphasize a more active role for the therapist and others encourage the client to do most of the work. Likewise, each therapist has evolved a somewhat personal style that (hopefully) best suits his or her personality and creates sufficient space for the clients to share whatever is on their minds. This could include anything that arose during the week, things that are bothersome or confusing, or perhaps just something that comes up in the moment. The whole idea of therapy that makes it so wonderful and special is that you can talk about absolutely anything without fear of critical judgment. It is, perhaps, the one safe place where you can unload anything that is upsetting or worrisome, talk about any subject on your mind, or bring up any issue that is confusing.

What should you talk about in therapy?

Whatever you want. But especially whatever you *don't* want to talk about.

3. How do I find not just a good therapist, but a truly great one—and how will I know the difference?

Unfortunately, it is really, really hard to tell a good therapist from a lousy one, much less identify one who is truly extraordinary. Famous therapists, or those like me who write books or give lectures, aren't necessarily the best ones by any means. It may very well be that we reduced clinical practice to move into other areas because we weren't very good at it, or grew tired or bored from the routines. Whereas I'd like to think that I was (and am) pretty good at clinical work, I also admit that I diversified my professional life precisely because I didn't want to do sessions all day anymore.

Our field is extremely confusing, not only because there are so many different theoretical orientations and treatment approaches numbering in the hundreds, but also because there are so many disciplines in this profession. Should you see a social worker or a psychologist or a counselor or a family therapist or a psychiatrist? Should you see someone with a masters degree or someone with a doctorate or medical degree? And what about the particular license that the clinician holds? It turns out that although each of these degrees and disciplines comes from a different academic tradition, there really isn't much evidence to support that one is superior to the others, although it depends on the client needs and complaints. Psychiatrists should be considered as a first option for those who may require medication or medical treatments for a problem that has organic origins such as biologically based depression, panic disorder, or a similar diagnosis. But even these problems still require therapy along with any prescribed drugs. Likewise, each of the other professional specialties may be more suitable for certain issues. For instance, a couple that is having difficulties would often be advised to seek a couples therapist to work on the relationship as a first option rather than seeing an individual therapist.

If you can't rely on reputation, then how do you find a professional who is exceptional? Therapy is all about relational connections, and that is a highly personal level of engagement that is often hard to predict. It is usually a good idea to ask a friend, or someone you trust, to offer a referral—but that is only a place to begin since each person has different preferences.

Master therapists, those who are truly exceptional in what they do and how they do it, are indeed unusual because of several things they tend to do on a regular basis (Kottler & Carlson, 2015). It turns out that a lot of things don't really predict excellence very well, such as the particular approach that is favored, the particular degree or license, or even the number of years in the field. What does matter the most is that the therapist takes the time and effort to find out from you regularly and systematically what is working best for you and what is not working much at all. Soliciting meaningful feedback from clients is often a hallmark of the best outcomes (Duncan, 2010; Duncan, Miller, Wampold, & Hubble, 2010; Miller, Duncan, Brown, Sorrell, & Chalk, 2006; Miller, Hubble, & Duncan, 2007).

Truly exceptional therapists are not just masters of technique, brilliant theoreticians, and extremely knowledgeable about human experience, they also hold certain personal characteristics that empower their influence and interventions. You will notice, almost immediately, that they exude an aura of wisdom and reassurance. They are compassionate and caring, utterly composed, even in the face of crises you discuss. They have the ability—and the willingness—to remain completely and fully present in the moment, often in such a way that it feels like they are reading your mind and heart. They are highly flexible and pragmatic, which makes them well equipped to continually adapt what they are doing, and how they are responding, depending on exactly what is required. Just as importantly, they are able to model and demonstrate in their own lives what they consider most critical to teach you. And yet . . . and yet . . . even with all these skills and capabilities, they remain modest and humble, recognizing that, ultimately, it's the client who deserves most of the credit for any progress gained.

Really great practitioners also don't limit themselves to options that are embedded in a single approach, regardless of their preferred orientation. They combine and integrate features and interventions from a wide assortment of approaches that may include relational engagement (humanistic), unconscious desires (psychodynamic), beliefs and attitudes (cognitive), unresolved attachment issues (emotionally focused), family dynamics (systemic), story reconceptualization (narrative), issues of meaning and purpose (existential), issues of oppression and cultural indoctrination (feminist), as well as task facilitation (behavioral) and several others. In each and every case, the clinician is continuously making assessments regarding what is best indicated, what is most effective, and what is not. What distinguishes master therapists from the rest more than anything else is their willingness to experiment with a variety of strategies, according to what is needed most.

4. How do I know which therapeutic approach is best for my case?

You don't necessarily know the answer to this question—although, in all fairness, depending on the presenting problem there are certain interventions and strategies that are considered optimal, often supported by empirical research. You should keep in mind that although therapists do sometimes identify strongly with a particular theory or model, most of us are fairly flexible in adapting what we do, and how we do it, to fit each client and issues. Nevertheless, there are indeed some approaches that are a better fit for certain concerns, depending on how much the person is in crisis, or how much interest there is in exploring the past, or whether there is time to delve into one area or another. It's a good idea to ask the therapist to explain his or her approach, as well as to do some research on your own.

5. Among other options besides the style or approach, is individual, group, or family therapy preferred?

That depends. I know you are tired of these evasive answers (although that's often what therapists do), but the reality is that it's difficult to determine which theoretical orientation, or which delivery system, is ideal for a particular client. In one sense, depending on the practitioner, almost any particular approach can be suitable for a particular case. Yet it is also true that some kinds of issues respond best to certain modalities. For instance, group therapy provides all kinds of opportunities to deal with interpersonal issues, receive lots of honest feedback from others, and to actually try out and rehearse new behaviors. We live and operate in a world of groups most of the time, so this structure provides the best possible simulation to practice new skills. On the other hand, for those who are shy and reticent, or those who may have what are called more "florid" styles of personality, meaning they can be overbearing and controlling, groups may not be the best option.

There are many practitioners who think of *all* therapy as taking place within a family context, no matter who actually attends sessions. Nevertheless, when the main difficulty is related to family disputes or conflicts, it makes sense to get as many parties into the room as possible to deal with the underlying systemic dysfunctions and patterns that are contributing to the impasse. Finally, ongoing individual therapy sessions are almost a luxury these days with such an emphasis on cost-effectiveness, efficiency, and delivering services that are most culturally appropriate, although they do provide excellent opportunities to address an individual's self-defeating behaviors.

6. What about doing therapy online or via video conference?

This is a mixed blessing. Clearly it is the wave of the future, offering increased convenience and efficiency. I can imagine a time in the not-too-distant future when perhaps most therapy and services will be delivered via avatars, simulations, or distance-based systems. Therapists especially appreciate the flexibility of these options because they can just schedule sessions from anywhere they have Internet access. Likewise, clients can save commuting time and expense and also access more qualified professionals from anywhere in the world. Many clients also report anecdotally that they are often willing to share things online or via video or audio conferences that they likely wouldn't be able to do in person.

Although I do see (and have seen) a few clients online and enjoy the experience, I also find it quite different. I acknowledge all the advantages and yet still see definite limitations to this modality, however convenient it might be. There is something to be said for being in a room with someone, including access to all the cues, nonverbal behavior, sights, sounds, smells, and feelings that may not be nearly as visible on a screen. I've also never really conceived therapy as being limited to the actual sessions—I think so much of the work takes place when people are on the way to the appointment, considering what they want to talk about, reviewing the last session, planning how they want to best use the time. And on the way home, clients also review what was said, consider what it all means, and continue to process the conversation afterwards. Can this happen anyway after the client disconnects online? Of course. But I still think that the more we invest of ourselves in a process, including commitment of time and energy, the more we often get out of it.

In summary, seeking out a therapist for distance-based treatment is becoming increasingly popular, but, as yet, there are a number of ethical, procedural, and legal issues still being sorted out considering the different licensing jurisdictions and lack of solid empirical research (and training) on best practices. In addition, many insurance and third-party payers will not support online or video-based treatment, so it is best to check. Finally, there are confidentiality and privacy issues that have yet to be fully addressed and remain a concern.

7. What do I do if my financial resources are limited and I can't afford much of a fee?

See above. There is often far more leverage and negotiating room in fees if you are not limited by your local options. In addition, almost any good therapist has a sliding scale based on ability to pay and financial resources; many practitioners take pro bono cases for those who can only afford a few dollars.

Most schools, institutions, and communities offer virtually free mental health services for students, employees, or residents. Whether through religious affiliated organizations (Catholic Social Services, Jewish Family Services, Muslim Family Services, Institute for Buddhist Studies, Christian Counseling Services, etc.), state or county mental health services, or those agencies supported by grants, charters, public donations, or charities, there are a host of options available for those who can't afford private pay or don't have health insurance that covers part or all of the cost.

In other words, some people may use money as an excuse for not seeking the help they need, but there are always affordable and viable options available.

8. How do I know if my therapist is a good match for me?

If you are already in therapy and asking that question, there very well could be some concerns about whether the relationship is compatible. Ideally, a therapeutic relationship is one in which you can talk about most anything. You would trust your therapist to the point that almost nothing is off limits and you feel you can reveal any part of yourself. You feel respected by your therapist and allowed to move at your own pace. In addition, you genuinely like this person and admire him or her.

Therapeutic relationships are delicate matters, at least during their inception and initial negotiation. Patterns are established. Rules and boundaries are established. And sometimes what clients agree to do, and how they were told things would go, are not necessarily what they want and desire. That isn't usually much of a problem as long as it feels like there is an opportunity to renegotiate the contract, so to speak. Just to be able to say, "I'm not happy with the way this is structured," is usually enough to change the established template. But often clients don't speak up for a variety of reasons. They don't feel safe doing so. They don't want to disappoint their therapist. Because of the perceived inequity of power, they don't feel comfortable challenging an authority figure who is supposedly an expert.

If something doesn't feel right, then it is absolutely critical to say so. Every time someone complains to me about their therapist, that they don't feel heard or understood, that their therapist seems quirky or confusing, that they aren't making progress, my first reaction is to ask if they'd said something about that in session. Of course, maybe if it felt safe and comfortable to do so, then there wouldn't be a problem. But perhaps the single most important thing a client can do to maintain control of his or her own therapy is to tell the therapist when things aren't working out as anticipated or hoped. Sometimes that is the result of unrealistic expectations, but at other times it can mean that there is some misunderstanding or disconnection in the relationship.

As awkward and uncomfortable as it felt at the time, I recall a few instances when I was confronted by clients telling me they weren't happy with the way things were going and were ready to quit. I resisted trying to talk them out of that, or becoming defensive, and instead simply asked them what we could be doing—or should be doing—instead. Inevitably such discussions led to breakthroughs that allowed us to alter the path we were taking and instead to head in a different direction that was more suitable. But without such honest and direct input, nothing much will change, the client will drop out, perhaps give up the search for help, and the therapist will never find out what he or she was doing (or not doing) that proved so ineffective.

9. How do I know if therapy is working or not?

This is an easy one: if you are getting better, and feeling better, then therapy is working—and that should start happening within a relatively short period of time, often just a few weeks. Clients often report they already feel much better just making a first appointment, making an effort to get help. The first few meetings usually instill some hope and provide some structure for work to be done. If that is not the case, it's time to reassess.

On the other hand, it is sometimes the case that you might feel worse before you start to feel better. After all, growth, learning, and change are often uncomfortable, so there can be a transitional period of disorientation when symptoms may not improve right away until new skills and knowledge are mastered and put to work. It is important to be patient, but only within reasonable limits before considering other options.

It isn't enough to rely solely on your own judgment regarding how you feel. Ask the therapist about his or her own impressions of initial progress. It's just as valuable to solicit input from significant others who know you best: What have they noticed has changed or is different about you? One of the legitimate criticisms of therapy over the years is that some people report that they feel better, that they thoroughly enjoy their sessions after attending diligently for months, if not years, and yet there is little noticeable change in their self-defeating behaviors. They may have fantastic insight into their problems, talk up a storm during sessions, and appear cooperative and responsive, but nothing has fundamentally been adjusted in the outside world. They continue to engage in the same kinds of ways that got them in trouble in the first place.

Feeling better and enjoying sessions is important. So, too, is the therapist's assessment that definite progress is being made. But, ultimately, the true test is whether you have actually internalized what you've learned and started applying those new skills and ideas on a daily basis. Talk is fine, but it's action that counts most.

10. What might I be doing—or *not* doing—that is curtailing the potential progress I could be making?

It's one thing to blame your therapist because you aren't getting what you want and quite another to examine your own contributions to the impasse. Keep in mind that virtually all interpersonal disagreements or conflicts represent a collective effort; it is never exclusively one person's fault. As easy it might be to accuse your therapist of incompetence or cluelessness (which could possibly be the case), it is usually far more helpful to examine your own role in the struggle, particularly with regard to what you are doing to make things difficult.

What might you be doing to deliberately/unconsciously/inadvertently sabotage therapy? Try out a few of these to see how they fit.

- You want and ask for a quick cure to a problem or issue that is both long-standing and complex, and then get frustrated and disappointed when your therapist can't fix it for you right away.
- You aren't being completely frank and honest about what is really going on, which is why your therapist isn't responding to your greatest needs.
- You are playing games, obfuscating, stalling, withholding, and being less than genuine and authentic in your interactions, pretending to be someone you are not.
- You are cut off from your feelings and only report safe reactions.
- You overreact and overpersonalize everything. You ruminate constantly about what your therapist said to you, what was *really* meant, and how that may indicate how little he or she likes and respects you.
- You are trying *way* too hard to read what your therapist wants to hear and then providing that as best you can.
- You are having strong personal reactions (transference, projections, overidentification) to your therapist because he or she reminds you of someone else.
- You keep begging the therapist to tell you what to do, give you advice, make decisions for you, and then end up feeling frustrated when that doesn't happen (because that's not what good therapists do).
- You aren't following through between sessions on actions you promised to take or homework you intended to complete.
- You are scared, terrified actually, of the deeper issues you are avoiding and so are doing your best to keep the discussions on safe ground.

- You constantly argue, make excuses, defend, and explain away any input or challenges that you may find threatening instead of exhibiting curiosity to explore what might be going on.
- There are some consistently annoying, self-destructive patterns that you have engaged in for a long time—which is why you are in therapy in the first place. The problem, however, is that what you typically do to push others away you are also doing with your therapist.
- There are others in your world who are actively working to sabotage your progress because they are threatened by what you are attempting to do, which could lead to changes in their lives they would prefer to avoid.

What is sometimes operating during impasses is that clients may very well be enjoying benefits or payoffs as a result of remaining stuck. That may sound strange, but it is actually quite common that all of us avoid change if it is at all possible because it's so much damn work to learn new coping strategies. Even when behaviors are clearly counterproductive or self-defeating, human beings are still inclined to continue them in order to avoid the unknown or possible alternatives they believe could be worse. People stay in abusive, neglectful, or limiting situations because they have learned to tolerate the present circumstances (with complaints), however unpleasant, and fear that things could become far worse. Clients may also slow things down in sessions, sabotage progress, deceive, play games, engage defenses, in order to distract from other issues or control things on their own terms. They have a ready excuse for behaving badly ("I can't help it. That's just the way I am"), can blame others for the problems ("It's not my fault they don't understand me"), and avoid responsibility for their plight. Until such time that people become aware of what they're doing, even if unconsciously (which is often the case), it's pretty hard to address the underlying ambivalence that is undermining the therapy.

11. What are some things that you might not realize can heighten the impact of therapy and help you get more out of the experience?

If the examples above are some of the reasons why you are not getting the most from therapy, then there are certainly some things you can do to alter that scenario. It is important to understand, for example, that what you do outside of therapy is even more important than what you talk about during sessions.

A second suggestion, if your therapist has not yet mentioned this, is that it really helps a lot to keep a journal in which you continue the work on your own. This is the place where you can process and apply the things you are learning, keep a record of themes and issues you are addressing, set goals for future sessions or your life, and continue the conversations with your therapist—and yourself. Years in the future it will be fascinating to go back and follow the threads of your journey. This is quite different from posting updates on social media for the benefit of others; a journal is a private space to wrestle with the questions and concerns that concern you the most.

If you wish to intensify and magnify the effects of therapeutic work, it really helps to write about your own internal thoughts as well as what you might be holding back during sessions. What are the issues you are avoiding? What are some of the topics you wish you could bring up—if only you felt more trust and greater safety and were willing to take additional risks? Now, imagine that you did feel increased courage and commitment: What would you talk about that you are avoiding? What's stopping you from doing so? What would it take for you to be more open, honest, and forthcoming? And if the answer to these questions is that you just aren't getting what you want and need, or that you just can't go there, maybe it's time to take a break or try something else.

12. When is it time to quit?

I like this question a lot because I find it so endlessly interesting and complex. When is it time to stop therapy? Maybe when you first start contemplating this question? Or perhaps that's a sign that you are avoiding something important that you wish to escape?

My standard response to such an inquiry usually challenged a client's resolve: "So just when things are getting tough you want to quit?" That might instill a certain amount of guilt and then invite a discussion between us about the work left to do before closure could and should be considered. But over the years I've changed my tactics: when a client wonders if it is time to quit, I usually support that choice immediately: "Maybe that's an excellent idea! Why don't we take a break for awhile and see how things go?"

I want clients to assume complete responsibility for their sessions, and so I put them in charge of what we do and how we do it, even how often we meet. It's not like I don't have my own opinions and expertise on these matters, but I also think it's more important that clients remain in charge of their own recovery and treatment. Of course I don't like to see clients leave; it hurts in its own way. I also don't like to see people abandon ship, especially when there is so much work left to do.

Traditionally, therapy is ended mutually after the treatment goals have been met, however those were identified and operationally defined. Yet there are often two levels of therapeutic work, the first of which includes the so-called presenting problems. These are the symptomatic concerns that were disruptive enough for the person to seek help. Depending on the issue or problem or disorder, treatment usually lasts a few weeks or months, at least during this era of brief therapy and empirically supported treatments. However, aside from what was initially presented, therapeutic explorations often excavate other issues that may be worth examining. These can involve existential questions such as, "What is the meaning of my life?" "What do I want to do before I die?" "How can I take more responsibility for my life choices?" "What can I do to make life more satisfying?" These sorts of questions represent the meaning-making efforts that can be investigated once initial problems are resolved—assuming you want to stick around long enough to get into these areas.

13. What do I do if I relapse or fall back after my sessions end?

A better question might ask: What do I do *when* I relapse? It is a virtual certainty that even after spectacular progress there will inevitably be some backsliding. It is almost impossible to avoid setbacks and not slip back into old, familiar patterns. This is not necessarily a problem—unless you are unprepared and unrehearsed for how to handle the relapse.

Prior to ending sessions, there is often some discussion of aftercare. The conversation is not about what will you do *if* you "forget" and fall into previous patterns but rather what you will do and how you will handle matters *when* that assuredly occurs. Some therapists help their clients to role-play and practice failure scenarios, recovering almost effortlessly to demonstrate that such fears are unwarranted: "So what if you slip up and lose your temper again? That is only a temporary lapse which you can easily recover from by practicing the self-talk strategies that we've gone over so often. Let's practice that again now. I want you get mad at me over something, anything, just the way you used to during our early meetings. And then I'm not going to respond at all because I want *you* to regain control on your own, just as we've practiced."

Common Reasons Why Clients Drop Out of Therapy

There are varied estimates about how often clients end therapy prematurely, ranging from 8 to 60%, depending on the therapist and the kind of treatment offered. It is a difficult figure to settle on, considering that clients may end their sessions for all kinds of reasons that don't necessarily signal a problem. Maybe they relocated to another area. Heck, maybe they already got what they wanted and didn't feel the need to return. So much of the time, therapists don't find out why clients never returned and are left to wonder. After all, it is so much easier for someone to just cancel an appointment and say they'll reschedule—or just send a text, email, or leave a message saying that he or she intends to take a little break but will call back when ready and available so you can continue the work together.

Personally, I'm not much of a fan for the excuses I hear from some therapists that when their clients cancel or don't return it's because they already got what they needed—and that counts as another success! If a solid working relationship was established in the first place, then it is not really a healthy way to end it by just canceling or not showing up. I believe that endings are important and that the way therapy ends reveals something about what was learned during the experience.

In ideal circumstances, several sessions are devoted to termination issues. There would first be a summary of what was accomplished, comparing those outcomes to what was expected and planned. There are always unresolved issues that can be identified and described, even if there is a choice not to deal with them at this time. In such an intimate relationship, with deep feelings by both parties, it is important to have a ritual for saying goodbye in a caring, supportive way. As mentioned, it is also critical that time is spent preparing for what follows next so that clients can internalize what was learned and function independently without needing the therapist's support any longer.

Even with all this planning during optimal circumstances, the reality is that somewhere around one-quarter to maybe one-third of clients prematurely (according to the therapist's perspective) end sessions before goals have been (apparently) attained. There are several very good reasons why clients might choose not to return, at least according to their own views.

My Therapist Doesn't Understand Me

This would indeed be a serious problem if it feels like all the therapist is interested in doing is talking, advising, lecturing, instructing, challenging, but doesn't seem to demonstrate much compassion, empathy, and hovering attention. People often go to therapy in the first place because they don't feel heard and understood by others in their lives. So apart from anything else that happens related to the presenting problems, it is really important that you feel like your therapist really and truly hears and understands you in a way that has never quite happened previously.

One corollary of this theme is not so much connected to feeling misunderstood as the realization that the therapist doesn't seem to agree with you about certain matters. I would say this is not only a frequent complaint but one that is normal. *Of course* the therapist doesn't necessarily agree with the client's view of what's wrong and what needs to be done, especially given that this perspective usually involves blaming others. There is usually some negotiation that takes place in the beginning, with the client presenting his or her take on things: "It's not my fault I'm in this situation. If only. . . ." Then the therapist presents an alternative view, one that usually emphasizes greater self-responsibility and personal control. Naturally, this is disappointing to hear when you hoped the therapist was on your side. And of course the therapist *is* on your side, which is why he or she disagrees with any assessment that means a further loss of control.

I Feel Judged

Feeling judged, versus actually *being* judged, might be two different entities. But if someone's feeling judged by another, whether that is an accurate assessment or not, that doesn't make it feel any less real. Therapy is all about sharing secrets, some of them shameful, others very difficult to even mention. It is easy to imagine that when talking about a sensitive subject for the first time that the person listening must be repulsed by the disclosure. "I'm having an affair." "I drink almost every night." "I hate my father."

The truth of the matter is that most therapists have heard it all before, usually many times before in every imaginable permutation, so we really aren't thinking to ourselves that you are naughty or unlovable. Clients disclose the most unusual, interesting, and yet uniquely human foibles, most of which they feel terrible shame. We try to normalize these feelings as much as possible, communicate acceptance and understanding, as well as help the person make different choices if that behavior is counterproductive in some way.

But this is an easy one to address: if you feel judged, speak up and say something! That is a very inhibiting obstacle to being more authentic, honest, and genuine, which, after all, is the purpose of attending sessions in addition to solving problems.

It Hurts Too Much

I don't know about "too much," but therapy does hurt. Sometimes a lot. After all, you are digging up the past, talking about the forbidden, scrutinizing every aspect of your behavior, processing conflicts, talking about failures. You are constantly being challenged, sometimes confronted vigorously.

The tender places that are touched, the wounds that still have scabs, the unresolved issues of the past, all bring with them a certain discomfort, if not pain. But, hopefully, it is the kind of suffering that ultimately leads to growth and deeper understanding. As you well know, some of the healthiest things that we must do—exercise, diet, complete chores, or resolve conflicts—involve sacrifice and hurt. That's how healing takes place.

My Therapist Talks Too Much . . . or Doesn't Talk at All

Some therapists do talk a lot, maybe even most of the time. There are certain approaches that emphasize instruction, tutoring, coaching, learning new skills and ways of being, just as there are others where the therapist takes a far more measured role, listening, cuing, facilitating, but perhaps speaking mainly to offer an interpretation, analysis, or summary. It's up to you to locate a therapist whose style matches your preferences and particular needs. Once you find such a professional, it's also up to you to negotiate a pattern of interaction that is most helpful and fits best. If you find yourself talking all the time in session and rarely getting anything back, that could reflect a particular therapeutic style that might be worth exploring further or else looking elsewhere for something more compatible. And if your therapist talks too much and doesn't appear to want to listen, interrupting you constantly, telling stories you've heard before, lecturing you in a condescending way, then it may also be time to seek help elsewhere.

I Don't Understand What Is Expected—or Where This Is Going

Ask. Just ask. Often the most interesting, stimulating, and impactful conversations are those in which you take a risk and reach beyond what is initially uncomfortable. There may be several times, in every single session, when your therapist will do or say things that you don't quite understand, but you nod your head anyway, pretending you grasp where things are going. I encourage every client to think of him- or herself as a therapist-in-training as well as a client, which means thinking critically about what has worked best and what hasn't worked much at all. Therapists should have a clear rationale for everything they say or do, one they can articulate or explain if you take the time to ask them.

My Therapist Keeps Asking Me to Do Things I Can't (or Won't) Do

One of the most frequent mistakes that therapists make is to ask clients to do something for which they are not yet ready or prepared. We do become impatient and want things to move along. We are under pressure to get this work done as quickly as possible. And we understand how important it is to take the talk during sessions and convert it into constructive action.

Some therapists prescribe homework assignments: "Why don't you make a point of talking to several of your friends to find out what they think about your new decision?" Some therapists push, persuade, or challenge clients to experiment with new behaviors: "Let's try that now. I'm going to ask to borrow something from you and I want you to stay no—and then not feel badly about that." Other therapists suggest courses of action directly related to the presenting problem: "Given that your anxiety seems much worse when you have to speak in front of large groups, maybe it would be best if you avoided putting yourself in those situations for awhile."

However well intended, clients—and their therapists—become frustrated when the assignments are not actually completed. Excuses abound: "I forgot." "I didn't have time." "The opportunity never came up." "I changed my mind." That last comment is probably pretty accurate in that no matter what people say is important, if they don't actually do it then it wasn't very important in the first place. We find the time and opportunities to do the things that really matter most to us. Therapists also sometimes need reminders from their clients that they may not feel ready to do what is in their best interests.

It's Too Expensive

Even if the fee is paid by a third party or a free service, time is money. It is a major commitment to devote priorities and energy to therapy sessions. It often feels like a luxury that takes time away from other things that are also important. Yet people squander their time and money on all kinds of things that are far less helpful, spending hours each day watching mindless television or playing video games, adding to their wardrobe collection, blowing limited funds on empty entertainment that does nothing but use up time.

Therapy is as much an investment in your future as any stock, savings, or retirement account. It represents a commitment to continued growth and an improved sense of well-being and life satisfaction. It is just about the most useful and practical education that anyone could possibly desire.

It Takes Too Much Time

Speaking of time, most people are in a hurry to get better. The good news is that, depending on the issue, there are now therapy options that can be completed in just a few months, or sometimes just a few sessions. One of the first questions I want to know from a prospective new client is how much time we have to get the work done. Do we have just a few weeks, a few months, or is our contract open-ended? It's important to be clear about expectations. If you've been going for a while (whatever that means to you) and not feeling—or getting—much better, then it is time to reassess the situation and have a conversation about other options. This could mean taking a sabbatical for a while, soliciting a referral to someone else, or perhaps trying to change the way the therapy has been proceeding in order to make it more helpful.

I'm Actually Becoming Worse

The vast majority of therapists are highly professional and competent, not to mention really nice people. But we have a few colleagues within our midst who engage in dubious or unethical behavior. Let's be clear on the rules: *everything* that a therapist does is supposed to be designed to protect your welfare and promote your best interests. Therapists are not permitted to meet their own needs in any way. If you experience your therapist as self-indulgent, manipulative, dishonest, or seductive, if you have some qualms about his or her professionalism, then those are definite warning signs that it may be time to end the relationship.

"They" Don't Want Me to Come Back Any More

Many clients don't necessarily want to stop therapy but they are being pressured or blackmailed into doing so by another family member. It is often the case that significant others feel confused, disoriented, or even threatened by changes that are made in sessions. When one person in a family or system changes in some way, it requires others to accommodate and adapt to this shift. That usually involves some degree of discomfort and work, something they would prefer to avoid. Given a choice between sabotaging the therapy and pulling the family member back into the fold—however dysfunctional the system—or allowing the growth to continue, it is far easier just to end the therapy. Partners or significant others may forbid the client from returning or do their level best to undermine the progress. In such cases, that is a strong indicator that a joint family session would be desirable to work on these issues.

I Just Don't Feel Comfortable; I Don't Know Why

This is a catch-all category that covers everything else that may be hard to explain or put into words. It just feels like the therapy isn't "right," or some intuitive feeling is warning that the timing just isn't ideal. Or you just decide you don't want to return. Those are all legitimate feelings. As your therapist, I might challenge these reactions and wonder if maybe your ambivalence and uncertainty reflect some fears of the unknown and reluctance to pursue things further. I happen to believe those are legitimate reasons to take a break and would try to avoid talking you into continuing the sessions. But I also know that other practitioners might handle this differently and call this resistance that should continue to be worked through.

How Do We Say Goodbye?

Regardless of the reasons why, when, and how therapy ends, this is usually a challenging transition to manage. There is an understandable fear of backsliding once regular support and sessions are finished. If a solid relationship has been established over time, then it can also be a painful time of grieving and adjustment—for *all* the participants involved. I will confess that although I act joyful and prideful when clients are about to be sent on their way, I also feel my own sense of loss. I miss the regular, intimate conversations, and since it is quite rare that ex-clients remain in touch, I frequently wonder how they are doing

From the client's perspective, there are often increased feelings of freedom and independence—not to mention banking time and money—but also reoccurring fears and setbacks. When this last stage of therapy is handled well, there is considerable time devoted to planning for this process. This may include relapse-prevention strategies as well as rehearsal of predicted problems that may inevitably arise. Just as important is an open discussion of some feelings that were yet to be brought into the open, unresolved issues that may be addressed in the future, and simply saying goodbye in a meaningful way. Finally, there are sometimes plans made for follow-up sessions in the future just to make sure that progress and growth continues.

Some Secrets About What Therapists Like Best in Their Clients

Parents are known to respond to a certain thorny question by answering, "Well, my kids are all different but I love them all the same." That's not quite the case, even if it is the only truly acceptable answer. Of course the same is true about the way that therapists feel about their clients—some are loved differently than others.

Let's face it, the people who often end up in therapy do so because they may do some spectacularly annoying things. Some were referred in the first place because everyone else is tired of dealing with their antics. While it is certainly true that many clients, attending sessions for learning and growth, are among the most interesting, joyful, and fun people you could ever meet, others are seriously disturbed and constantly play games, lie, manipulate, and otherwise do their best to make everyone around them as miserable as possible.

It is clearly important to be liked by your therapist, or at least *feel* liked by him or her. As you might imagine, that's not always easy to do, especially when the particular client is doing his level best to be as difficult as possible. Nevertheless, ask a therapist who her favorite clients might be, theoretically speaking, and you will usually get a carefully crafted response something like this: "I do specialize in ________________ (fill in the blank) and like working with those issues, but I pretty much enjoy seeing almost anyone." Of course that's not quite accurate.

It used to be that therapists in the olden days were quite clear about who they preferred as ideal clients. Given that a few decades ago almost all therapists were older white males, it probably isn't surprising that their stated preference for clients included individuals very much like themselves (educated, intelligent, white, middle class, and highly verbal). Things haven't changed much over the years considering that therapy *is* an endeavor that involves a certain degree of insight and verbal fluency. Nevertheless, in a survey in which therapists were asked to supply three adjectives to describe their ideal client, most of them could be easily guessed (Howes, 2009). Therapists want their clients to be completely honest and forthcoming, open-minded and flexible, highly motivated and determined, with a high tolerance for both pain and ambiguous, uncertain issues. Yeah, who wouldn't want to hang out with someone like that?

Of course, therapists like particular clients for different reasons—because they remind them of someone, because they appear similar in values and interests, because they are seen as attractive or interesting in some way. Yet there are also some stated preferences that vary considerably. For instance, I've always enjoyed working with rebellious adolescents, the kind who are defiant and (perceived as) obstructive even though I find them wildly entertaining. My office partner would refer all her adolescent referrals to me, perhaps not surprisingly because she had three teenage children of her own. Likewise, as the parent of a toddler at the time, I would refer all my young kids to her because I was so tired of playing *Candyland*, hide-and-seek, and other games at home at night.

Many clients don't return to therapy after a session or two because they don't feel their therapists truly grasp the nuances of their cultural backgrounds. There is considerable research supporting these reports considering that the majority of people of color don't last very long in sessions because they didn't feel comfortable or understood by their therapists, especially when they were members of the majority culture. In some cases, the perceived slights, often called "microaggressions," were inadvertent but nevertheless offensive and off-putting.

Each therapist develops a specialty based not only on interests and training but also on personal preferences. There are specialists who work exclusively with eating disorders, multiple personality disorder, panic disorder, addictions, or trauma, not only because of their expertise but also because of what they are drawn to personally. Therapists who most enjoy working with drug and alcohol clients talk about how much they appreciate the drama of these cases. Some therapists admit that their stated preference is based on efforts to continue self-healing or explorations that parallel the issues of their clients. For instance, at this stage in life my perfect client is a mature adult who wants to explore and find meaning in new life challenges; in other words, my perfect client is just like me!

Although many therapists do have their favorites, other client characteristics that are most appreciated include a willingness to be patient as results might accrue slowly and unpredictably. We like our clients to be driven and desperate for change but also willing to be patient and forgiving with us when things don't necessarily proceed according to plan. We want clients to be responsible and dependable, at least with respect to showing up on time and paying their bills. We like them to be curious and reflective, interested and willing to look critically at their own behavior and its impact on others. We'd definitely prefer clients to be upbeat, joyful, and funny (who wouldn't?), but that is often not likely until perhaps the end, considering that most clients are either highly anxious, confused, and/or depressed.

Here's the bottom line if you are comparing your own "condition," personality, and style to this ideal and are feeling definitely inadequate in these areas: therapists want their clients deeply invested in the process and willing to work hard on themselves; the rest of these factors don't matter much at all if motivation and commitment are present. This is more than a little difficult to assess considering that everyone feels ambivalence about changes that are contemplated—they may be desirable, but they also involve a lot of discomfort, unfamiliarity, and hard work.

Initiating Difficult and Really, Really Honest Conversations

Most relationships eventually become entrenched into patterns that can become both predictable and often limiting. During therapy sessions those habits become established rather quickly. Clients almost always sit in the same spot, just as therapists always sit in their favorite chair. Sessions usually begin ("What would you like to talk about today?") and end ("Let's reschedule for next week. Same time?") the same way. The participants fall into routines that are, at once, comforting as well as restrictive. This sometimes makes it difficult to abruptly change the subject and bring up something that is disturbing or bothersome but not necessarily on the planned agenda.

Clients are often reluctant to challenge or confront their therapists due to the power inequity posed by the therapist's status as expert and authority figure. There are exceptions, of course, especially with those clients who are rather flamboyant and aggressive. Generally speaking, therapy gets stuck, and stays that way, until one or both participants decide to change the trajectory of the process. This means stirring things up, taking risks, and bringing up a subject that has been neglected but is clearly the unspoken elephant in the room.

How Do I Know That You Are the Best Therapist for Me?

You can't possibly know the answer to this question until a few weeks into the process, any more than you can determine after a single blind date that the relationship will live happily ever after. However, you can invest a little time during the initial contact, whether on the phone or during the intake interview, to find out some basic information that helps you make a more informed decision about whether to continue with this professional or not.

You likely wouldn't want to turn the tables interviewing the therapist for too long or you'll end up using up all your time. Nevertheless, there are several questions you might address:

- Would you please tell me about your background, training, and credentials?
- What kind of therapy and approach do you favor, and why do you think it is appropriate for what I'm experiencing?
- Given what you already know about me and my issues, how would you propose to help me and what would this look like over time?
- I'm Christian/Muslim/Jewish/gay/homeless/vegan/a lawyer . . . (fill in the blank). How do your own values mesh with my background?
- What are some of your rules related to paying fees, late or canceled appointments, and other such issues?

What makes this type of conversation a little awkward is that you are deliberately altering the nature of the interaction to make it clear that you are an an informed consumer who intends to take your own clear responsibility for the encounter. You aren't willing to make a commitment to the process until such time that your questions and concerns are adequately addressed. This could become excessive if the interrogation went on more than a few minutes beyond these basic questions, but most therapists would actually appreciate that you took the time and effort to determine whether this was a good fit for you.

This Isn't Working and I Want to Quit

This would be a difficult and disappointing declaration for any therapist to hear (unless they are also anxious to get rid of you). It's really hard to tell someone that you don't like what they are doing and don't much appreciate the way things have been going. That's one reason why many clients don't bother being honest at all about their feelings and instead just cancel their appointment and don't call again. As mentioned previously, this is *not* an ideal way to manage an unsatisfactory relationship, just to go away without any explanation or closure. In fact, it's likely that if a client does this with a therapist it is probably an ongoing life pattern that is less than effective.

However anxious you might feel about telling a therapist you are unhappy with the service, at the very least it provides an opportunity to share feedback, come to a deeper understanding of what happened, and bring things to a more satisfying closure. When sharing such honest (and possibly awkward) input, along the lines of, "I don't much like what we are doing and have not been getting much out of it," it is entirely possible you could find yourself stuck in further disagreement about who is at fault and then subject to persuasive arguments regarding why you should give things more time. If this is the case, then you clearly have the answer to your questions about whether this therapist hears and understands you.

On the other hand, sometimes such a difficult conversation can lead to a major breakthrough, whether you remain with this therapist or not. Just to be able to assert yourself in an honest way, to say what you don't like or appreciate, and to do so with a powerful authority figure, can very well change ongoing patterns in other relationships. In addition, it is quite possible that after bringing up complaints and disappointments there is still an opportunity to renegotiate the ways you work together and customize the process to better meet your needs. This all begins with you speaking up.

I Wasn't Exactly Truthful

People lie. A lot. They lie to their family, their friends, colleagues, everyone. They lie to their dentist when they say they floss every day. They lie to their boss when they say they can't come into work because they aren't feeling well. They especially lie to themselves about their real capabilities and flaws. They even lie to their therapists, which seems rather strange if you consider that they can't improve or get much from the experience until they are prepared to be open and honest. Nevertheless, lying, deceiving, exaggerating, minimizing, and misleading are part of the reality of human interaction during the objective of managing one's image. No client in his right mind would simply blurt out all his foibles, secrets, difficulties, and shameful behavior to someone he just met. It takes time to build this trust.

What I'm saying is that although it is certainly desirable, if not imperative, to be as honest as possible with your therapist, it is also normal and common to shade the truth at times, at least until such time that you feel truly accepted and comfortable. One client says that although she likes and trusts her therapist, she admits she has been frequently lying in her sessions. She finds him rather detached and emotionally unavailable to her, so she does her best to shock him into some genuine reaction. "I have yelled and cursed at him," she says. "He said that he would never fire me because I am only one hour in his week and he accepts his limits. I interpreted this that he doesn't really care about me. It's also weird to say but I don't want to hurt his feelings. Despite everything I have done to shock him I don't want to tell him that almost everything I told him is a lie."

I collected stories from therapists about the most spectacular lies their clients have ever told them in which they had been thoroughly duped. While somewhat amusing, the experiences were also painfully disturbing because of the extent to which some people would intentionally manipulate, disguise, and hide their true selves in order to play games. In all their various forms and styles, psychotherapy is essentially an interaction built upon mutual trust; once that is compromised, the work will inevitably become stalled. So if you are aware that you have been less than honest about certain things in sessions, it is time to reassess what that might mean.

I'm Really Hurt and Offended

Of course there are times you would feel this way, especially if you consider that the therapist's job is to push you into areas that you have been trying to avoid. Some therapists can be rather direct, telling you things that you may not wish to acknowledge. There are times when you will hear things that are wounding, or perhaps more than you can handle, and you may very well feel hurt or misunderstood. This happens a lot in everyday life as well. But here's the interesting growth experience: in therapy with a safe professional you have the opportunity to speak your feelings aloud. It doesn't matter if they were "justified" or represent "overreactions"—it is very important to be able to tell someone that you don't like what they said. This gives both of you the chance to work things through, to explain your positions, and come to some mutual understanding of what happened and why.

As a therapist I sometimes take risks with clients, meaning I challenge them and say things that I know will be difficult to hear. Sometimes I experiment with strategies though I'm not sure where they will end up. I may offer interpretations or explanations that are just plain misguided, if not wrong. And there are also times when I just say something that might be construed as insensitive or rude, even when I try to be careful. I'm not surprised when this happens, or when a client may be offended by something I've said or done. If this doesn't happen, then it means I'm being way too cautious and conservative in my approach. I say this because in a solid, trusting relationship we sometimes make mistakes, apologize, and then move forward. I actually love it when a client confronts me because it presents such a great opportunity for us to be more direct and honest with one another. Oops. That was a lie. Of course I don't "love" it when someone, anyone, confronts me. It's scary and unnerving and triggers for me feelings of inadequacy. What I mean to say is that although I don't initially "enjoy" being confronted, I do love where it can eventually lead if we stick with the feelings. Those can become the most magical and helpful moments in a therapeutic relationship.

What Did You Really Mean By That?

It isn't unusual that there are times we don't understand someone, especially someone who is well educated and uses lots of big words and jargon. A doctor, lawyer, electrician, computer technician, therapist, or other professional is explaining something to us and we nod our heads in acknowledgment, pretending we understand even though we don't have the slightest clue what he or she is talking about. Often in therapy, as well, clients find themselves carefully scrutinizing their therapists' reactions and the meaning of what they said, searching for the hidden clues. Since therapists go to great lengths to maintain the most neutral and blank expressions possible, this would certainly lead to a lot of confusion. That's why it's so important whenever you don't understand something, or are puzzled by what a therapist says or does, that you ask. Every single time. We are actually quite grateful for those queries, assuming they are genuine, since it provides valuable feedback that we aren't being as clear as we would like. These sorts of questions actually lead to far more interesting interactions.

"When you said that I'm kind of person who would do something like that, you kind of laughed. Was there something funny about that I missed?"

"Absolutely not. I was just remembering when you told me that story earlier about when your mother called to interrupt you and you told her you couldn't talk right then because you had just poured milk on your cereal. I thought that was pretty hilarious, and it reminded me how you were less than candid with your friend who wanted to get together with you. It just gets me wondering how you might be holding back with me as well."

It was precisely the probe and search for clarification that may very well be a game changer in terms of understanding, at a deeper and more meaningful level, the dysfunctional patterns of behavior.

First Look at Your Own Behavior Rather Than Blaming the Therapist

As I've mentioned previously, very few people really want to change unless they absolutely have to—and hardly anyone really wants to go to therapy unless they are somewhat desperate and have run out of other options. Being a client in therapy is a very difficult "job" because the rules appear to be so elusive and the process so mysterious. It's not always clear what's expected, much less whether you are actually "performing" as expected. It's not evident much of the time whether it's even helping.

Impasses, conflicts, and unsatisfactory progress in therapy are almost always the result of an interactive effect, meaning that both (or all) parties have some share of responsibility for the outcome. Therapists tend to blame their clients for being resistant, obstructive, or difficult when things get tough; likewise, clients blame their therapists for not doing their jobs properly. Of course, in one sense both are correct in that they each have a role in somehow perpetuating the difficulty.

Generally speaking, people tend to avoid changing if they can continue to get away with it. It just takes too much time and energy. It takes too long. It's too damn hard. In some cases, they simply "enjoy" the benefits that result from staying stuck, the so-called "secondary gains." This allows them to avoid responsibility for their problems and blame others for their plight, whether parents, siblings, the weather, economy, or the therapist. They have a great excuse for continuing to behave badly and engage in self-destructive behavior: "I can't help it!" They are able to distract themselves from other issues that may be even more frightening. They can avoid the unknown and, in one sense, control things on their own terms.

The experience of being in therapy (in either role) is one of the most interesting, exciting, stimulating, confusing, overwhelming, and challenging things you can do in your lifetime. It is absolutely incredible to sit with someone, a trained professional, whose only job is help you improve your life in a multitude of ways. This person listens with an intensity that is unimaginable in any other setting and relies on expertise, experience, and knowledge that allows her to observe and hear things that would be inaccessible to anyone else without this training. You can (hopefully) talk about *anything* without fear of judgment. Each week you have a completely open space and forum to delve into the issues and concerns that weigh on you the most. Who wouldn't want such an opportunity to learn more about themselves and the source of their difficulties? Who wouldn't want a structure that helps them to consistently improve their functioning across a wide spectrum of areas?

If you are currently seeing a therapist, or contemplating doing so, I applaud your commitment to personal growth and refusing to settle for mediocrity, much less unnecessary suffering. As any decent therapist will mention, *you* are the one who determines the value of the experience and how much you get from it. Likewise, if things are not proceeding the way you want, it is time to take a stand and change the direction that things have been going. That begins not just with pointing out your therapist's perceived inadequacies but also examining what you are doing—or not doing—that is getting in your own way.

Final Thoughts

As should be clear throughout this book, like many professional services, one size hardly fits all. Every therapist operates in slightly different ways, even if they subscribe to the same approach. Likewise, each person who seeks help has particular needs, expectations, and desires that can't be met by just anyone. Fit is everything. This means feeling like you have chosen the kind of person who truly understands you and responds to your needs. If this isn't yet the case, or you having some doubts, then I highly recommend that before you consider quitting, much less just canceling your next appointment and calling that the end, you begin an honest conversation about your frustrations and dissatisfactions. Even if this doesn't resolve the difficulties, it provides you with excellent practice in taking initiative and making a more concerted effort to better meet your needs.

Regardless of whether you are a prior client, currently attending sessions, or contemplating doing so, I hope that you now have a better understanding of what is involved, how the process often works, and definite steps you can take to get the most from your experience.

APPENDIX A

Discussion Questions

1. What are some things you learned about being a therapist that surprised you most?
2. Kottler talks extensively about the power of storytelling to promote change and transformation, and even included a chapter on the subject. What's one story in the book that haunts *you* the most and you think will stick with you?
3. What are some of the ideas presented in the book that you are inclined to disagree with? Instead of basing this criticism solely on personal opinion, supply some compelling evidence to support your position.
4. Different cultures have their own unique traditions related to helping and healing, not all of which place the same emphasis on "talk therapy." What are some other healing traditions that you know of that might complement (or conflict with) the practice of Western psychotherapy?
5. Kottler introduces the idea from the beginning that people choose to become therapists in our culture, not only for altruistic reasons but also, in part, to save themselves. What do you make of that idea?
6. Self-care is discussed at length in this book, in recognition of our increased understanding of secondary traumatic stress, transference, burnout, and other risks inherent in this work. What are some of the ways you take time for yourself, and what support systems do you have available when you need help?
7. If you've ever been in therapy yourself, what do you wish your therapist could have—or should have—done differently that would have been helpful to you?
8. There is some discussion in the book about the ways that therapy, as well as our larger culture, are becoming transformed because of advances in technology and knowledge. What are some things you might predict will continue to impact the way that therapy is practiced during the next decade? What is your best prediction about what you think therapy will actually be like in 10 years?

9. What are some ways you might take some of the ideas, thoughts, or content from this book and apply them to quite different contexts of your life?
10. There is a chapter in the book about the reciprocal nature of helping relationships, how the clients who attend therapy often have tremendous impact, for better or worse, on the therapist as well. What is an instance in your life in which you helped, guided, or assisted someone in a helping relationship and this experience had a huge influence or effect on you?
11. What's your own best guess about why you think therapy works and why it sometimes doesn't work out too well?
12. In the chapter on failure, there is a convincing case made about the ways that mistakes, errors, and lapses can often be our greatest teachers. What is an example of a major failure in your life that actually turned out to be an important lesson for you?
13. The point was made in the book that a so-called "difficult client" is in the eye of the beholder, meaning that not all therapists struggle with the same kinds of individuals or problems; much depends on their own experience, personality, training, specialty, values, and interests. Who do you imagine would be *your* most difficult person to help during a time of crisis?
14. According to Kottler (and some research), boredom and burnout often occur not just when we are stressed, but also when our work becomes stale and predictable. What are some routines and patterns that you have slipped into in your life that actually prevent you from becoming more actively engaged, taking more constructive risks, and living your life more intensely?
15. Kottler talks a lot about the paradoxes of the profession, for example, the need to get close, but not too close . . . caring, yet detached . . . supportive without fostering dependency. Can you recognize some of these same tensions in your own relationships, and are there differences in professional and personal dynamics?

References

Adams, M. (2014a). Therapists are human too. *Therapy Today, 25*(9), 22–25.

Adams, M. (2014b). T*he myth of the untroubled therapist.* New York: Routledge.

Adler, J. M. (2013). Clients' and therapists' stories about psychotherapy. *Journal of Personality, 81*(6), 595–605. http://dx.doi.org/10.1111/j.1467-6494.2012.00803.x

Aldarondo, E. (2007). Rekindling the reformist spirit in the mental health professions. In E. Aldarondo (Ed.), *Advancing social justice through clinical practice* (pp. 3–18). Mahwah, NJ: Erlbaum.

Aleksandrowicz, D. R., & Aleksandrowicz, A. O. (Eds.). (2016). *Countertransference in perspective.* Sussex, U.K.: Sussex Academic Press.

Alexander, B. (2011). *The new digital storytelling: Creating narratives with new media.* Santa Barbara, CA: Praeger.

Alexander, F. G., & Selesnick, S. T. (1966). *The history of psychiatry*. New York: Mentor.

Anderson, C. (1987, May/June). The crisis of priorities. *Family Therapy Networker*, pp. 19–25.

Appel, M. (2008). Fictional narratives cultivate just-world beliefs. *Journal of Communication, 58*, 62–83.

Appel, M., & Richter, T. (2007). Persuasive effects of fictional narratives increase over time. *Media Psychology, 10*, 113–134.

Arana, M. (2008, July 3). Five life stories that changed my life. *The Washington Post.* Retrieved from http://voices.washingtonpost.com/shortstack/2008/03/five_life_stories_that_changed.html

Arnold, D., Calhoun, L. G., Tedeschi, R. G., & Cann, A. (2005). Vicarious posttraumatic growth in psychotherapy. *Journal of Humanistic Psychology, 45*(2), 239–263.

Austen, B. (2012, July 23). The story of Steve Jobs: An inspiration or a cautionary tale? *Wired.* Retrieved from http://www.wired.com/business/2012/07/ff_stevejobs/all/

Bandura, A. (1977). *Social learning theory*. Upper Saddle River, NJ: Prentice-Hall.

Banerjee, P. (2014). Locating countertransference in the psychotherapy process: A review. *Journal of the Indian* Acad*emy of Applied Psychology, 40*(1), 27–37.

Barnett, M. (2007). What brings you here? An exploration of the unconscious motivations of those who choose to train and work as psychotherapists and counselors. *Psychodynamic Practice, 13*, 257–274.

Barraclough, S. (2015). The myth of the untroubled therapist: Private life, professional practice. *British Journal of Guidance and Counselling, 43*(3), 375–378.

Bartoskova, L. (2015). Research into post-traumatic growth in therapists: A critical literature review. *Counselling Psychology Review, 30*(3), 57–68.

Bates, Y. (Ed). (2006). *Should I be feeling better by now? Client views of therapy.* New York: Palgrave.

Bauer, J. J., & McAdams, D. P. (2004). Personal growth in adults' stories of life transitions. *Journal of Personality, 72*, 573–602.

Beaulieu, D. (2006). *Impact techniques for therapists.* New York: Routledge.

Beersma, B., & Van Kleef, G. A. (2011). How the grapevine keeps you in line: Gossip increases contributions to the group. *Social Psychological and Personality Science, 2*(6), 642–649.

Beersma, B., & Van Kleef, G. A. (2012). Why people gossip: An empirical analysis of social motives, antecedents, and consequences. *Journal of Applied Social Psychology, 42*(11), 2640–2670.

Bemak, F., & Chung, R. (2008). New professional roles and advocacy strategies for school counselors: A multicultural/social justice perspective to move beyond the nice counselor syndrome. *Journal of Counseling and Development, 86*, 372–381.

Bercier, M. L. (2015). Interventions for secondary traumatic stress with mental health workers: A systematic review. Resea*rch on Social Work Practice, 25*(1), 81–89.

Bercier, M. L., & Maynard, B. R. (2015). Interventions for secondary traumatic stress with mental health workers: A systematic review. *Research on Social Work Practice, 25*(1), 81–89.

Berg, H., Antonsen, P., & Binder, P. E. (2016). Vistas in the relational matrix of the unfolding "I": A qualitative study of therapists' experiences with self-disclosure in psychotherapy. *Journal of Psychotherapy Integration.* Retrieved from http://dx.doi.org/10.1037/a0040051

Berger, B., & Newman, S. (Eds.). (2012). *Money talks: In therapy, society, and life.* New York: Routledge.

Bergese, R. (2013). In the spaces between—sustaining creativity in child psychotherapy. *Journal of Child Psychotherapy, 39*, 319–333.

Bergner, R. M. (2007). Therapeutic storytelling revisited. *American Journal of Psychotherapy, 61*(2), 149–162.

Beutler, L. E. (1983). *Eclectic psychotherapy: A systematic approach.* New York: Pergamon Press.

Bitter, J. R., & Byrd, R. (2011). Human conversations: Self-disclosure and storytelling in Adlerian family therapy. *Journal of Individual Psychology, 67*(3), 305–313.

Bloom, M. (1975). *The paradox of helping.* Hoboken, NJ: Wiley.

Bloomgarden, A., & Mennuti, R. B. (Eds.). (2015). *Psychotherapist revealed: Therapists speak about self-disclosure in psychotherapy*. New York: Routledge.

Blume-Marcovici, A. C., Stolberg, R. A., & Kahademi, M. (2013). Examining our tears: Therapists' accounts of crying in therapy. *American Journal of Psychotherapy, 69*(4), 399–421.

Blume-Marcovici, A. C., Stolberg, R. A., Khademi, M. K., & Giromini, L. (2015). When therapists cry: Implications for supervision and training. *The Clinical Supervisor, 34*(2). 164–183.

Boorstein, D. (1983). *The discoverers*. New York: Random House.

Boynton, R. S. (2003, January). The return of the repressed: The strange case of Masud Khan. *Boston Review*. Retrieved from http://bostonreview.net/archives/BR27.6/boynton.html

Brems, C. (2000). *Dealing with challenges in psychotherapy and counseling*. Pacific Grove, CA: Brooks/Cole.

Bucay, J. (2013). *Let me tell you a story: Tales along the road to happiness.* New York: Europa.

Buechler, S. (2012). *Still practicing: The heartaches and joys of a clinical career.* New York: Routledge.

Bugental, J. F. T. (1976). *The search for existential identity: Patienttherapist dialogues in humanistic psychotherapy*. San Francisco: Jossey-Bass.

Bugental, J. F. T. (1978). *Psychotherapy and process*. Reading, MA: Addison-Wesley.

Bugental, J. F. T. (1990). *Intimate journeys: Stories from life-changing therapy.* San Francisco: Jossey-Bass.

Burns, G. W. (Ed.)(2007). *Healing with stories: Your casebook for using therapeutic metaphors.* New York: Wiley.

Burton, A. (1972). Healing as a lifestyle. In A. Burton & Associates (Eds.), *Twelve therapists: How they live and actualize themselves*. San Francisco: Jossey-Bass.

Butler, M. (2014). The impact of providing therapy on the therapist: A student's reflection. *Journal of Clinical Psychology: In Session, 70*(8), 724–730.

Cafferky, B. M. (2015). Simple story structure intervention. *Journal of Family Psychotherapy, 26*, 157–162.

Carson, D. K., & Becker, K. W. (2003). *Creativity in psychotherapy*. New York: Haworth.

Clark, J. Z. (1991). Therapist narcissism. *Professional Psychology: Research and Practice, 22*, 141–143.

Colvin, G. (2010). *Talent is overrated: What really separates world-class performers from everybody else*. London: Portfolio.

Connor, D. R., & Callahan, J. L. (2015). Impact of psychotherapist expectations on client outcomes. *Psychotherapy, 52*(3), 351–362.

Corey, M. S., & Corey, G. (2016). *On becoming a helper* (7th ed.). Belmont, CA: Cengage.

Corey, G., Corey, M. S., Corey, C., & Callanan, P. (2015). *Issues and ethics in the helping professions* (9th ed.). Belmont, CA: Cengage.

Csikszentmihalyi, M. (1975). *Beyond boredom and anxiety: The experience of play in work and games*. San Francisco: Jossey-Bass.

Csikszentmihalyi, M. (1998). *Finding flow: The psychology of engagement with everyday life*. New York: Basic Books.

Cummings, J. (2011). Sharing a traumatic event: The experience of the listener and the storyteller. *Nursing Research, 60*(6), 386–392.

Davis, M., Eshelman, E. R., & McKay, M. (2012). *The relaxation and stress reduction workbook* (6th ed.). Oakland, CA: New Harbinger.

Delehanty, J. P., & Omin, R. R. (2014). When the therapist becomes the patient. *Journal of Social Work in End-of-Life & Palliative Care, 10*, 209–218.

Dembosky, A. (2016, June 30). How therapy became a hobby of the wealthy, out of reach for those in need, *National Public Radio*. Retrieved from http://www.npr.org/sections/health-shots/2016/06/30/481766112/how-therapy-became-a-hobby-of-the-wealthy-out-of-reach-for-those-in-need

Dinnage, R. (1989). *One to one: Experiences of psychotherapy*. New York: Penguin.

Doherty, W. (2008, November/December). Beyond the consulting room. *Psychotherapy Networker*, pp. 28–35.

Dunbar, R. I. M. (2004). Gossip in evolutionary perspective. *Review of General Psychology, 8*(2), 100–110.

Duncan, B. L. (2010). *On becoming a better therapist.* Washington, DC: American Psychological Association.

Duncan, B. L., Miller, S. D., and Sparks, J. (2004). *The heroic client: Principles of client-directed, outcome-informed Therapy* (rev.). San Francisco: Jossey-Bass.

Duncan, B. L., Miller, S. D., Wampold, B. E., & Hubble, M. A. (2010). *The heart and soul of change: Delivering what works in psychotherapy* (2nd ed.). Washington, DC: American Psychological Association.

Edelstein, L. N., & Waehler, C. A. (2011). *What do I say? The therapist's guide to answering client questions.* New York: Wiley.

Edelwich, J., & Brodsky, A. M. (1980). *Burnout.* New York: Human Sciences Press.

Ellis, A. (1972). Psychotherapy without tears. In A. Burton & Associates (Eds.), *Twelve therapists: How they live and actualize themselves* (pp. 103–126). San Francisco: Jossey-Bass.

Ellis, A. (1984). How to deal with your most difficult client—you. *Journal of Rational Emotive Cognitive Behavior Therapy, 1*(1), 3–8.

English, O. S. (1972). How I found my way to psychiatry. In A. Burton & Associates (Eds.), *Twelve therapists: How they live and actualize themselves*. San Francisco: Jossey-Bass.

Ericsson, K. A. (2014). Why expert performance is special and cannot be extrapolated from studies of performance in the general population: A response to criticisms. *Intelligence, 45*, 81–103.

Farber, B. A. (1990). Burnout in psychotherapists: Incidence, types, and trends. *Psychotherapy in Private Practice, 8*(1), 35–44.

Farber, B. A. (2006). *Self-disclosure in psychotherapy*. New York: Guilford Press.

Feinberg, M., Willer, R., Stellar, J., & Keltner, D. (2012). The virtues of gossip: Reputational information sharing as prosocial behavior. *Journal of Personality and Social Psychology, 102*(5), 1015–1030.

Figley, C. (2002). *Treating compassion fatigue*. New York: Routledge.

Fine, H. J. (1980). Despair and depletion in the therapist. *Psychotherapy: Theory, Research, and Practice, 17*(4), 392–395.

Fish, J. M. (1973). *Placebo therapy: A practical guide to social influence in psychotherapy*. San Francisco: Jossey-Bass.

Fish, J. M. (1996). *Culture and therapy*. Northvale, NJ: Aronson.

Flowers, J. V., & Frizler, P. (2004). *Psychotherapists on film*. Jefferson, NC: McFarland.

Forrest, G. G. (2012). *Self-disclosure in psychotherapy and recovery*. New York: Jason Aronson.

Fox, G. (2000). *Mockingbird years: A life in and out of therapy*. New York: Basic Books.

Frank, J. D. (1993). *Persuasion and healing* (3rd ed.). Baltimore: Johns Hopkins University Press.

Frank, R. (1979). Money and other trade-offs in psychotherapy. *Voices, 14*(4), 42–44.

Freud, S. (1912). The dynamics of transference. In *Collected papers*, Vol. 8. London: Imago.

Freud, S. (1954). *The origins of psychoanalysis*. New York: Basic Books.

Freud, S. (1955). Letter to Ferenczi, Oct. 6, 1910. In E. Jones, *The life and work of Sigmund Freud* (Vol. 2, pp. 221–223). New York: Basic Books.

Freudenberger, H. J. (1975). The staff burn-out syndrome in alternative institutions. *Psychotherapy: Theory, Research, and Practice, 12*(1), 73–82.

Freudenberger, H. J., & Robbins, A. (1979). The hazards of being a psychoanalyst. *Psychoanalytic Review, 66*, 275–296.

Fryer, B. (2003, June). A conversation with screenwriting coach Robert McKee. *Harvard Business Review*, pp. 51–55.

Gabriel, L. (2005). *Speaking the unspeakable: The ethics of dual relationships in counseling and psychotherapy*. New York: Routledge.

Gallup. (2015). Honesty/ethics in professions. Retrieved from http://www.gallup.com/poll/1654/honesty-ethics-professions.aspx

Gazzaniga, M. (2008). *Human: The science behind what makes your brain unique*. New York: Harper Perennial.

Gelso, C. J., & Hayes, J. A. (2007). *Countertransference and the therapist's inner experience: Perils and possibilities*. Mahwah, NJ: Erlbaum.

Gerson, B. (Ed.). (2009). *The therapist as a person*. New York: Routledge.

Ghent, E. (1999). Masochism, submission, surrender: Masochism as a perversion of surrender. In S. Mitchell & L. Aron (Eds.), *Relational psychoanalysis: The emergence of tradition* (pp. 211–242). Hillsdale, NJ: Analytic Press.

Gil, S. (2015). Secondary trauma among social workers treating trauma clients: The role of coping strategies and internal resources. *International Social Work, 58*(4), 551–561.

Gladding, S. T. (2008). The impact of creativity in counseling. *Journal of Creativity in Mental Health, 3*(2), 97–104.

Gladding, S. T. (2016). *Counseling as art: The creative arts in counseling* (5th ed.). Alexandria, VA: American Counseling Association.

Gmelch, W. (1983). Stress for success: How to optimize your performance. *Theory into Practice, 22*(1), 7–14.

Goh, M. (2005). Cultural competence and master therapists: An inextricable relationship. *Journal of Mental Health Counseling, 27*, 71–81.

Goldberg, A. (2007). *Moral stealth: How correct behavior insinuates itself into psychotherapeutic practice.* Chicago: University of Chicago Press.

Goldberg, A. (2012). *An analysis of failure: An investigation of failed cases in psychoanalysis and psychotherapy.* New York: Routledge.

Gonzalez, D. M. (2016). Client variables and psychotherapy outcomes. In D. J. Cain, K. Keenan, & S. Rubin (Eds.), *Humanistic psychotherapies: Handbook of research and practice* (2nd ed.). Washington, DC: American Psychological Association.

Goodyear, R., Lichtenberg, J. W., Bang, K., & Graff, J. B. (2014). Ten changes psychotherapists typically make as they mature into the role of supervisor. *Journal of Clinical Psychology: In Session, 70*(11), 1042–1050.

Gottschall, J. (2012). *The storytelling animal: How stories make us human.* New York: Houghton Mifflin.

Grant, M. (2010–2012). *The newsflesh trilogy: Feed, Deadline, and Blackout.* New York: Orbit.

Greenberg, R., Constantino, M., & Bruce, N. (2006). Are patient expectations still relevant for psychotherapy processes and outcomes? *Clinical Psychology Review, 26*, 657–678.

Gregoire, C. (2014, March 3). 18 things highly creative people do differently. *Huffington Post.* Retrieved from http://www.huffingtonpost.com/2014/03/04/creativity-habits_n_4859769.html?view=print&comm_ref=false

Griswell, G. E. (1979). Dead tired and bone weary. *Voices, 15*(2), 49–53.

Groman, M. (2009). Lowering fees in hard times: The meaning behind the money. Retrieved from http://www.psychotherapy.net/article/lowering_fees_in_hard_times

Gross, D., & Kahn, J. (1983). Values of three practitioner groups. *Journal of Counseling and Values, 28*, 228–333.

Guy, J. D. (1987). *The personal life of the psychotherapist.* Hoboken, NJ: Wiley.

Haley, J. (1973). *Uncommon therapy.* New York: W. W. Norton.

Hamman, J. J. (2001). The search to be real: Why psychotherapists become therapists. *Journal of Religion and Health, 40*, 343–356.

Hantoot, M. S. (2000). Lying in psychotherapy supervision. *Academic Psychiatry, 24*, 179–187.

Hardiman, P., & Simmonds, J. G. (2013). Spiritual well-being, burnout, and trauma in counsellors and psychotherapists. *Mental Health, Religion, and Culture, 16*(10), 1044–1055.

Hayes, J. A., Nelson, D. L., & Fauth, J. (2015). Countertransference in successful and unsuccessful cases of psychotherapy. *Psychotherapy, 52*(1), 127–133.

Heatherington, L., Friedlander, M. L., & Diamond, G. M. (2014). Lessons offered, lessons learned: Reflections on how doing family therapy can affect therapists. *Journal of Clinical Psychology: In Session, 70*(8), 760–767.

Heide, F. J. (2013). Easy to sense, hard to define: Charismatic nonverbal communication and the psychotherapist. *Journal of Psychotherapy Integration, 23*(3), 305–319.

Heineman, T. (2016). *Relational treatment of trauma: Stories of loss and hope.* New York: Routledge.

Heinonen, E., & Orlinsky, D. E. (2013). Psychotherapists' personal identities, theoretical orientations, and professional relationships: Elective affinity and role adjustment as modes of congruence. *Psychotherapy Research, 23*(6), 718–731.

Henretty, J. R., Currier, J. M., Berman, J. S., & Levitt, H. M. (2014). The impact of counselor self-disclosure on clients: A meta-analytic review of experimental and quasi-experimental research. *Journal of Counseling Psychology, 61*(2), 191–207.

Henry, W. E., Sims, J. H., & Spray, S. L. (1973). *Public and private lives of psychotherapists.* San Francisco: Jossey-Bass.

Herlihy, B., & Corey, G. (2014). *Boundary issues in counseling: Multiple roles and responsibilities* (3rd ed.). Alexandria, VA: American Counseling Association.

Hersoung, A. G., Hoglend, P., Havik, O. E., von der Lippe, A., & Monsen, J. T. (2009). Therapist characteristics influencing the quality of alliance. *Clinical Psychology and Psychotherapy, 16*, 100–110.

Hess, M. (2012). Mirror neurons, the development of empathy and digital storytelling. *Religious Education, 107*(4), 401–414.

Hoglend, P. A., Monsen, J. T., & Ronnestad, M. H. (2013). The contribution of the quality of therapists' personal lives to the development of the working alliance. *Journal of Counseling Psychology, 60*(4), 483–495.

Howes, R. (2009, December 30). The ideal psychotherapy client. *Psychology Today.* Retrieved from https://www.psychologytoday.com/blog/in-therapy/200912/the-ideal-psychotherapy-client

Howes, R. (2015, January/February). Losing our war on stress. *Psychotherapy Networker*, pp. 57–58.

Hoyt, T., & Yeater, E. A. (2011). The effects of negative emotion and expressive writing on posttraumatic stress symptoms. *Journal of Social and Clinical Psychology, 30*(6), 549–569.

Hsu, J. (2008). The secrets of storytelling: Our love for telling tales reveals the workings of the mind. *Scientific American Mind, 19*(4), 46–51.

Iacoboni, M. (2008). *Mirroring people: The new science of how we connect with others.* New York: Farrar, Straus & Giroux.

Ingemark, C. A. (Ed.). (2013). *Therapeutic uses of storytelling.* Lund, Sweden: Nordic Academic Press.

Iyer, P. (2014). *The art of stillness.* New York: Simon & Schuster.

Khair Badawi, M. T. (2015). The countertransference: When painful traumatic traces sustain the countertransference and reveal themselves to the psychoanalyst 14 years later. *International Journal of Psychoanalysis, 96*(6), 1477–1489.

Kantrowitz, J. L. (2015). Reflections on becoming an older and more experienced psychotherapist. *Journal of Clinical Psychology: In Session, 71*(11), 1093–1103.

Karakurt, G., Anderson, A., Banford, A., Dial, S., Kokow, H., Rable, F., & Doslovich, S. F. (2014). Strategies for managing difficult clinical situations between sessions. *American Journal of Family Therapy, 42*, 413–425.

Keen, S. (1977, May). Boredom and how to beat it. *Psychology Today*, pp. 78–84.

Keeney, B. P. (1991). *Improvisational therapy*. New York: Guilford Press.

Keeney, B. P. (1996). *Everyday soul: Awakening the spirit in daily life.* New York: Riverhead.

Keeney, B. P. (2003). *Ropes to God: Experiencing the Bushmen spiritual universe.* Philadelphia: Ringing Rocks Press.

Keeney, B. (2009). *The creative therapist.* New York: Routledge.

Kegel, A. F., & Fluckiger, C. (2015).Psychotherapy dropouts: A multilevel approach. *Clinical Psychology and Psychotherapy, 22*(5), 377–386.

Kirsch, I., Wampold, B., & Kelley, J. M. (2015). Controlling for the placebo effect in psychotherapy: Noble quest or tiling at windmills? *Psychology of Consciousness: Theory, Research, and Practice, 3*(2), 121–131. http://dx.doi.org/10.1037/cns0000065

Kirschenbaum, H. (2009). *The life and work of Carl Rogers*. Alexandria, VA: American Counseling Association.

Kiser, L. J., Baumgardner, B., & Dorado, J. (2010). Who we are, but for the stories we tell: Family stories and healing. *Psychological Trauma: Theory, Research, Practice, and Policy, 2*(3), 243–249.

Koestler, A. (1964). *The act of creation*. New York: Dell.

Kooperman, D. (2013). When the therapist is in crisis: Personal and professional implications for small community psychotherapy practices. *American Journal of Psychotherapy, 67*(4), 385–403.

Kopp, S. (1985). *Even a stone can be a teacher*. Los Angeles: Tarcher.

Korkki, P. (2014). The science of older and wiser. *New York Times*, March 12. Retrieved from http://www.nytimes.com/2014/03/13/business/retirementspecial/the-science-of-older-and-wiser.html?_r=0

Kottler, J. (1990). *Private moments, secret selves: Enriching our time alone*. New York: Ballantine.

Kottler, J. (1991). *The compleat therapist*. San Francisco: Jossey-Bass.

Kottler, J. (1992). *Compassionate therapy: Working with difficult clients*. San Francisco: Jossey-Bass.

Kottler, J. (1993). Facing failure as a counselor. *American Counselor, 2*(4), 14–19.

Kottler, J. (1997). *Travel that can change your life*. San Francisco: Jossey-Bass.

Kottler, J. A. (2006). *Divine Madness: Ten Stories of Creative Struggle.* San Francisco: Jossey-Bass.

Kottler, J. (2008, September/October). Transforming lives. *Psychotherapy Networker*, pp. 42–47.

Kottler, J. (2010). *The assassin and the therapist: An exploration of truth and its meaning in psychotherapy and in life*. New York: Routledge.

Kottler, J. A. (2012). *The Therapist's workbook: Self-assessment, self-care, and self-improvement exercises for mental health professionals* (2nd ed.). New York: Wiley.

Kottler, J. A. (2014). *Change: What leads to personal transformation*. New York: Oxford University Press.

Kottler, J. A. (2015a). *The therapist in the real world: What you never learn in graduate school (but really need to know)*. New York: W. W. Norton.

Kottler, J. A. (2015b). *Stories we've heard, stories we've told: Life-changing narratives in therapy and everyday life*. New York: Oxford University Press.

Kottler, J., & Blau, D. (1989). *The imperfect therapist: Learning from failure in therapeutic practice*. San Francisco, JosseyBass.

Kottler, J. A., & Carlson, J. (2002). *Bad therapy: Master therapists share their worst failures*. New York: Routledge.

Kottler, J. A., & Carlson, J. (2003). *The mummy at the dining room table: Eminent therapists reveal their most unusual cases*. San Francisco: Jossey-Bass.

Kottler, J. A., & Carlson, J. (2006). *The client who changed me: Stories of therapist personal transformation*. New York: Routledge.

Kottler, J., & Carlson, J. (2007). *Moved by the spirit: Discovery and transformation in the lives of leaders*. Atascadero, CA: Impact.

Kottler, J. A., & Carlson, J. (2008). *Their finest hour: master therapists share their greatest success stories* (2nd ed.). Bethel, CT: Crown Publishing.

Kottler, J. A., & Carlson, J. (2009). *Creative breakthroughs in therapy: Tales of transformation and astonishment*. New York: Wiley.

Kottler, J., & Carlson, J. (Eds.). (2011). *Duped: Lies and deception in psychotherapy*. New York: Routledge.

Kottler, J. A., & Carlson, J. (2015). *On being a master therapist: Practicing what we preach*. New York: Wiley.

Kottler, J. A., & Carlson, J. (2016). *Therapy over 50: Aging issues in psychotherapy and the therapist's life*. New York: Oxford University Press.

Kottler, J., Carlson, J., & Keeney, B. (2004). *American shaman: An odyssey of global healing traditions*. New York: Routledge.

Kottler, J. A., Englar-Carlson, M., & Carlson, J., & (Eds.). (2013). *Helping beyond the 50 minute hour: Therapists involved in meaningful social action*. New York: Routledge.

Kottler, J., & Marriner, M. (2009). *Changing people's lives while transforming your own: Paths to social justice and global human rights*. Hoboken, NJ: Wiley.

Kovacs, A. L. (1976). The emotional hazards of teaching psychotherapy. *Psychotherapy: Theory, Research, and Practice, 13*(4), 321–334.

Kuchuck, S. (Ed.). (2014). *Clinical implications of the psychoanalyst's life experience: When the personal becomes professional*. New York: Routledge.

Kugelmass, H. (2016). Sorry, I'm not accepting new Patients: An audit study of access to mental health care. *Journal of Health and Social Behavior*, *57*(2), 168–183.

Lambert, M. J. (Ed.). (2013). *Bergin and Garfield's handbook of psychotherapy and behavior change* (6th ed.). New York: Wiley.

Lambert, M., & Shimokawa, K. (2011). Collecting client feedback. In J. Norcross (Ed.). *Psychotherapy relationships that work* (2nd ed., pp. 203–223). New York: Oxford University Press.

Levy, F. J. (2014). Integrating the arts in psychotherapy: Opening the doors of shared creativity. *American Journal of Dance Therapy*, *36*(1), 6–27.

Lindner, R. (1960). *The fifty-minute hour.* New York: Bantam.

Linley, P. A., & Joseph, S. (2004). Positive change following trauma and adversity: A review. *Journal of Traumatic Stress*, *17*(1), 11–21.

Linley, P. A., & Joseph, S. (2007). Therapy work and therapists' positive and negative well-being. *Journal of Social and Clinical Psychology*, *26*(3), 385–403.

Loy, D. R. (2010). *The world is made of stories*. Boston: Wisdom Publications.

Lyman, E. L. (2014). Reflections on intrapersonal and interpersonal changes in a beginning (psychodynamically-oriented) psychotherapist. *Journal of Clinical Psychology: In Session*, *70*(8), 731–740.

Macdonald, J., & Mellor-Clark, J. (2015). Correcting psychotherapists' blindsidedness: Formal feedback as a means of overcoming the natural limitations of therapists. *Clinical Psychology and Psychotherapy*, *22*, 249–257.

Maeder, T. (1989, January). Wounded healers. *Atlantic Monthly*, pp. 37–47.

Mahoney, M. J. (1997). Psychotherapists' personal problems and self-care patterns. *Professional Psychology: Research and Practice*, *28*, 14–16.

Malikiosi-Loizos, M. (2013). Personal therapy for future therapists: Reflections on a still debated issue. *European Journal of Counselling Psychology*, *2*(1), 33–50.

Malinowski, A. J. (2013). Characteristics of job burnout and humor among psychotherapists. *International Journal of Humor Research*, *26*(1), 117–133.

Mar, R. A., Oatley, K., Djikic, M., & Mullin, J. (2011). Emotion and narrative fiction: Interactive influences before, during, and after reading. *Cognition and Emotion*, *25*(5), 818–833.

Marar, Z. (2008). *Deception.* Stocksfield, U.K.: Acumen Publishing

Maslach, C. (2003). *Burnout: The cost of caring.* Cambridge, MA: Malor Books.

Maslach, C., & Leiter, M. P. (1997). *The truth about burnout.* San Francisco: Jossey-Bass.

Maslow, A. (1968). *Toward a psychology of being.* New York: Van Nostrand Reinhold.

Masterson, J. F. (2014). *Countertransference and psychotherapeutic technique: Teaching seminars.* New York: Routledge.

Mathieu, F. (2012). *The compassion fatigue workbook.* New York: Routledge.

McAdams, D. P. (2006). *The redemptive self: Stories Americans live by.* New York: Oxford University Press.

McAndrew, F. T., & Milenkovic, M. A. (2002). Of tabloids and family secrets: The evolutionary psychology of gossip. *Journal of Applied Social Psychology*, *32*, 1064–1082.

Mennuti, R. B. (Eds.). (2009). *Psychotherapist revealed: Therapists speak about self-disclosure in psychotherapy*. New York: Routledge.

Messer, S. B. (2015). How I have changed over time as a psychotherapist. *Journal of Clinical Psychology: In Session*, *71*(11), 1104–1114.

Messer, S. B., & Gurman, A. (Eds.). (2013). *Essential psychotherapies: Theory and practice* (3rd ed.). New York: Guilford.

Miller, S. D., Duncan, B. L, Brown, J., Sorrell, R., & Chalk, B. (2006). Using outcome to inform and improve outcomes. *Journal of Brief Therapy*, 5, 5–22.

Miller, S., & Hubble, M. (2011, March/April). The road to mastery. *Psychotherapy Networker*, pp. 22–31.

Miller, S., Hubble, M., & Duncan, B. (2007, Nov./Dec). Supershrinks: What's the secret of their success? *Psychotherapy Networker*, pp. 27–35.

Miller, S. D., & Rousmaniere, T. (2014). Why most therapists are just average (and how we can improve). *International Journal of Psychotherapy*, *18*(2), 39–49.

Moltu, C., & Binder, P. E. (2013). Skilled therapists' experiences of how they contributed to constructive change in difficult therapies: A qualitative study. *Counselling and Psychotherapy Research*, *14*(2), 128–137.

Morgan, W. P. (1978, April). The mind of the marathoner. *Psychology Today*, pp. 38–47.

Morris, R., & Picard, R. (2012, April). Crowdsourcing collective emotional intelligence. *Proceedings of CoRR*. Retrieved from http://arxiv.org/abs/1204.3481v1

Murphy, S. (2012, Sept.). The power of story. *Counseling Today*, pp. 38–41.

Myers, D., & Hayes, J. A. (2006). Effects of therapist general self-disclosure and countertransference disclosure on ratings of the therapist and the session. *Psychotherapy*, *43*, 173–185.

Neff, K. (2015, Sept./Oct.). The five myths of self-compassion. *Psychotherapy Networker*, pp. 31–35, 47.

Neimeyer, R. A. (2004). Fostering posttraumatic growth: A narrative contribution. *Psychological Inquiry*, *15*, 53–59.

Newbury, R., Hayter, M., Wylie, K. R., & Riddell, J. (2012). Sexual fantasy as a clinical intervention. *Sexual and Relationship Therapy*, *27*(4), 358–371.

Nigam, S. K. (2012). The storytelling brain. *Science and Engineering Ethics*, *18*, 567–571.

Nissen-Lie, H. A., Havik, O. E., Hoglend, P. A., Monsen, J. T., & Ronnestad, M. H. (2013). The contribution of the quality of therapists' personal lives to the development of the working alliance. *Journal of Counseling Psychology*, *60*(4), 483–495.

Nissen-Lie, H. A., Ronnestad, M. H., Hoglend, P. A., Havik, O. E., Solbakken, O. A., Stiles, T. C., & Monsen, J. T. (2015). Love yourself as a person, doubt yourself as a therapist? *Clinical Psychology and Psychotherapy*. Retrieved from http://onlinelibrary.wiley.com.lib-proxy.fullerton.edu/store/10.1002/cpp.1977/asset/cpp1977.pdf;jsessionid=7DEA8B73283D2A79BF54A58BDBACCFC8.f02t03?v=1&t=isoekyse&s=67c096c3ffd1f42b27b2160c905b71cea5ba0a92

Norcross, J. C. (2000). Psychotherapist self-care: Practitioner-tested, research informed strategies. *Professional Psychology: Research and Practice*, *31*(6), 710–713.

Norcross, J. C., Bike, D. H., & Evans, K. L. (2009). The therapist's therapist: A replication and extension 20 years later. *Psychotherapy: Theory, Research, Practice, Training, 46*(1), 32–41.

Norcross, J. C., & Connor, K. A. (2005). Psychotherapists entering personal therapy. In J. D. Geller, J. C. Norcross, & D. E. Orlinsky (Eds.), *The psychotherapist's own psychotherapy* (pp. 192–200). New York: Oxford University Press.

Norcross, J. C., & Guy, J. D. (2005). The prevalence and parameters of personal therapy in the United States. In J. D. Geller, J. C. Norcross, & D. E. Orlinsky (Eds.), *The psychotherapist's own psychotherapy* (pp. 165–176). New York: Oxford University Press.

Norcross, J. C., & Guy, J. D. (2007). *Leaving it at the office: A guide to psychotherapist self-care*. New York: Guilford Press.

Olarte, S. W. (1997). Sexual boundary violations. In *The Hatherleigh guide to ethics in therapy* (pp. 195–209). New York: Hatherleigh Press.

Orlinsky, D. E., Norcross, J. C., Ronnestad, M. H., & Wiseman, H. (2005). Outcomes and impacts of the psychotherapist's own psychotherapy. In J. D. Geller, J. C. Norcross, & D. E. Orlinsky (Eds.), *The psychotherapist's own psychotherapy* (pp. 214–230). New York: Oxford University Press.

Orlinsky, D. E., & Ronnestad M. H. (2005). *How psychotherapists develop: A study of therapeutic work and professional growth*. Washington, DC: American Psychological Association.

Owen, J., Tao, K. W., Imel, Z., Wampold, B. E., & Rodolfa, E. (2014). Addressing racial and ethnic microaggressions in therapy. *Professional Psychology: Research and Practice, 45*(4), 283–290.

Paul, A. M. (2012, March 17). Your brain on fiction. *New York Times*. http://www.nytimes.com/2012/03/18/opinion/sunday/the-neuroscience-of-your-brain-on-fiction.html?pagewanted=all&_r=0

Pipher, M. (2013, March/April). Many faces of wisdom. *Psychotherapy Networker*.

Polman, R. (2010). Type D personality, stress, and symptoms of burnout: The influence of avoidance coping and social support. *British Journal of Health Psychology, 15*, 681–696.

Pomerantz, K. A. (2007). Helping children explore their emotional and social worlds through therapeutic stories. *Educational and Child Psychology, 24*(1), 46–55.

Pope, K. S., & Bouhoutsos, J. C. (1986). *Sexual intimacy between therapists and patients*. New York: Praeger.

Pope, K. S., Sonne, J. L., & Greene, B. (2006). *What therapists don't talk about and why*. Washington, DC: American Psychological Association.

Probst, B. (2015). The other chair: Portability and translation from personal therapy to clinical practice. *Clinical Social Work, 43*, 50–61.

Puig, A., Yoon, E., Callueng, C., An, S., & Lee, M. (2014). Burnout syndrome in psychotherapists: A comparative analysis of five nations. *Psychological Services, 11*(1), 87–96.

Rainer, T. (1978). *The new diary*. Los Angeles: Tarcher.

Ram Dass & Gorman, P. (1985). *How can I help? Stories and reflections on service*. New York: Knopf.

Reamer, F. G. (2015). Ethical misconduct and negligence in social work. *Social Work Today, 15*(5), 20–25.

Reese, E. (2013). *Tell me a story: Sharing stories to enrich your child's world*. New York: Oxford University Press.

Remley, T., & Herlihy, B. (2015). *Ethical, legal, and professional issues in counseling* (6th ed.). Upper Saddle River, NJ: Pearson.

Revell, S., & McLeod, J. (2016). Experiences of therapists who integrate walk and talk into their professional practice. *Counselling and Psychotherapy Research, 16*(1), 35–43.

Reynolds, G. (2012). *Presentation Zen: Simple ideas on presentation design and delivery*. Berkeley, CA: New Riders.

Riggar, T. F. (2016). Counselor burnout. In I. Marini & M. Stebnicki (Eds.), *The counselor's desk reference* (2nd ed.). New York: Springer.

Rizzolatti, G., & Craighero, L. (2004). The mirror-neuron system. *Annual Review of Neuroscience, 27*, 169–192.

Rogers, C. R. (1972). My personal growth. In A. Burton & Associates (Eds.), *Twelve therapists: How they live and actualize themselves* (pp. 28–77). San Francisco: Jossey-Bass.

Rojano, R. (2007). The practice of community family therapy. In E. Aldarondo (Ed.), *Advancing social justice through clinical practice* (pp. 245–264). Mahwah, NJ: Erlbaum.

Roos, J., & Werbart, A. (2013). Therapist and relationship factors influencing dropout from individual psychotherapy: A literature review. *Psychotherapy Research, 23*(4), 394–418.

Rosenthal, H. (2011). When therapists lie to promote their own agendas. In J. Kottler & J. Carlson (Eds.), *Duped: Lies and Deception in Psychotherapy* (pp. 39–46). New York: Routledge.

Rosenthal, H. (Ed.). (2001). *Favorite counseling and therapy homework assignments: Leading therapists share their most creative strategies*. New York: Routledge.

Rothschild, B., & Rand, M. L. (2006). *Help for the helper: The psychophysiology of compassion fatigue and vicarious trauma*. New York: Norton.

Rowan, J., & Jacobs, M. (2002). *The therapist's use of self*. Philadelphia: Open University Press.

Roy, B. (2007). Radical psychiatry: An approach to personal and political change. In E. Aldarondo (Ed.), *Advancing social justice through clinical practice* (pp. 65–90). Mahwah, NJ: Erlbaum.

Rupert, P. A., & Morgan, D. J. (2005). Work setting and burnout among professional psychologists. *Professional Psychology: Research and Practice, 36*, 544–550.

Rupert, P. A., Stevanovic, P., & Hunley, H. (2009). Work-family conflict and burnout among practicing psychologists. *Professional Psychology: Research and Practice, 40*, 54–61.

Rzeszutek, M., & Schier, K. (2014). Temperament, traits, social support, and burnout symptoms in a sample of therapists. *Psychotherapy, 51*(4), 574–579.

Sands, A. (2000). *Falling for therapy: Psychotherapy from a client's perspective.* London: Palgrave Macmillan.

Schaler, K. (2009). *Travel therapy: Where do you need to go?* Berkeley, CA: Seal Press.

Schoener, G. R. (2015). Treating impaired psychotherapists and wounded healers. In D. Geller, J. C. Norcross, & D. E. Orlinsky (Eds.), *The psychotherapist's own psychotherapy* (pp. 322–341). New York: Oxford University Press.

Schor, J. B. (1992, March/April). Work, spend, work, spend: Is this any way to live? *Family Therapy Networker*, pp. 24–25.

Schroder, T., Wiseman, H., & Orlinsky, D. E. (2009). "You were always on my mind": Therapists' intersession characteristics, professional characteristics, and quality of life. *Psychotherapy Research, 19*, 42–53.

Schroeder, D. A., & Graziano, W. G. (Eds.). (2015). *The Oxford handbook of prosocial behavior.* New York: Oxford University Press.

Schwartz, B., & Flowers, J. V. (2006). *How to fail as a therapist.* Atascadero, CA: Impact.

Schwartz, R. (2015, Sept./Oct). Facing our dark sides. *Psychotherapy Networker*, pp. 19–23, 42.

Simmons, A. (2006). *The story factor: Inspiration, influence, and persuasion through the art of storytelling.* New York: Basic Books.

Skovholt, T. M. (2001). *The resilient practitioner: Burnout prevention and self-care strategies for counselors, therapists, teachers, and health professionals.* Boston: Allyn & Bacon.

Skovholt, T. M. (2012). *Becoming a therapist: On the path to mastery.* New York: Wiley.

Somers, A. D., Pomerantz, A. M., Meeks, J. T., & Pawlow, L. A. (2014). Should psychotherapists disclose their own psychological problems? *Counselling and Psychotherapy Research, 14*(4), 249–255.

Spaulding, A. E. (2011). *The art of storytelling: Telling truths through telling stories.* Lanham, MD: Scarecrow Press.

Spense, D. P. (1982). *Narrative and historical truth.* New York: Norton.

Steingard, S. (2015). The placebo effect in clinical practice. *Psychiatric Services, 66*(9), e3.

Stewart, A. E., & Neimeyer, R. A. (2007). Emplotting the traumatic self: Narrative revision and the construction of coherence. In S. Krippner, M. Bova, & L. Gray (Eds.), *Healing stories: The use of narrative in counseling psychotherapy* (pp. 41–62). Charlottesville, VA: Puente.

Stewart, R. E., & Chambless, D. L. (2008). Treatment failures in private practice: How do psychologists proceed? *Professional Psychology: Research and Practice, 39*, 176–181.

Strange, J. J. (2002). How fictional tales wag real-world beliefs. In M. C. Green, J. J. Strange, & T. C. Brock (Eds.), *Narrative impact: Social and cognitive foundations* (pp. 263–286). Mahwah, NJ: Lawrence Erlbaum.

Strean, H. S. (2002). *Controversies on counter-transference.* Northvale, NJ: Aronson.

Sue, D. W., & Sue, D. (2015). *Counseling the culturally diverse* (6th ed.). New York: Wiley.

Sussman, M. B. (1995). *A perilous calling: The hazards of psychotherapy practice.* Hoboken, NJ: Wiley.

Sussman, M. B. (2007). *A curious calling: Unconscious motivations for practicing psychotherapy.* New York: Aronson.

Theriault, A., & Gazzola, N. (2005). Feelings of inadequacy, insecurity, and incompetence among experienced therapists. *Counselling and Psychotherapy Research, 5*(1), 11–18.

Theriault, A., & Gazzola, N. (2006). What are the sources of feelings of incompetence in experienced psychotherapists? *Counseling Psychology Quarterly, 19*, 313–330.

Thoreson, R. W., Miller, M., & Krauskopf, C. J. (1989). The distressed psychologist: Prevalence and treatment considerations. *Professional Psychology: Research and Practice, 20*, 153–158.

Timulak, L. (2014). Witnessing clients' emotional transformation: An emotion-focused therapist's experiencing of providing therapy. *Journal of Clinical Psychology: In Session, 70*(8), 741–752.

Tower, G. (2005). *Fish in a barrel: A true story of sexual abuse in therapy.* Salt Lake City, UT: Millennial Mind.

Trachtman, R. (2011). *Money and psychotherapy: A guide for mental health professionals.* Washington, DC: National Association of Social Work.

Treadway, D. (2000, November/December). How involved is too involved? *Psychotherapy Networker*, pp. 32–35.

Trosclair, G. (2015). *I'm working on it in therapy: How to get the most out of psychotherapy.* New York: Skyhorse Publishing.

Turkle, S. (2015). *Reclaiming conversation: The power of talk in the digital age.* New York: Penguin.

Turner, J. A., Edwards, L. M., Eicken, I. M., Yokoyama, K., Castro, J. R., & Tran, A. N. (2005). Intern self-care: An exploratory study into strategy use and effectiveness. *Professional Psychology: Research and Practice, 36*, 674–680.

van der Kolk, B. (2014). *The body keeps score: Brain, mind, and body in the healing of trauma.* New York: Penguin.

Vandenberghe, L., & Silvestre, R. L. (2013). Therapists' positive emotions in-session: Why they happen and what they are good for. *Counselling and Psychotherapy Research, 14*(2), 119–127.

Vanderbes, J. (2013). The evolutionary case for great fiction. *The Atlantic.* Retrieved from http://www.theatlantic.com/entertainment/archive/2013/09/the-evolutionary-case-for-great-fiction/279311/

Wang, S. S. (2008). Ethics lapses usually start small for therapists. *Health Blog.* Retrieved from http://blogs.wsj.com/health/2007/10/17/ethics-lapses-usually-start-small-for-therapists/

Warkentin, J. (1972). Paradox of being alien and intimate. In A. Burton & Associates (Eds.), *Twelve therapists: How they live and actualize themselves.* San Francisco: Jossey-Bass.

Waters, D. (1992, September/October). Therapy as an excellent adventure. *Family Therapy Networker*, pp. 38–45.

Welfel, E. R. (2015). *Ethics in counseling and psychotherapy*. Belmont, CA: Brooks/Cole.

White, M. (2007). *Maps of narrative practice*. New York: W. W. Norton.

Wicker, A. W. (1985, October). Getting out of conceptual ruts. *American Psychologist*, pp. 1094–1103.

Wicks, R. J. (2008). *The resilient clinician*. New York: Oxford University Press.

Wilson, E., & Harris, C. (2006). Meaningful travel: Women, independent travel and the search for self and meaning. *Tourism*, *54*(2), 161–172.

Wiseman, S., & Scott, C. D. (2003). Hasta la vista baby, I'm outta here: Dealing with boredom in therapy. In J. A. Kottler and W. P. Jones (Eds.), *Doing better*. New York: Brunner/ Routledge.

Wood, B., Klein, S., Cross, H. J., Lammes, C. J., & Elliot, J. K. (1985). Impaired practitioners: Psychologists' opinions about prevalence, and proposals for intervention. *Professional Psychology: Research and Practice*, *16*, 843–850.

Wright, R. H. (2005). The myth of continuing education: A look at some intended and (maybe) unintended consequences. In R. H. Wright and N. A. Cummings (Eds.), *Destructive trends in mental health: The well-intentioned path to harm* (pp. 143–151). New York: Taylor & Francis.

Wylie, M. S., & Markowitz, L. M. (1992, September/October). Walking the wire. *Family Therapy Networker*, pp. 19–30.

Yalom, I. (1989). *Love's executioner and other tales of psychotherapy*. New York: Basic Books.

Yalom, I. (2000). *Momma and the meaning of life: Tales of psychotherapy*. New York: Basic books.

Yalom, I. D. (2002). *The gift of therapy*. New York: HarperCollins.

Yalom, I. (2015). *Creatures of a day and other tales of psychotherapy*. New York: Basic Books.

Yalom, I. D. (2008). *Staring into the sun: Overcoming the terror of death*. San Francisco: Jossey-Bass.

Yalom, I., & Elkin, G. (1974). *Every day gets a little closer: A twice-told therapy*. New York: Basic Books.

Yashinsky, D. (2004). *Suddenly they heard footsteps: Storytelling for the twenty-first century*. Jackson, MS: University Press of Mississippi.

Zerubavel, N., & Wright, M. O. (2012). The dilemma of the wounded healer. *Psychotherapy*, *49*(4), 482–491.

Zimmerman, M. S., & Strouse, D. V. (2002). *Choosing a psychotherapist*. San Jose, CA: Writers Club Press.

Zipes, J. (2006). *Why fairy tales stick*. New York: Routledge.

Zur, O. (2014). Not all multiple relationships are created equal. *Independent Practitioner*, *34*(1), 15–22.

About the Author

Jeffrey A. Kottler is one of the most prolific authors in the fields of counseling, psychotherapy, and education, having written over 90 books about a wide range of subjects. He has authored a dozen texts for counselors and therapists that are used in universities around the world and a dozen books each for practicing therapists and educators. Some of his most highly regarded works include *Creative Breakthroughs in Therapy; The Mummy at the Dining Room Table: Eminent Therapists Reveal Their Most Unusual Cases and What They Teach Us About Human Behavior; Bad Therapy; The Client Who Changed Me; Divine Madness; Change: What Leads to Personal Transformation; Stories We've Heard, Stories We've Told: Life-Changing Narratives in Therapy and Everyday Life;* and *Therapy Over 50.*

Jeffrey has been an educator for 40 years, having worked as a teacher, counselor, and therapist in preschool, middle school, mental health center, crisis center, nongovernmental organization, university, community college, private practice, and disaster relief settings. He has served as a Fulbright scholar and senior lecturer in Peru and Iceland, as well as worked as a visiting professor in New Zealand, Australia, Hong Kong, Singapore, and Nepal. Jeffrey is currently Professor Emeritus of counseling at California State University, Fullerton.

Name Index

Subject Index